LEADERSHIP
FOR
GLOBAL
CITIZENSHIP

BARBARA C. CROSBY

LEADERSHIP FOR GLOBAL CITIZENSHIP

Building Transnational Community

SAGE Publications
International Educational and Professional Publisher
Thousand Oaks   London   New Delhi

For information:

SAGE Publications, Inc.
2455 Teller Road
Thousand Oaks, California 91320
E-mail: order@sagepub.com

SAGE Publications Ltd.
6 Bonhill Street
London EC2A 4PU
United Kingdom

SAGE Publications India Pvt. Ltd.
M-32 Market
Greater Kailash I
New Delhi 110 048 India

Printed in the United States of America

Library of Congress Cataloging-in-Publication Data

Crosby, Barbara C., 1946–
    Leadership for global citizenship: Building transnational
community / by Barbara C. Crosby.
       p. cm.
    Includes bibliographical references and index.
    ISBN 0-7619-1746-2 (cloth: acid-free paper)
    ISBN 0-7619-1747-0 (pbk.: acid-free paper)
    1. Leadership I. Title.
    HD57.7 .C73 1999
    658.4′092—dc21   98-40149

99 00 01 02 03 04 05 7 6 5 4 3 2 1

Acquisition Editor:	Catherine Rossbach
Editorial Assistant:	Heidi Van Middlesworth
Production Editor:	Denise Santoyo
Editorial Assistant:	Patricia Zeman
Typesetter:	Lynn Miyata
Cover Designer:	Candice Harman
Indexer:	Teri Greenberg

Contents

Preface

We travel together, passengers in a little spaceship, dependent upon its vulnerable resources of air and soil; all committed for our safety to its security and peace; preserved from annihilation only by the care, the work, and I will say the love we give our fragile craft.

—Adlai Stevenson

We live in an era in the history of nations when there is a greater need than ever for coordinated political action and responsibility.

—Gro Harlem Brundtland

In many ways, today's world is not a pretty place. Newspapers, television, and other media reveal the yawning disparities between the world's rich and poor, the haves and the have-nots. Communications media also recount egregious abuses of power and disregard for human rights that abound in every country. Added to these causes for concern and outrage is a growing global awareness that the very future of the earth may be in danger from the proliferation of nuclear weaponry and pollution by nuclear and other wastes.

At the same time, today's world remains a place where human hearts leap at sunstruck maple leaves in autumn; where our souls gasp in awe at pictures of earth from space; where the miracle of human intimacy can exist across all kinds of boundaries, from the simplest to the most formidable and complex; where creativity, passion, play, and humor can offer us respite from our destructive urges. It is a world that harbors a growing consensus that all people are entitled to the security, freedom, and material foundation they need to lead lives of dignity and self-determination.

We inhabitants of the earth also are developing a sense of our interconnectedness with each other and with the earth itself. This awareness grows in part from technological innovations. Thanks to spaceship explorations, we are now able to view our planet from space, and we notice that political boundaries are invisible on our cloud-swathed blue, green, and brown home. Thanks to telephones, faxes, e-mail, and satellites, we can communicate with each other almost instantaneously, though separated by continents. Global television networks allow us to view major events almost anywhere on earth as they happen. Global commercial airline service, even with its hitches, can deliver people from every corner of the world to global conventions such as the UN environmental conference in Rio de Janeiro in 1992, the UN economic development conference in Brussels in 1995, and the UN women's conference in Beijing, also in 1995.

We are being pulled toward world community, world citizenship, but with no clear understanding of what world citizenship is all about, especially in the absence of world government. What are the rights and responsibilities of world citizenship? How are they learned and practiced? How can a sense of world citizenship be spread more broadly?

Partial answers to these questions, I believe, can be derived from considering the work of people I call leaders in the global commons, people who are building world community through creation of transnational citizen organizations or exchange programs. Another way to think of this world community is as a "global civil society" (de Oliveira, 1995) in which the world's inhabitants can come together to discover the common good (usually by focusing on public problems that spill beyond national boundaries).

For most of the 1980s, I worked with colleagues at the Reflective Leadership Center at the University of Minnesota's Humphrey Institute of Public Affairs to develop a comprehensive understanding of leadership. A result of that collaboration was *Leadership for the Common Good: Tackling Public Problems in a Shared-Power World* (Bryson & Crosby, 1992). The book presents a leadership framework, illuminated by U.S. case studies. The framework has been the basis of numerous midcareer leadership seminars and workshops that John Bryson and I have conducted at the Humphrey Institute and elsewhere.

Even as we completed the book, I became interested in applying the framework to global public problems. What is different, I wondered, about promoting "leadership for the common good" within the United States and promoting such leadership transnationally? To explore this question, I studied leadership in several transnational citizen organizations, focusing especially on two—Amnesty International and the International Women's Rights Action Watch (IWRAW). (I have labeled these organizations *transnational* rather than *international* to emphasize that the founders of these organizations did not see themselves or their constituents as mainly representing or connected to nations, but rather as people reaching out across national boundaries to solve global problems.) I also drew on my experience, starting in 1990, coordinating an international fellows program at the Humphrey Institute. The fellows were outstanding civil servants, educators, and business executives from Africa, Asia, Latin America, and Central Europe who were in the United States for a year of study and professional development. Some fellows, especially those from countries with nondemocratic governments, were skeptical about the existence of a shared-power world, but all wanted to resolve public problems within and among their countries, and most knew that they would be, or already had been, called to leadership in some fashion in their societies.

It may seem odd that I concentrated on leadership in citizen organizations instead of analyzing international leadership by heads of state or the occupants of top positions in the United Nations and associated agencies. I agree that these highly visible and powerful officials can contribute to leadership in the global commons, especially in establishing global policies, standards, and governance structures. Focusing on these officials, however, obscures the vital role that citizen initiatives and organizations play in prompting official actions and in ensuring that those actions have widespread impact. The need for citizen groups to be involved in implementing official policies is especially strong at the global level, where official enforcement powers are often extremely weak.

PURPOSE OF THIS BOOK

This book is the result of my exploration, over the last several years, of citizen leadership across national boundaries. Through it, I seek to strengthen the emerging global civil society by offering potential and existing leaders insights about how they can hear the call to world citizenship themselves and enlist others in accepting the call and engaging in successful mutual efforts to solve global problems. I want to further develop the "leadership for the common good" framework to increase its usefulness in situations involving people from different cultures and regions of the world. In addition, I hope to connect my exploration of leadership to the work of numerous other scholars and researchers who are calling for leadership approaches attuned to the challenges of the 21st century.

AUDIENCE

This book is for people who feel a concern and responsibility for connecting with citizens in other countries in order to promote the well-being of the earth and its inhabitants. They may be working to connect the citizens of only two countries, or they may be trying to link citizens in countries around the world. These people can come from a wide array of vocational backgrounds: They may be business entrepreneurs, lawyers, health care workers, farmers, teachers, grassroots organizers, clergy, union representatives, diplomats and other civil servants, elected officials, homemakers, artists, or journalists. I think especially of the participants in the Humphrey Institute's midcareer leadership seminars for people from numerous countries. Many of these people have leadership responsibility in a voluntary group, a government agency, or a business. They are concerned about their personal development, the well-being of their organizations, and the future of their countries. They also realize that their lives and work are increasingly affected by global developments, although the participants from outside the United States probably have the stronger sense of global interdependence.

I hope that this book can help people like these to hear the call to world citizenship more clearly and provide them with tools for exercising leadership in the global commons. I also will speak to people who have less experience in managing and leading organizations but who want to be involved in transnational citizen initiatives. In addition, this book should be helpful to people already providing leadership in transnational citizen organizations and to national and international officials who view these organizations as partners in tackling global public problems.

This book will probably be most helpful to people with some familiarity and comfort with personal and group assessment, democratic process, multiple perspectives on team and organizational dynamics, systems thinking, or the search for cross-cultural ethical principles. Although the main ideas and methods in the book have been refined as I have worked with people from many different countries and cultures, I recognize that the ideas and methods are strongly shaped by my mainly U.S. experience and my work in a field—leadership studies—that is the province mainly of U.S. scholars. Thus, the book will be most accessible to people from the United States, but it should have usefulness for globally minded people from many societies.

This book speaks most directly to those who want to be *leaders* in the global commons. It does not directly address the "other side" of the leadership relationship—that is, the people often identified as followers. Because I join colleagues such as Michael Winer (1996) in thinking that the word *follower* is burdened with connotations of apathy and uncritical compliance, I actually see "followers" more as members, constituents, or citizens—fully engaged and contributing to the leadership work. I offer guidance for world citizens only by implication. At the same time, I emphasize that the people I identify as leaders are not always acting as leaders. Often they act as citizens inspired and mobilized by another leader. I have a fluid view of leadership: That is, some people may be leaders in one or more contexts for a time, but they are not leaders in all the contexts in which they find themselves. Moreover, people, public problems, organizations, projects, and communities change. The person who is called to lead during the early stages of dealing with a public problem, founding an organization, starting a project, or organizing a community may be more suited to being a contributing member in later stages.

INFLUENCES

In preparing this book, I am taught by all the people—from many countries, many occupations, and cultural backgrounds—who have participated with me in courses, seminars, and workshops. I draw on the wisdom of my colleagues, friends, and family. I benefit especially from the insights of other scholars who have analyzed leadership, cross-cultural communication, and social movements. I am buoyed by the example of all those people who share my concerns for the world and who often are engaged in highly courageous service related to those concerns. Although my guides are highly diverse, I am fully aware that they do not represent all experiences, all groups, or all points of view. I do believe, however, that as conversation partners they can help me think out ways of promoting social justice for human beings in very diverse situations around the world.

I also draw on my life as a woman born and raised in the deep, luscious, troubled South of the United States. I am the granddaughter of South Carolina sharecroppers and Kentucky tobacco farmers. I have been a journalist, teacher, and administrator; I have lived in many U.S. states and in London and Oxford, England. I am married to John Bryson, a wonderful partner, colleague, and coparent; our children, Kee and Jessica, keep us grounded and offer us multiple delights and challenges. I have lived on the economic margins but now have relative economic security. For a time, I was very active in an organization that is part of international peace and social justice movements, but now I am mainly an interested member of such organizations. As for religious roots, I might best describe myself as a Zen Presbyterian and backslidden Baptist; thus, I am alive to the world's contradictions. I am a fixer who tries to remember that the world cannot be fixed.

My perspective doubtless reflects various privileges: my being a descendant of fair-skinned European Americans, my heterosexual orientation, my middle-class status, my usually healthy body. It also reflects the marginalized experience and insights of girls and women in my country and in the rest of the world. While I am aware of lines (such as color, class, and gender) that demarcate my experience, I have considerable experience crossing those lines. Two examples are especially important to me. The first is my household—my spouse, my children, and myself—who combine European and Asian heritage; the second is the international fellows program I have already described.

I gather hope from the photographs showing me with my family or groups of fellows. The photographs of my spouse, my children, and me show people of different ethnic and national origins; the photographs of the fellows show people of many national, ethnic, linguistic, and religious backgrounds. These photographs seem so ordinary to me, yet they were almost outside the realm of possibility in the social milieu of my youth. This is not to say that there are no ethnic or national tensions among the people with whom I work, nor is it to say that I am unaware of cultural differences in my family, but there all of us are, together in the photographs, smiling for the cameras and meaning it.

OUTLINE OF THE BOOK

Chapter 1 of this book begins the inquiry into leadership in the global commons by presenting my leadership framework and the shared-power perspective that supports it. Each of the next eight chapters will be devoted to one of the main types of leadership in the global commons: leadership in context (Chapter 2), personal leadership (Chapter 3), team leadership (Chapter 4), organizational leadership (Chapter 5), visionary leadership (Chapter 6), political leadership (Chapter 7), and ethical leadership (Chapter 8). A final chapter will explain how the main types of leadership are linked together in change cycles and will offer concluding counsel and caveats. Every chapter will include extensive examples from my case studies of Amnesty International and IWRAW; an explanation of how the studies were conducted is in Appendix A. Interested readers may obtain the contextual essay "A Framework and Methodology for Developing Leadership in the Global Commons" (Crosby, 1996b), which further elucidates the literature and methods used to produce the book, by contacting me at the University of Minnesota.

Acknowledgments and Dedication

Many people have helped me clarify my thinking and writing about leadership in the global commons. I especially appreciate the contribution of those who carefully read my original manuscript, asked constructive questions, and made suggestions for improving my arguments and explanations. These intrepid readers are Rosita Albert, Sharon Anderson, John Bryson, Martha Crunkleton, Michael Hopkins, Milne Kintner-Dee, Helena Meyer-Knapp, Michael Miner, Tom O'Connell, Jurandyr Passos, Michael Patton, Suleha Suleman, Robert Terry, Néné Traoré, and Michael Winer. Elizabeth Minnich was a valued advisor in the early stages of developing this book. Arvonne Fraser and Marsha Freeman were extremely helpful in preparation of my case study of the International Women's Rights Action Watch, and Andrew Blane, Maggie Bierne, and David Weissbrodt generously commented on the case study of Amnesty International. John Bryson, my partner in domestic as well as professional endeavors, deserves additional heartfelt recognition for the abundant support he has given me throughout the creation of this book.

I dedicate this book to Jessica Ah-Reum Crosby Bryson and John Kee Crosby Bryson, my children and adventurous world travelers. May their ears be alert to the call for world citizenship.

CHAPTER 1

Leadership and Global Problems

Without a genuine sharing of authority and power, of concerns and fears, of hopes and dreams, little can be done to alleviate human suffering.
—Jimmy Carter

THE FOUNDING OF AMNESTY INTERNATIONAL

Riding the train to his office one day in 1960, a London barrister named Peter Benenson read a newspaper account of two Portuguese students who had been sentenced to 7 years in prison for raising a toast to "freedom" in a Lisbon restaurant. Here was an especially outrageous example of the government repression that Benenson had long opposed. He considered lodging a protest with the Portuguese Embassy but decided that such an individual gesture could be too easily ignored.

Instead, he developed the idea of a 1-year international campaign for the release of all political prisoners around the world. He soon enlisted several colleagues and friends in support of the idea, and together they launched "Appeal for Amnesty, 1961." They publicized the appeal through an extensive article in the London *Observer* (Benenson, 1961) and a report in *Le Monde*, followed by a press conference in London.

The appeal's organizers promised to focus attention on "prisoners of conscience" selected impartially from around the world and to provide information to other groups fighting for freedom of opinion or religion. They encouraged people to write to them with offers of help and information. The subsequent outpouring of support led the appeal's organizers to set up a permanent organization, which in 1962 was named Amnesty International.

By 1997, Amnesty International had more than 1 million members, subscribers, or regular donors in over 100 countries and territories, along with 4,287 local groups and several thousand school, university, professional, and other groups around the world. It had received the Nobel Prize for peace and was the preeminent human rights organization in the world.

THE FOUNDING OF IWRAW

As the 1985 Nairobi conference marking the end of the UN Decade for Women drew near, Arvonne Fraser and Rebecca Cook wondered how they could sustain the international campaign for women's rights after the decade was over. Fraser, who directed a women's project at the University of Minnesota in the United States, had been deeply involved in international women's issues throughout the decade. Cook was a lawyer working with a development law and policy program at Columbia University in the United States and had worked with the International Planned Parenthood Federation for several years.

The two women focused on the Convention on the Elimination of All Forms of Discrimination Against Women (usually called the Women's Convention), an international treaty adopted during the UN Decade that spelled out principles and standards for achieving equality between men and women while promoting secure and healthy families (United Nations, 1979/1983a). By the time of the Nairobi conference, 78 countries had ratified it, but the means of enforcing it were extremely weak. Fraser and Cook decided to hold a series of workshops at the Nairobi conference that would both explain the Women's Convention and consider ways to make it effective.

With the help of two more women—Norma M. Forde, a member of the law faculty of the University of the West Indies, and Jane Connors, a consultant for the Commonwealth Secretariat in London—Fraser and Cook conducted the workshops, which attracted large, enthusiastic audiences. Over 250 people from 52 countries signed workshop sheets indicating an interest in being a part of a larger international network seeking to implement the Women's Convention. Several workshop participants held extra meetings to hammer out the contours of such a network, which they named the International Women's Rights Action Watch (IWRAW). They decided that IWRAW should help educate women and men about the Women's Convention, promote legal and policy changes within countries, and monitor countries' compliance with the convention.

IWRAW was officially launched in 1986. Twelve years later, the network includes 5,000 individuals and groups spread around the world. The network has become a foremost advocate of women's human rights, and members work at local to global levels.

LEADING IN THE GLOBAL COMMONS

The founders of Amnesty International and IWRAW answered the call to world citizenship and became leaders in the global commons. By *leadership,* I mean "the inspiration and mobilization of others to undertake collective action in pursuit of the common good" (Bryson & Crosby, 1992, p. 31). I think of the global commons as a shared public space, analogous to the "free spaces" identified by Evans and Boyte (1986). In the global commons, people from many countries and cultures can come together in formal and informal groups to claim their mutual rights and responsibilities and work on common problems. Such groups include community organizations, cooperatives, advocacy groups, service organizations, political parties, schools, charitable organizations, and professional groups. With the exception of political parties and schools, these groups are often thought of as the voluntary, nonprofit, independent, or nongovernmental sector. Although these groups thrive best where governments are democratic, they are not the invention of one country or one region. They are rooted in the diverse traditions of mutual obligation, communal cooperation, and charity that exist the world over. These groups jointly constitute an emerging global civil society, which is undergirded by and sustains the idea that every human being rightfully participates in public decision making and should have the necessities of life.

Cleveland (1990) and others have talked about the global commons mainly in terms of natural environments that are the "common" property of humankind. I am referring to spaces, from the Internet to the UN headquarters, to village squares, where the world's citizens secure their shared political, economic, social, and cultural rights.

The overarching aim and contribution of leadership in the global commons is to strengthen the emerging global civil society, or world community. The founders of Amnesty International and IWRAW committed themselves to solving specific problems that spill across national boundaries, but the organizations that they began foster world citizenship in the course of working on those problems.

To begin unfolding the main types of leadership in the global commons, this chapter will present an orienting framework, illustrated by examples from my study of Amnesty International and IWRAW. The "shared-power" worldview, which inspired the framework, also will be discussed. I will explain how my view of leadership in the global commons fits with popular and academic leadership perspectives. Finally, I will consider the special challenges of inspiring and mobilizing citizens to tackle global public problems.

A FRAMEWORK FOR LEADERSHIP IN THE GLOBAL COMMONS

The main tasks of leadership in the global commons are

- Understanding the social, political, economic, and technological "givens" (leadership in context)

- Understanding the people involved, especially oneself (personal leadership)

- Building teams (team leadership)

- Nurturing effective and humane organizations, interorganizational networks, and communities (organizational leadership)

- Creating and communicating meaning in formal and informal forums (visionary leadership)

- Making and implementing legislative, executive, and administrative policy decisions in formal and informal arenas (political leadership)

- Sanctioning conduct—that is, enforcing ethical principles, laws, and norms and resolving residual conflicts in formal and informal courts (ethical leadership)

- Coordinating leadership tasks in change cycles (putting it all together)

In illustrating this framework with examples from the Amnesty International and IWRAW stories, it may be most helpful to focus first on *personal leadership* because leadership springs up at the intersection of personal passions and public problems. Peter Benenson had a passion for the human freedom to think and believe, and that passion intersected with specific denials of that freedom. Arvonne Fraser and Rebecca Cook had a passion for women's rights that intersected with the second-class (or worse) treatment of women around the world. These people brought to their leadership efforts an array of personal qualities and skills, from legal knowledge, to religious faith, to communications skills, to organizing experience, to self-understanding. They would use their skills to inspire and mobilize others.

But although leadership is most visibly attached to persons, it cannot be separated from its *context.* Amnesty was founded in a country that upholds, however imperfectly, the values of political and religious freedom. IWRAW was founded at the peak of an international celebration of women's accomplishments and concern with their needs, a celebration sponsored by the most visible international political institution, the United Nations. Both Amnesty and IWRAW are outgrowths of the international human rights political culture established most authoritatively by the Universal Declaration of Human Rights in 1948 (United Nations, 1948/1983d).

Team leadership is obviously important in an organization's embryonic stage, when a team may be all there is. The founders of Amnesty International and IWRAW had to keep their purposes clear, encourage creative problem solving, and sort out which team members were responsible for what. As the organizations matured, the original team reorganized and new teams were added, but the importance of teamwork continued.

Perhaps the most crucial element of *organizational leadership* within Amnesty and IWRAW has been clarity of mission. In the decades since its founding, through many internal debates, Amnesty has never veered far from its founders' original mission of working for better treatment and release of political prisoners or prevention of their detention in the first place. IWRAW's leaders, meanwhile, have focused steadfastly on promoting ratification and implementation of the Women's Convention.

People in Amnesty and IWRAW have exercised *visionary leadership* by organizing or joining many forums (i.e., conferences, meetings, publications) in order to create shared understandings of human rights. Amnesty International framed, or interpreted, the imprisonment of people for expressing their religious or political beliefs as a violation of internationally accepted human rights principles and carved out a new path—citizen action and putting a face on political prisoners—for achieving the vision of a world in which everyone can freely express his or her beliefs. IWRAW, meanwhile, interpreted women's rights as human rights and envisioned a path for achieving women's rights through the methods presented in the Women's Convention.

Activists in Amnesty International and IWRAW exercised *political leadership* by exerting pressure on policy makers in national governments and international bodies in ways carefully geared to alienate these people as little as possible while pressing them for change.

The founders of both organizations exemplify *ethical leadership.* Peter Benenson and colleagues emphasized ideals of justice and fairness and particular articles of the Universal Declaration of Human Rights as they worked for fair trials in the formal courts and appealed to the worldwide court of public opinion to sanction government actions. IWRAW's founders continually espoused the principles in the Women's Convention and even translated it into less legalistic terms so that ordinary people could better understand it. They have appealed to formal courts and the court of public opinion for redress of rights violations.

Putting it all together requires linking all the types of leadership in a change cycle, the multiphase process of tackling a complex public problem. These phases are the initial agreement or plan, problem definition, the search for solutions, policy or plan formulation, proposal review and adoption, implementation and evaluation, and policy or plan maintenance, succession, or termination. Different types of leadership are more important in some phases than others. For example, visionary leadership is most important in the first three. Thus, the founders of Amnesty and IWRAW had to pay particular attention to creating and communicating shared meaning about the problems that concerned them as they tried to initiate collective action on the problems, understand them more fully, and choose the most promising solutions.

This framework reveals the tasks of leadership in the global commons as multiple and complex. No one can perform them all; shared leadership is required to achieve the common good.

THE SHARED-POWER WORLD

The leadership framework that I have just outlined is basically a recipe for leadership that can contend with a "shared-power, no-one-in-charge world." In this world, no single individual, group, or organization has the power to dictate solutions to major public problems, yet many individuals, groups, and organizations have some responsibility to act on the problems.

At the global level, public problems such as AIDS, desertification, refugee migrations, and discrimination against women spill beyond organizational, governmental, and geographic boundaries. If we could draw a line fully encircling one of these problems, it would encompass many power centers: national, local, and midlevel governments as well as supranational quasi-governmental bodies such as the UN General Assembly, UNICEF, or the World Health Organization. The territory of the problem might also include projects sponsored by the World Bank or the International Monetary Fund. It might encompass economic enterprises, including portions of transnational corporations. Also within the territory might be warring clans, political factions, even organized crime. An array of media enterprises would be included, from global television networks to local newspapers. Finally, the territory would include numerous organizations variously called voluntary, nonprofit, charitable, religious, independent, or nongovernmental. Some of these organizations would be very small and narrowly focused; others might be national or transnational operations such as the International Red Cross, Greenpeace, Oxfam, or Bread for the World.

Some power centers within the problem territory would be linked in informal networks, formal alliances, or contractual agreements. Some individuals, groups, and organizations would favor maintaining the status quo, others would seek change, and others would be relatively neutral. Regardless, even the most powerful alliances would be unable to dictate solutions to the problem.

This shared-power perspective does not mean that power is shared equally (either among or within these groups). The leadership challenge is how to pool enough power to develop and implement solutions that are morally sound as well as technically and politically feasible—in other words, that promote the common good.

The first step for those accepting this challenge is to understand the deep dynamics of power and the most effective level of intervention in a shared-power world. Power (as explained in Bryson & Crosby, 1992) plays out through three main social practices:

- Creating and communicating meaning (the focus of visionary leadership)

- Making and implementing policy decisions (the focus of political leadership)

- Sanctioning conduct (the focus of ethical leadership)

Each of these practices, in turn, has three overlapping, interacting dimensions: *observable action* (first dimension); *mediating structure,* or ideas, rules, modes, media, and methods (second dimension); and *deep structure* (third dimension) (see Figure 1.1). These dimensions can be illustrated by the example of an

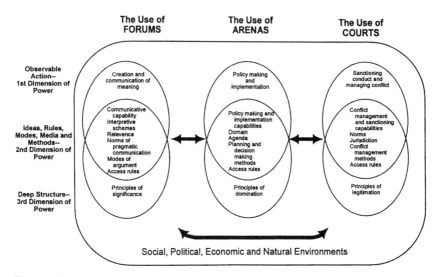

Figure 1.1. Dimensions of Power and the Use of Forums, Arenas, and Courts

SOURCE: From *Leadership for the Common Good: Tackling Public Problems in a Shared-Power World* (p. 91), by J. M. Bryson & B. C. Crosby, 1992, San Francisco: Jossey-Bass. Copyright 1992 by Jossey-Bass. Adapted by permission.

election. The observable action would include the campaigning, the voting, the tallying of the votes, and announcement of the results. Beneath this surface level, however, would be a second level: the ideas, rules, modes, media, and methods that govern the election—by, for example, controlling access to candidacy, establishing polling places and voter qualifications, and interpreting the voting act. Below the second level would be deep structure: widely shared assumptions about human nature, social action, and the distribution of resources. For example, the election rules might be based on the assumption that some humans, because of their education or property ownership, are true citizens and that others are not. Another fundamental assumption might be that resources (such as campaign funds) are or should be distributed evenly.

Each social practice also occurs in a characteristic setting: *forums* (creating and communicating meaning), *arenas* (making and implementing decisions), and *courts* (sanctioning conduct). Indeed, creating and communicating meaning can be understood as the design and use of formal and informal forums, making and implementing decisions as the design and use of formal and informal arenas, and sanctioning conduct as the design and use of formal and informal courts (see Figure 1.1).

It is difficult in a shared-power world to dictate observable actions or outcomes (first dimension of power). Also difficult is direct alteration of deep structure (third dimension of power). Leaders should instead concentrate on the second dimension of power, which mediates between deep structure and action. By altering ideas, rules, modes, media, and methods at this intermediate level, leaders can have considerable impact on observable action, which in turn reinforces or alters the deep structure. (This approach can also be an effective strategy for change agents in a world in which many outcomes are controlled by a very powerful individual or group.)

The next section will present examples and important characteristics of forums, arenas, and courts. The incident that sparked the founding of Amnesty International will be used as an illustration.

Forums, Arenas, and Courts

Forums include task forces, conferences, public hearings, town meetings, tribal councils, staff meetings, brainstorming sessions, luncheon conversations, computer networks, newspapers, documentaries, plays, and television shows. The characteristic observable action is the use of signs and symbols, usually through dialogue, debate, or discussion, to create shared meaning and values among participants. Important ideas, rules, modes, media, and methods include communicative ability, modes of argument, access rules, and interpretive schemes and modes of deciding among them. (Interpretive schemes are shared ways of looking at the world that link values, beliefs, assumptions, and past experience to observed phenomena.) The basic structure of forums is a speaker and an audience (of at least one) who share at least a minimum set of common linguistic rules and resources.

In the case of the incident that led to Amnesty's founding, two young men who presumably shared an understanding of the sounds and syntax of Portuguese, as well as elements of nonverbal communication, were in a restaurant. They raised their glasses and made a toast to freedom. Government authorities either observed the act or were told about it. The two young men were creating with their words and gestures a shared understanding of, and tribute to, freedom. They had the ability to speak and move. They probably shared an interpretive scheme, based on their studies and other experiences, that personal liberty was a good thing, and therefore, that the repressive practices of the Salazar regime were objectionable. Meanwhile, Salazar sympathizers who observed the toast interpreted it as an unacceptable challenge to the Salazar regime's authority. The two young men were unable to explore possible shared values with the Salazar supporters, who in a sense imposed their values on the two students. The students had access to the restaurant but probably did not count on Salazar supporters' being there as well. The outcome of the operation of this forum was that any dialogue or debate about freedom was thwarted. This issue would not be carried forward to legislative arenas, which presumably had passed laws supporting censorship in Portugal.

Arenas include legislatures, parliaments, local elected councils, boards of directors, executive committees, markets, and cartels. The characteristic observable action is making and implementing decisions establishing principles, laws, policies, plans, rules, standards, norms, or prices that apply to a population or a category of actions. Important ideas, rules, modes, media, and methods are the arena's domain; agendas; permitted methods of planning, budgeting, decision making, and implementation; and access rules. The basic structure of an arena is a policy maker and at least one other participant operating in a framework of basic social assumptions about the distribution of political, economic, and cultural resources. The policy maker must be able to affect a shared resource base that makes policy making necessary and possible.

In the case of the Portuguese students, the making and implementing of laws was dominated by Salazar supporters. The national government's domain extended to everyone within the nation's borders and encompassed citizen behavior that international human rights law deems outside legitimate government interference. Although the government's domain extended to all citizens, only supporters of the regime had significant access to government arenas, the capacity to establish the agendas in those arenas, and the capacity to decide which policy-making methods would be permitted. Any laws that the parliament passed, any decrees that António Salazar himself issued, could only be expected to reinforce the existing unequal distribution of political and economic resources that benefited supporters of the regime.

Courts include the International Court of Justice, national supreme courts, local and midlevel courts, military tribunals, ecclesiastical courts, licensing bodies, and the court of public opinion. The characteristic observable action in courts is moral evaluation and sanctioning of conduct, and especially conflict management and dispute resolution. The basic structure of a court is two disputants and a third party to resolve their dispute on the basis of shared assumptions about legitimate authority. Important ideas, rules, modes, media, and methods are conflict management and sanctioning capabilities, norms, jurisdiction, conflict management methods, and access rules.

In the case of the Portuguese students, the formal courts could be counted on to impose negative sanctions on the conduct of the two students in keeping with the anti-free-speech provisions of the laws passed by the national arenas. Indeed, the students were sentenced to 7 years in jail. Portuguese judges could ignore the provisions of the UN Declaration of Human Rights because the European Human Rights Commission, which had technical jurisdiction over human rights abuses in Europe, had extremely weak enforcement powers.

Peter Benenson had several options for responding to the Portuguese incident and similar cases. He might have lodged a protest with Portugal's London Embassy and had some slim hope of affecting the political arenas that issued decrees or passed laws restricting freedom of speech, or he might have kept attending individual trials, hoping that his presence and inquiries would prompt court officials to observe judicial norms such as due process.

It was the realization, however, that different versions of the Portuguese incident were occurring all over the world that set Benenson on course to launch the Appeal for Amnesty. Instead of continuing to act on abuses one by one, he could recruit others to join him in highlighting the general problem, as well as specific abuses, in the global mass media. This use of far-reaching forums was designed to activate the court of public opinion and channel its verdict to the officials responsible for abuses.

CRITIQUE OF SHARED POWER

The idea of a shared-power world is most comprehensible to those of us who live in democratic societies. In the United States, we are used to a government in which powers are shared among the executive, legislative, and judicial branches and among the various levels of our federalist system. Democracies, of whatever form, rest on the assumption that ultimate power resides in the people, even though the people may grant considerable power to members of parliament, a prime minister, or a president. A shared-power world may make less sense to citizens of countries governed by a dictator or an autocratic single party. Even in such cases, however, the citizens have considerable latent power, as Communist Party officials in the former Soviet Union found out. In China, the most prominent current example of continued single-party rule, top party officials have recognized the benefits of moving to an economic system in which decision-making power is much more dispersed, even as they try to maintain tight political controls.

In working with midcareer people from the United States and many other countries, I have encountered two main types of resistance to the idea of a shared-power world. The first is from those who think some individuals or groups are so powerful that the power of everyone else is nearly insignificant. This view is expressed in statements such as "The politicians just do what they want, regardless of what the citizens say," "The Clinton administration is the real power in Haiti," "The World Bank and International Monetary Fund are calling the shots in my country," and "Multinational companies really run the world." The second type of resistance comes from those who question the desirability or effectiveness of shared-power arrangements. They have experienced schools, businesses, and even countries that operate effectively as hierarchical systems in which power is highly concentrated at the top. Conversely, they are skeptical of shared-power arrangements because the ones they know about—for example, "old-boy networks"—are being employed to undermine the common good.

Both forms of resistance carry some truth, but I do not think they negate the helpfulness of a shared-power perspective. Yes, some individuals and organizations are more powerful than others, but that power depends on the acquiescence, acceptance, or contribution of other groups. As my colleague Robert Terry is fond of saying, the only completely powerless people are in cemeteries. Benjamin Barber (1984) even argued that the dead remain powerful because of the institutions, policies, and perspectives they bequeath the living.

Meanwhile, people considered extremely powerful must confront formidable limitations. The U.S. president cannot for long pursue a course of action that is unsupported by the majority of U.S. voters or foreign allies, even when the United States is the only remaining nation widely accorded superpower status. The secretary general of the United Nations cannot unilaterally end strife in the former Yugoslavia. A transnational corporation cannot easily market a product that does not meet the needs, wants, or legal requirements of a society.

I also agree that hierarchical organization has some advantages. In a crisis, for example, it is helpful to have an individual or small executive committee issuing clear directives that are promptly carried out by others (although even then, individuals need to exercise judgment as they interpret and apply the directives). A wise chief elder or a monarch can provide considerable stability and cohesion for his or her society. A business that concentrates power at the top can function well as long as its top management is competent, benevolent, and wise; its market is relatively secure; its product is standardized; its access to suitable workers is ensured; and its technology remains adequate. This type of organization, however, does not provide the flexibility and creativity that is needed to cope with many of the demands of a global economy, the telecommunications revolution, or a disaffected citizenry. Management and leadership gurus such as Margaret Wheatley (1992), James Kouzes and Barry Posner (1987, 1993), and David Osborne and Ted Gaebler (1992) champion more decentralized structures and empowerment of employees and other stakeholders. (It also is important to acknowledge that the best structure for a particular organization will be a blend of centralized and decentralized control. See Chapter 5 on organizational leadership.)

There is a definite democratic bias to my argument for a shared-power world. That is, not only do I think that the power to solve global public problems *is* dispersed among many individuals and groups, but I believe that it *should* be, and I hope it will be even more widely shared. The solutions to global public problems can be developed best by involving a wide array of affected parties, or their representatives, in working out the solutions because useful knowledge is dispersed among these groups, and their support will be needed to implement solutions that are adopted.

This is not an argument for anarchy. In addition to recognizing that power already is shared and advocating increased sharing, I emphasize that the key to promoting the common good is developing shared-power arrangements that constitute "regimes of mutual gain" (Bryson & Crosby, 1992, p. 14). These regimes comprise the principles, norms, rules, and decision-making procedures that guide the framing of a public problem, adoption of solutions, and accountability for implementing solutions. They are likely to include a variety of organizational structures, formal and informal, hierarchical and fluid.

In establishing such regimes, the most important focal point may be the groups often considered least powerful—that is, the voluntary sector (including charitable, advocacy, educational, professional, and religious groups). These groups have less secular authority than government and less economic power than business. They usually struggle for tangible resources such as money, office space, equipment, and personnel.

To be sure, solving public problems is within the purview of governments, but governments typically cannot do so by themselves. They need help from voluntary organizations, businesses, and individual citizens. Officials in a democracy must convince a majority of the citizens or their elected representatives that a problem is worth tackling and that certain solutions are worth pursuing. Nondemocratic governments have little incentive to tackle public problems that pose no immediate threat to their hold on power. Businesses, meanwhile, are likely to be too focused on making profits (including capturing benefits and exporting costs to the society at large) and perpetuating themselves to worry about the common good.

Citizen organizations are founded to deal with public problems that government or business is ignoring or even causing. This does not mean that citizen organizations do it all themselves. One of their prime methods may be prodding and assisting government and business to do their part in solving the problem (see, e.g., Fisher, 1998).

When a citizen organization creates or joins a social movement, the organization becomes even more powerful. The core of the movement is one or more organizations seeking a specific sociopolitical change. The movement also embraces allied organizations, a "penumbra" of people (see Freeman, 1983, p. 2) who support the organizations but are not necessarily controlled by them, and linkages among the core and supportive organizations. Amnesty International founded a global "prisoners of conscience" movement and helped create the global human rights movement. IWRAW was an outgrowth of the worldwide women's movement and now helps shape that movement as well as the global human rights movement.

OTHER LEADERSHIP PERSPECTIVES

My view of leadership embraces people who may or may not occupy top positions in government, business, or voluntary organizations. It includes women and men from all cultural backgrounds. It considers leadership a force for the common good. I have encountered very different perspectives, however, both in academic studies, in the mass media, and in my conversations with people in my courses, seminars, and workshops. Some people simply define leaders as the occupants of top political or tribal office or the heads of organizations. They may be interested in how to improve the quality of those leaders, cope with their demands, or become a leader themselves. In this view, leaders are a small, elite group. Accordingly, many books on leadership have focused on chief executives—for example, *Leaders: The Strategies of Taking Charge* (Bennis & Nanus, 1985) or *The President as World Leader* (Kellerman & Barrilleaux, 1991).

Some people identify leaders not only as a powerful elite but as irrelevant or antithetical to efforts to achieve the common good. These people argue along these lines: If Pol Pot and Adolph Hitler are called leaders, how can leadership precepts be helpful in efforts, say, to protect women's property rights?

My response to elitist views of leadership is twofold. First, I think the quality of organizational and civic life can be improved by widespread sharing of leadership tasks. Second, I join James MacGregor Burns (1978) in arguing that mere power wielding is not leadership. Thus, a person could be in a powerful position and influence thousands of people's actions but would more appropriately be called a tyrant, dictator, demagogue, or empire builder than a leader. Authentic leadership, I argue, arises from democratic leader-follower interactions and arrangements, such as the free operation of public forums that allow diverse voices and perspectives to be heard. Such leadership promotes the well-being of a particular group or community but practically and ethically must consider the well-being of connected groups or communities. Thus, I would consider a chief executive of a large business a leader only if he or she sought the well-being of employees, customers, and the larger society, as well as of stockholders.

The shared-leadership perspective is becoming prominent among U.S. leadership scholars, who have published a spate of books in the late 1980s and early 1990s that emphasize the relational, social, and ethical aspects of leadership. Many of these writers argue explicitly or implicitly that the "Western," and especially U.S., celebration of individualism (and associated models of leadership) is becoming ineffective and dysfunctional, if not downright destructive. They insist that the well-being of organizations, local communities, nations, and the entire world requires more socially minded and democratic visions of social life and leadership. Examples (besides Bryson & Crosby, 1992) are Sally Helgeson's *The Female Advantage* (1990), Joseph Rost's *Leadership for the Twenty-First Century* (1991), Margaret Wheatley's *Leadership and the New Science* (1992), Robert Terry's *Authentic Leadership* (1993), James Kouzes and Barry Posner's *Credibility* (1993), and Ronald Heifetz's *Leadership Without Easy Answers* (1994).

Even though I emphasize the merits of a shared-leadership perspective, I do not want disputes about the nature of leadership to get in the way of promoting collective action in pursuit of the common good. If what I call leadership in the global commons is called collaborative problem solving or simply right action by someone else, I still hope he or she can gain helpful insight from this book.

SPECIAL CHALLENGES OF LEADING
IN THE GLOBAL COMMONS

The remaining chapters of this book will describe further the main types of leadership in the global commons. They will focus especially on the added challenges of leading across national boundaries. For now, I will briefly state what I consider the most important of these challenges.

Leadership in Context

It is hard enough to understand the social, political, economic, and technological "givens" that constitute a local or national context for public problem solving. It is even harder to understand those "givens" for a group of countries or the world as a whole. The central challenge is to identify what aspects of the global context help and hinder efforts to tackle a public problem. Once these aspects are identified, leaders in the global commons must decide how to benefit from the helpful aspects and overcome the hindrances.

Personal Leadership

The most difficult challenge at the personal level for leaders in the global commons may be understanding themselves as the product of particular national and ethnic cultures. They should ask: How does my nationality, ethnicity, gender, class, religion, sexual orientation, and physical ability facilitate my connection with some people and separate me from others? What can I do to understand and appreciate people very unlike me?

Leadership usually requires personal courage. Does leading across national boundaries demand special reserves of courage?

Team Leadership

In assembling a team that initiates, sustains, or oversees work on a global public problem, leaders should strive to represent multiple perspectives and different cultures. Yet how can leaders help such a diverse team agree on and accomplish a common purpose?

Organizational Leadership

How can leaders in the global commons build transnational citizen organizations or networks that spark and sustain social movements involving large numbers of people in developing and implementing solutions to public problems? How do these organizations connect to business and government organizations?

Visionary Leadership

How can leaders in the global commons overcome barriers of language, culture, and physical distance to create and communicate shared meaning? In particular, what kind of forums can these leaders convene at the local, national, global, and intermediate levels to frame and reframe the problems that concern them and to develop solutions?

Political Leadership

Leaders in the global commons must cope with differing political systems. They also must build coalitions or alliances that can bring optimal pressure to bear on pertinent decision-making arenas, from local to global levels.

Ethical Leadership

The thorny question of ethical leadership is: Which ethical principles, treaty provisions, laws, or norms have global legitimacy? How do leaders in the global commons enforce and reinforce principles, treaty provisions, laws, and norms in formal and informal courts in support of the public policy changes they are seeking?

Putting It All Together

How do leaders script dramas on the world stage so that policy conflicts are heightened, reframed, or resolved? How can these dramas produce trans-national regimes of mutual gain?

All the elements of leadership are important in efforts to resolve global public problems. Linking the different types of leadership becomes even more complex as leaders try to coordinate action across many societies. How do leaders become global systems thinkers? How do they ensure that leadership is widely shared?

SUMMARY

This chapter has introduced the stories of Amnesty International and IWRAW as examples of leadership in the global commons. I also have outlined the leadership framework that I use to gain insights from these stories and other sources. I have discussed the shared-power worldview that supports the leadership framework, and I have considered how my view of leadership in the global commons relates to other leadership perspectives. Finally I have outlined special challenges confronting leaders who answer the call to world citizenship.

The next chapter begins the elaboration of the main types of leadership in the global commons by focusing on leadership in context. This chapter and the following seven will have a common format. I will describe first the main aspects of each leadership type, using illustrative examples from Amnesty International and IWRAW. I will then present additional resources and guidance for those seeking to exercise this type of leadership.

CHAPTER 2

Leadership in Context

Nothing endures but change.
—Heraclitus

Plus ça change, plus c'est la même chose.
—Alphonse Karr

Leaders such as Peter Benenson, Arvonne Fraser, and Rebecca Cook demonstrate an understanding of the larger context of their efforts—that is, the social, political, economic, and technological "givens" and what can be changed. To identify possible and desirable changes in social, political, economic, and technological arrangements, those seeking to follow their example should ask: What shifts in these arrangements offer new opportunities for leadership connected to the global problem that concerns me? Which aspects of the global context might help efforts to tackle this problem, and which aspects hinder those efforts? How can I take advantage of the helpful aspects and overcome the hindrances?

This chapter will examine the main aspects of leadership in context, using examples from Amnesty International and IWRAW. It also will offer resources and guidance for practicing leadership in context at the turn of the millenium.

POLITICAL CONDITIONS AND TRENDS

In the latter half of the 20th century, leaders in the global commons have had to recognize the continuing importance of the nation-state, the growth of international governance mechanisms, and the ideological and military alliances that formed in the wake of World War II. The most cataclysmic political change during this period has been the breakup of the former Soviet Union in the late 1980s.

Amnesty International

Peter Benenson and others who joined in launching Amnesty International as the 1960s began were very aware that the world was divided into nation-states, ranging from democratic to totalitarian. Moreover, the tradition of national sovereignty gave national governments considerable power over their citizens. The doctrine effectively prohibited governments from interfering in each others' domestic affairs and certainly provided no standing for foreign citizens who objected to a government's treatment of its own people.

The world of the 1960s also was gripped by the Cold War between two superpowers, the United States and the Soviet Union. International politics comprised three main camps: the United States and its allies, the Soviet Union and its allies, and the nonaligned states. Efforts to build ties or develop common cause between citizens of different countries were interpreted through a Cold War lens colored by demonology: That is, the prevailing ideology in both the U.S. and Soviet camps depicted governments and citizens of the other camp as evil or at best untrustworthy.

At the same time, shifts were occurring in these political conditions. A new international political culture was taking hold. The UN General Assembly was maturing as a setting where nations' representatives could debate and make decisions about international issues. Most significantly, from the perspective of Amnesty's founders, the UN charter had established the principle that all human beings around the world had certain rights that their countries could not legitimately deny. By signing the charter, what David Forsythe (1991) called "in effect a global constitution" (p. 4), the overwhelming majority of the world's nations committed themselves to the international protection of human rights.

These rights—those deemed essential to human freedom and security—were spelled out in the 30 articles of the Universal Declaration of Human Rights, adopted by the UN General Assembly in 1948. Some of the articles concentrate on what have been called civil and political rights, such as freedom from slavery or servitude, free elections, the right to a nationality, and the right to a public trial. Others declare social and economic rights, such as equal pay for equal work, unemployment protection, reasonable working hours, and adequate standard of living. Article 2 stipulates, "Everyone is entitled to all the rights and freedoms set forth in this Declaration without distinction of any kind, such as race, colour, sex, language, religion, political or other opinion, national or social origin, property, birth or other status" (United Nations, 1948/1983d, p. 64).

When the declaration was adopted, it was more an expression of hope than a codification of reality, but by the late 1950s, some enforcement mechanisms had been created, and important books on human rights had been published. When Peter Benenson (1961, p. 21) announced the "Appeal for Amnesty, 1961," he quoted two articles of the Universal Declaration:

> Article 18—Everyone has the right to freedom of thought, conscience and religion; this right includes freedom to change his religion or belief, and freedom, either alone or in community with others and in public or private, to manifest his religion or belief in teaching, practice, worship and observance.
>
> Article 19—Everyone has the right to freedom of opinion and expression; this right includes freedom to hold opinions without interference and to seek, receive and impart information and ideas through any media and regardless of frontiers. (quoted in Benenson, 1961, p. 21)

As the 1960s began, there also was some thawing in the Cold War. The combination of new top leaders in the United States and the Soviet Union and the spirit that Pope John XXIII brought to the Catholic papacy made 1960 to 1961 a hopeful period for improving international relations (Benenson, 1984). In addition, an important example of successful international cooperation, the World Refugee Year, had just been completed. This UN-sponsored intensive appeal, initiated by British humanitarian and political activists, found homes and provided rehabilitation for over a million refugees in Europe, Palestine, China, and Hong Kong.

The British democratic political system also provided favorable conditions for launching a campaign against the repression of speech and opinion. Citizens and resident foreigners had considerable leeway to organize voluntary organizations pursuing political or social reforms.

IWRAW

By the time of IWRAW's founding in 1985, the international human rights culture—based on the principle that certain basic individual rights supersede a national government's prerogatives—was much stronger than it had been almost 25 years before, when Amnesty was founded. The United Nations, national governments, and voluntary human rights groups such as Amnesty International had developed numerous mechanisms for implementing the provisions of the declaration. Among the significant UN actions was the adoption of two covenants—the International Covenant on Civil and Political Rights (United Nations, 1966/1983b) and the International Covenant on Economic, Social, and Cultural Rights (United Nations, 1966, 1983c)—that spelled out how countries should protect the rights enumerated in the declaration. The covenants were developed by the UN Commission on Human Rights and adopted by the General Assembly in 1966; enough countries had signed them by 1976 to make them operative. The United Nations also created internal agencies to monitor compliance with the covenants and other human rights laws and to adjudicate claims of rights violations.

As the covenants were being developed, the UN Commission on the Status of Women (actually a subcommission of the Commission on Human Rights) worked on a comparable document focusing on women's rights. The ultimate product, representing almost 30 years' work by the Commission on the Status of Women and international women's organizations, was the Convention on the Elimination of All Forms of Discrimination Against Women (United Nations, 1979/1983a). This international treaty, known as the Women's Convention, was adopted by the UN General Assembly on December 19, 1979, and became effective December 3, 1981. By 1985, 78 countries had ratified it.

The convention's first five articles define discrimination against women and outline general principles such as the need to guarantee women basic human rights and fundamental freedoms on an equal basis with men and the need to eliminate sex-role stereotyping. Articles 6 through 16 specify necessary actions in areas such as political and public life, employment, nationality, education, health care and family planning, and prostitution. The remaining articles focus on means of ensuring compliance with the convention.

At the same time that international mechanisms for protecting human rights had improved, the power and importance of national governments by no means had disappeared. Governments signed the international human rights treaties and were the main parties held accountable for violations. Some governments refused to sign important treaties or agreed to adhere only to parts of them.

Voluntary human rights groups, or nongovernmental organizations, also had grown in numbers and in influence on UN deliberations during the years after Amnesty's founding. Thus, the international political terrain already had considerable space into which IWRAW could fit, and it included many potential IWRAW allies.

SOCIAL CONDITIONS AND TRENDS

Throughout the second half of the 20th century, the world's peoples have continued to be separated, not only by national political boundaries, but by their diverse national and local cultures—a separation often reinforced by language differences. The easiest cross-cultural connections have been with people from similar cultures. At the same time, these peoples have increasingly been brought into contact with each other through expanding international air travel, telecommunications, and refugee flows. Leaders in the global commons must take advantage of the increasing ease of connecting the world's diverse inhabitants to each other, while appreciating the continued force of cultural difference.

These leaders also should recognize the continuing importance of class and caste structures in countries around the world. Class and caste structures invariably establish hierarchies that assign people status and power on the basis of economic assets, ethnicity, religion, gender, or some other criterion. Like culture, these hierarchies are powerful means of connecting large numbers of people while separating them from many other people. To serve or recruit members of varying levels in these structures, leaders in the global commons must understand the different groups' needs, desires, and resources. Leaders must remember that class and caste structures change. World War II's demand on human resources fostered more egalitarian arrangements. African troops, for example, fought side by side with their colonial masters. In the U.S. military, African Americans, American Indians, and Asian Americans served with distinction along with European Americans. In many countries, women moved into the workforce to fill production, management, and leadership roles left vacant by men who had gone to war. After the war, powerful men tended to reclaim their old positions, but women and other dominated groups had new images of themselves that would continue to erode the traditional structures. Powerful trade unions in the industrialized countries also ensured that more wealth would flow to the working class.

Leaders in the global commons also must attend to demographic conditions and shifts. For example, the movement of more and more of the world's people to cities may exacerbate global problems such as air pollution, but these people may be easier to organize to remedy the problems.

Amnesty International

When Peter Benenson and colleagues launched Amnesty International, they built on previous connections between their fellow Britons and other peoples. Before World War II, colonization, trade, missionary and humanitarian efforts, immigration, and even recreational travel were already bringing people from the United States and Europe into contact with people in African, Latin American, and Asian countries. The war brought large numbers of U.S. and European soldiers and officials to distant parts of the world.

British society of the 1960s was internationally minded, due in part to the country's imperialist history. This internationalism also had a humanitarian strain, however, which was strongly manifest in the work of voluntary organizations such as Save the Children and Oxfam. Such organizations also were rooted in a tradition of liberal philanthropy and social reform.

In the years immediately after World War II, British people were preoccupied with rebuilding their own country, but by the early 1960s, they were ready to look outward again. Opinion leaders such as David Astor, editor of the influential London *Observer,* were building public concern about repressive conditions in South Africa and European communist countries.

In launching Amnesty, Peter Benenson also drew on an understanding of the British upper middle class, which included his own family, his schoolmates, and his fellow lawyers. He used that understanding to find outlets for

Amnesty's message, to fund and staff the organization, and gather ideas for its strategies.

IWRAW

By 1985, thanks in part to the continued expansion of global telecommunications and transportation networks, the world's cultures were increasingly in contact, and in conflict. Some of the meetings convened as part of the UN International Decade for Women resulted in searing, sometimes brutal confrontations over religious and class differences within and between countries. Women from Western cultures and their priorities were especially challenged by other women who identified Western cultures with imperialism. At the same time, many women at these meetings were united by awareness that women had secondary status and were severely discriminated against in all countries of the world. By the time of the Nairobi conference concluding the decade, women overcame cultural and other differences sufficiently to agree on a platform of common strategies to promote women's equality and development.

An important result of the International Decade for Women and all the organizing of women's groups and initiatives during the decade was the creation of a global women's society that was the true locale of IWRAW's birth. IWRAW's headquarters would be located in the United States, which has an even stronger tradition of nurturing voluntary associations than Britain does.

ECONOMIC AND TECHNOLOGICAL CONDITIONS AND TRENDS

Leaders in the global commons must understand national economies and their links to national political systems, as well as the increasing importance of the global economy. They also should take advantage of opportunities resulting from technological innovation, while countering the threats that such innovation may pose to social well-being.

Amnesty International

At the time of Amnesty's founding, economic systems were linked to nations and wrapped up with prevailing political ideologies. Thus, the national government's control of economic planning and operations in the USSR or China was an essential part of the Marxist-Leninist political system. The mostly capitalist U.S. economy was intermeshed with the U.S. version of democratic government. Between the capitalist and communist economies were economies with varying degrees of state ownership and centralized planning (see Lindblom,

1977). Regardless of the economic system, a country's policy makers focused on expanding or protecting their own national economy.

At the same time, national policy makers were becoming more aware that national economies were interdependent. Following World War II, the victors committed themselves to rebuilding the economies of their defeated enemies. They had learned from the aftermath of World War I that stifling the economic restoration of defeated nations could backfire. The creation of the World Bank, the International Monetary Fund, and the General Agreement on Tarriffs and Trade following World War II was a concerted effort to foster increased international trade and more even economic development throughout the world.

In addition, by the 1960s a growing international airline and communications industry was bringing people together more easily across national boundaries. Amnesty members thus would be able to respond more and more rapidly to human rights violations around the world and bring far-flung members together for meetings.

IWRAW

The founders of IWRAW were alert to worldwide economic discrimination against women. In 1985 (as today), the world's women carried extra burdens, had lower incomes, had less access to capital, were excluded from top positions, or were otherwise disadvantaged compared to men. The major national economic systems—whether capitalist, socialist, communist, or some variation on these—all undervalued work done by women. Much of women's work—for example, child care, farming, and housekeeping—was unpaid and left out of economic calculations such as the gross national product (Waring, 1988).

Women also experienced new opportunities and threats as a result of the growing ability of companies to establish multinational operations. Say, for example, that a U.S. company opened a garment manufacturing plant in Thailand. Many Thai women would be hired to work in the plant at wages and working conditions much lower than those of their U.S. counterparts. Once the new plant was operating, the parent company might well shut down or drastically pare its U.S., mainly female, workforce.

At the same time, the ways in which economic arrangements harmed women were being directly challenged by the international women's movement, which promoted reforms in education, employment practices, insurance, pensions, and credit that would improve women's economic status. Economist Marilyn Waring (1988) and others promoted methods of valuing women's unpaid work.

The continued growth of the global telecommunications and transportation networks gave the founders of IWRAW tools for speedily exchanging information with supporters around the world and for convening meetings that included representatives from Asia, Africa, Europe, and both Americas. Another technological condition important for women's human rights advocates was the development of modern birth control technology. IWRAW's leaders faced the dilemma of ensuring women had access to safe and effective family planning methods while not being forced to accept birth control technologies.

ADDITIONAL RESOURCES AND GUIDANCE FOR LEADERSHIP IN THE GLOBAL CONTEXT

Understanding the political, social, economic, and technological context of a global problem is a formidable, almost unlimited task. The context cannot be fully understood by a single individual or group. Nevertheless, leaders in the global commons can improve their grasp of context by becoming students of culture; learning about their own countries' political, social, and economic systems; and studying global conditions and trends.

Becoming a Student of Culture

Any group that has some stability over time develops a culture, or distinctive way of doing things (Schein, 1992). The concept of culture is used most frequently in connection with nationality or ethnicity: For example, we speak of Japanese, U.S., or Chilean culture and of Native American, Afro-Caribbean, or Zulu culture. In addition, culture is associated with subnational regions, cities, neighborhoods, organizations, and other social groups. For example, analysts may explore the culture of Paris, the south of France, IBM, feminist organizations, or gay and lesbian communities. To exercise leadership in context, leaders in the global commons need, at the very least, a general understanding of culture, of pertinent national cultures including their own, and of the global culture.

General Understanding of Culture. A group's culture includes visible artifacts such as clothing, diet, and rituals as well as a set of espoused values, but most fundamentally it is a set of shared assumptions about reality and truth, time, space, and human nature. These assumptions, developed over time in response to the basic challenges facing the group, are interwoven to constitute a particular group's distinctive worldview or paradigm (Schein, 1992). Cultural analysts identify several important ways in which societies or groups differ in their assumptions about reality and truth, time, space, and human nature:

- *Reality and truth.* Is the culture what Edgar Hall (1959) called "low context" or "high context"? People in a low-context culture—for example, the dominant U.S. culture—rely a great deal on written and verbal messages to convey information and understand reality. People in a high-context culture analyze messages more expansively, paying attention not only to the words but to the status of the people communicating, their nonverbal behavior, and the situation they are in. Societies and groups also vary in whether they believe truth is based in moral authority or pragmatic experimentation.

- *Time.* Low-context cultures, Hall found, have a monochronic approach: That is, they tend to divide time into segments and organize these segments into rigid schedules. In high-context cultures, time is polychronic, or full of simultaneous happenings, and completing a transaction is more important than adhering to a schedule. Societies or groups also vary in whether they are oriented toward the future, present, or past (Kluckhohn & Strodtbeck, 1961).

- *Space.* What are the group's shared assumptions about appropriate interpersonal distance? How are living and working spaces arranged?

- *Human nature.* Does the society or group think that the proper role of human beings is to control or dominate nature? Does it assume that nature is really in control and that humans must accept natural occurrences? Or is the prevailing view that human beings should strive to harmonize themselves with the environment through, for example, meditation and self-control (Schein, 1992, p. 129)? Does the society or group see human beings as mainly good, as mainly evil, or as a mixture of good and evil? How does it view gender and ethnic differences? Does the society or group emphasize social hierarchy, or is it relatively egalitarian? Are individuals viewed mainly as separate personalities (as in individualist cultures such as the United States) or as part of a social group (as in collectivist cultures such as China)? Is a person's status determined mainly by his or her accomplishments or by family background or group membership? Does the society or group make strong distinctions among work, family life, and personal concerns, and if so, does it value them differently?

In a particular society or group, the assumptions around each of these dimensions become interwoven to constitute that society's or group's distinctive worldview or paradigm (Schein, 1992). Culture clash occurs when people from different groups come into contact with each other with little awareness of how their worldviews differ. A good simulation of this clash is the game BaFa BaFa (Shirts, n.d.).

Understanding National Cultures. Making extended visits, or what Brislin (1981) called "sojourns," to other countries for work, study, or recreation is especially helpful in understanding different national cultures and the ways that culture shapes economic and political systems. In the course of an extended visit, you can combine observation, written explanations of the culture, and personal interviews of people living in the country. If you cannot actually visit other countries, you still gain insights into their cultures by reading and talking to immigrants or visitors from those countries. You also can participate in experiential exercises called intercultural sensitizers, to be discussed in the next chapter.

A helpful guide for analyzing a society's culture is the approach that Schein (1992) has developed to probe organizational culture. To get at shared assumptions, using this approach, you would start with the artifacts—easily discernible manifestations such as dress, language, art, ritual, structural designs, and technology. Once you identified these, you would focus on the society's espoused values—that is, the philosophies and goals explicitly endorsed by the society. Finally, by considering matches and mismatches between the society's espoused values and the artifacts, you would try to discern the society's fundamental shared assumptions.

It is also important to recognize that societies are likely to embrace a number of "co-cultures" (see Samovar & Porter, 1994), the cultures of groups that, because of their ethnicity, gender, religion, or other characteristics, are excluded from the "mainstream." These cultures contribute to the national culture but are not dominant within it. The person who would understand a country's dominant culture and co-cultures must rely on diverse informants.

Understanding one's own national culture may be the most difficult contextual task because—intercultural scholars emphasize—it is very hard to understand something that is so pervasive and taken for granted in a society. Probably the best way to understand one's own culture has already been recommended—that is, making an extended visit to another culture. By watching how another society deals with basic human tasks, such as the ordering of time or interpersonal relations, sojourners can see more clearly how their home society approaches these tasks and perhaps question the assumption that the home society's approach is the only "right" way. They also learn how people in another society view the sojourners' society. My stays in England, for example, have made me very aware of the British view of U.S. people—namely, that we are energetic, boisterous, uncouth, boastful, often arrogant, and sometimes sleazy. In addition to foreign sojourns, it is possible to improve one's understanding of the contrasts between one's own culture and others through extended conversations with foreign visitors, participation in sensitization exercises, and study of cultural analyses.

There is still another way to understand one's own national culture: by being part of a co-culture—that is, an outsider in the dominant culture. In the United States, for example, the national culture has been strongly shaped by those with the most economic and political power, who tend to be male, middle to upper class, able-bodied, heterosexual, and of European heritage. These are the people who are most at home in the national culture, which emphasizes individualism, freedom, and competition, among other things. U.S. citizens who are female, poor, physically disabled, lesbian, gay, or from non-European heritage are at least partially outside the national culture and have access to their own distinctive co-cultures. Often, for purposes of survival, they develop acute understanding of how the ruling assumptions of the dominant national culture contrast with the assumptions of their co-cultures (see Anzaldúa, 1990; Hall, 1990). Similarly, Muslim citizens of India should have penetrating insights into the predominantly Hindu culture of their country, and Laplanders in Norway could help other Norwegians better understand that country's dominant culture.

Global Culture. Leaders in the global commons also should recognize the burgeoning global culture, which can be viewed from at least two angles. From one, it is a mélange of music, media images, and messages from different parts of the world, dominated by the global spread of English (the global culture's lingua franca), U.S. films, television series, music, and advertising. This U.S. influence, with its emphasis on individualism and consumerism, can undermine efforts to promote citizen cooperation on global problems, such as air pollution. From another angle, global culture is created and inhabited by the networks of people throughout the world who share an interest or project. They are familiar with the World Wide Web and international airports; they are employed by transnational corporations, UN agencies, churches, arts organizations, or other globally minded groups; they belong to international associations or they are involved in international research or volunteer efforts. For these people, the ability to speak more than one language will continue to be important even as English is the main common medium of communication. These people are used to thinking and acting across national boundaries; they and their networks can be prime resources in efforts to resolve global problems.

Understanding One's Own Political, Social, and Economic Systems

The importance of understanding one's own culture already has been noted. Developing an understanding of other social systems, as well as political and economic systems, in one's own society also prepares people to exercise leadership in the global commons. Peter Benenson's involvement with local and national Labour Party politics for many years before founding Amnesty supplied him with a network vital for founding a new organization but also gave him an extensive understanding of how one political system worked. As a young woman, Arvonne Fraser was active in Democratic politics in her home state of Minnesota, then went to Washington when her husband was elected to Congress. She worked in his office, became familiar with constituents' concerns, and found out how the congressional legislative process works. In the 1970s, she became active in the U.S. women's movement and turned her attention to women's economic condition. She helped found the Women's Equity Action League, which attacked discrimination against women in U.S. economic arrangements.

Global Conditions and Trends

Leaders who want to keep abreast of global conditions and trends can consult reports such as the annual *Human Development Report* issued by the United Nations Development Programme. The report provides comparative information about income, employment, health, literacy, political freedom, and other conditions around the world. Another assessment of the contemporary global picture is the annual *State of the World Report,* available in written and video format, issued by the Worldwatch Institute in Washington, D.C. The United Nations also publishes a catalogue update that announces recent UN reports on global political, social, economic, and technological affairs. The Organization for Economic Cooperation and Development and the World Bank issue numerous reports focusing on national and global economic conditions. Scholarly comparative analyses include *Women and Politics Worldwide* (Nelson & Chowdhury, 1994), *Comparative Politics Today: A World View* (Almond & Powell, 1992), *Handbook of Comparative Public Administration and Development* (Farazmand, 1990), and *Power and Choice* (Shively, 1995). In addition, leaders in the global commons can develop the habit of listening to or reading the analyses of a wide range of international observers, from government officials to academics to advocacy groups. These analyses can be found in books, international journals, newspapers and newscasts, or bulletins on the World Wide Web.

Several interrelated political, social, economic, and technological conditions and trends are prominent in such analyses of the current global context. One overarching condition also is important—the convergence of a number of analyses, sensibilities, and common understandings that put human civilization at an important turning point as a new millenium approaches.

Political Conditions. Nation-states remain important, despite continued erosion of their sovereignty over economic transactions and other matters. Cleveland (1993, pp. 38-39) described how power "leaks" out of national governments from the top, the sides, and the bottom. The continued importance of nations is underlined by the fierce determination of many groups around the world to break away from existing nations and establish their own. Nation-states provide (or hold the promise of) a larger community of shared heritage, purpose, governance, and achievement, a community beyond one's province but smaller than the globe. There are two main implications for leaders in the global commons. First, they usually will have to work with national government officials in some way to resolve the global problem at issue. Second, they will have to take national identity into account. I will discuss working with government officials in the chapter on political leadership; here I want to elaborate on the importance of national identity.

Leaders hoping to bring people together across national boundaries must be attuned to people's identification of their own being and interests with that of their country, or the country they hope to form. Two experiences have helped me understand the strength of national identity and pride (even for people like myself who find much to criticize about their countries). The first experience is working with international fellows visiting the United States, and the second is my own sojourning in the United Kingdom. In the cases of the international fellows, I recall especially the words of one, who said, "When I am in my country I may say many critical things about it. When I am away from my country, I express mainly my pride in it." This man was expressing his sense of attachment to, and psychological investment in, his country. My experience living in the United Kingdom taught me how deeply I am imprinted with my nationality. I realized how much I believed in the "rightness" of U.S. representative democracy (when authentically practiced) and how uncomfortable I was with the very idea of a monarchy, even a constitutional one. At the same time, I understood better, having lived in the United Kingdom, why having a queen and a parliamentary system seemed so right and even necessary to the British majority.

Though nation-states remain important, national political systems and alliances among nations are in considerable flux. As the Soviet Union crumbled in the late 1980s and the Cold War became history, the forces of democratization gained strength throughout the former Soviet empire. Many authoritarian regimes in South America and Asia also gave way to more democratic systems. Democracy is on the upswing throughout the world, as Cleveland (1993) and others have noted. Yet the structures of civil societies needed to sustain democratic practices are often in the early stages of development. As a result, many of the newly democratic regimes are highly imperiled. In addition, in many countries, such as China, the loosening of government control in one sphere is counterbalanced by government repression in another. Democratic governments are under threat from those who want to revive Soviet communism, reinstate military or authoritarian controls, or establish a state based on religious fundamentalism.

These national political trends in a post-Cold War world bring both good news and bad for leadership in the global commons. The good news is that as countries become more democratic, they provide more favorable environments for leadership in the global commons. The bad news is that the triumph of democracy is not assured and that numerous, often violent, ethnic and nationalist clashes have flared up in the ruins of the Soviet empire and old colonial regimes. In the United States, the end of the Cold War, along with rising public concern about domestic social ills such as crime and the national debt, has caused the government to focus inward. U.S. officials will continue to involve themselves in global affairs, but their strongest commitment is to strengthening the U.S. economy, controlling immigration, and supplying an international police force of last resort. The final years of the 20th century are a time when transnational citizen groups can hardly expect to drum up substantial U.S. government assistance for their efforts.

Meanwhile, at the international level, the UN system is attempting to exert more control over conflicts within and among nations and to expand its mechanisms for resolving global problems. The United Nations convenes important forums, such as the 1993 World Conference on Human Rights, in which national government representatives and citizen groups can attempt to define global problems and develop solutions. The General Assembly is an ongoing arena for deciding which of these solutions should become international law, and other

UN bodies serve as courts for sanctioning (however weakly) conduct that violates these laws. (*Basic Facts about the United Nations,* United Nations, 1995, provides an introduction to the United Nations and its specialized agencies.)

Other supranational governance bodies, such as the European Union, the World Bank, and the Organization of American States, also include forums, arenas, and courts that attempt to resolve transnational public problems. Leaders in the global commons should identify and use the parts of the United Nations and other supranational systems that can aid their efforts.

Social Conditions. Leaders in the global commons need to recognize the growing divergence between rich and poor groups around the world. About 1.3 billion of the world's 5.8 billion people live in "absolute poverty" (Crossette, 1995a). The income gap between the world's richest and poorest countries doubled between the mid-1960s and mid-1990s (Crossette, 1995b), and the income of the richest fifth of the world's inhabitants is 150 times that of the poorest fifth (UN Development Programme, 1995). Economic inequality in the United States has been rising since the 1970s. Today, the top fifth have more than 80% of the nation's wealth, a higher percentage than other industrial nations (Bradsher, 1995). In addition, social analysts have noted the emergence of a new worldwide elite of information workers (who will be described further in the section on economic conditions).

What is the effect of the growing gap between the rich and poor? It may be harder and harder for people from rich and poor countries to work together on common problems because their experiences and resources are so disparate. The elite information workers around the world may feel more connected to each other than to workers from their own countries who lack the competencies highly valued in the information age and are struggling to make a living. A crucial challenge for leaders in the global commons is persuading affluent groups that their fate is entwined with the poor and that economic systems must be altered to distribute resources more justly. Also, leaders may need to question their definitions of rich and poor. Is wealth only a matter of income, or should it include property, investments, family support systems, informal exchanges of goods and services, health and education levels, the status of women, volunteer service, and environmental quality? When these other factors are included, a more complete picture emerges of relative poverty and wealth. The Human Development Report published by the UN Development Programme provides such a picture annually.

Leaders in the global commons also confront other pernicious social hierarchies based on gender, ethnicity, religion, sexual orientation, and other characteristics. It is important to recognize that these hierarchies are also changing. For example, the world's women still make up a disproportionate percentage of poor people, yet growing numbers of women also are achieving economic parity with men. As a result, family structures are changing in many countries, rich as well as poor, around the world. Women are more likely to share responsibilities for producing family income with their husbands or to be the primary breadwinners. Women are also more likely to divorce and to have children outside marriage. Women who raise children alone, however, are much more likely to be poor than those who are in a two-parent household (see Bruce, Lloyd, & Leonard, 1995).

In addition to social divisions, the sheer numbers of people and the growth in industrial production increase the need for leadership in the global commons. For 30 years, scientists, citizen activists, religious leaders, and others have raised global awareness that human activities may be exceeding the earth's carrying capacity. Fish stocks are being depleted at a rapid rate, rain forests are being decimated, deserts are spreading, acid rain harms forests in many countries, and air pollution is causing worrisome climate changes. The growing awareness of earth's limits is definitely an asset for leaders seeking to resolve transnational environmental problems. For leaders working on other transnational problems, the need to protect or restore the earth must be a criterion in assessing problem solutions.

Migration to urban centers continues to be a worldwide trend, and many of the world's major cities have become vast megalopolises, increasingly independent of nation-states. In addition, analysts are predicting far-reaching impacts of a "graying globe," or the aging of populations around the world (Kristof, 1996). They foresee heightened intergenerational conflict, overburdened social security systems, and increased immigration of foreign workers into industrialized countries.

Economic Conditions. Global economic integration continues as free-market capitalism advances worldwide, more trade barriers fall (especially within regions), and sophisticated transportation and telecommunications networks facilitate the rapid flow of information, goods, services, and capital from country to country. The goods produced by a country's workers often must compete in a global marketplace. Entrepreneurs hoping to attract investors for their businesses must compete in global financial markets. Indeed, many analysts argue that global financial markets are the most important force affecting a nation's well-being today. Take Mexico's 1995 economic debacle, for example. When the government decided to devalue the peso (finally bringing it in line with its actual purchasing power), foreign investors who had poured their money into peso-denominated Mexican stocks and bonds in the early 1990s rushed to sell off their holdings, thus causing the peso to lose even more value. Facing a devastating cutback in production, employment, and wages and even more loss of foreign investment, the Mexican government desperately sought emergency loans from the U.S. government and other sources. In large part due to a $12.5 billion loan provided by the Clinton administration, the Mexican government avoided economic collapse, but not without severe reductions in most citizens' standard of living.

The most advantaged workers in the global economy are those called information, or knowledge, workers. In what Peter Drucker (1994) called "developed free-market countries," information workers are shoving aside industrial workers who were central to these countries' economies from 1900 to the 1960s. Some industrial workers will still be needed in these countries, but Drucker predicted that by the year 2010, industrial workers in all these countries will account for no more than an eighth of the workforce (p. 56). The rest of the world's countries also must develop a substantial population of knowledge workers, Drucker noted, but this task is daunting. Most of these countries—for example, China, India, and the sub-Saharan African states—"will have to find jobs for millions of uneducated and unskilled young people who are qualified for little except yesterday's blue-collar industrial jobs" (p. 64).

Another important aspect of global economic integration is the rise of the multinational corporation—that is, a corporation with branches in more than one country. The *Economist* (Emmott, 1993), citing UN sources, reported the existence of 35,000 such corporations, a fivefold increase in 20 years. The origins of these firms have also changed. In 1970, over half of the world's multinationals were from the United States and the United Kingdom; in 1993, a little less than half were from the United States, Japan, Germany, and Switzerland. Moreover, multinationals are now originating in countries outside the circle of industrial giants, including what the *Economist* (Emmott, 1993) called the "third world and the industrialising Asian dragons" (p. 6). Although some multinationals fit the popular image of a large corporation with branches throughout the world, many are small, and most are more accurately described as regional rather than global. The *Economist* predicted that this regional orientation would continue and noted that continued multinational expansion depends on the willingness of national governments to continue reducing barriers to cross-border investment.

For leaders in the global commons, global economic integration along capitalist lines has several implications. Any economic arrangements that are vital for solving a transnational public problem are likely to be affected by global market forces and government responses. Many commentators—for example, Daly and Cobb (1989), Mies and Shiva (1993), and Korten (1995), and advocacy groups such as the Minneapolis-based Institute for Agriculture and Trade Policy—worry that the advance of worldwide capitalism, with its pervasive emphasis on profits, growth, and consumption, will widen gaps between the rich and poor, threaten the earth's carrying capacity even further, and foment severe social upheaval. In response, leaders in the global commons can champion appropriate market controls, workplace democracy, credit unions, producer-consumer cooperatives, barter schemes, and other means of enabling workers and citizens to counter the harmful effects of the global economy.

While recognizing that global economic forces create problems, leaders in the global commons also can find opportunities in the global economy. For example, humanitarian organizations such as Oxfam can take advantage of global transportation and telecommunication networks to market goods from crafts cooperatives in low-income communities. Multinational companies, given adequate citizen pressure, may become powerful partners in efforts to resolve public problems, such as apartheid in South Africa. Workers may find common cause across national boundaries. For example, some U.S. steelworkers in recent years have begun forging ties with counterparts in Japan and Brazil.

Technological Conditions. The telecommunications revolution is not over. Computer technology is spreading even to the most isolated and poor countries. The power of both personal and mainframe computers continues to increase, and the price for a given level of computational power continues to drop. The ability to communicate images and words over long distances continues to grow. These technological advances enable leaders in the global commons to communicate with existing and potential supporters around the world, to publicize problems and successes rapidly, and even to organize teleconferences. Nevertheless, the expense of installing and using computer equipment and accessing communications networks can be a barrier that these leaders have to overcome. They also should remember that too much reliance on sophisticated technology may keep them from reaching the technological "have-nots" and cause them to overlook useful but simple technologies.

Leaders in the global commons also should be alert for additional technological developments that assist their efforts. For example, technological breakthroughs may help control environmental damage, feed the hungry, or combat AIDs.

End of the Millenium. Hillel Schwartz (1990) noted that the end of a century, much less a millenium, is an important psychological marker. As the end of an era approaches, fear and foreboding are much in evidence, along with glimmers of optimism. As the current millenium closes, most of the pessimistic assessments about human conditions focus on the massive and unprecedented threat of humans' destructive power, either through nuclear and other weapons or through depletion of the earth's rich resources. Analysts also wonder how human societies can cope with the rapid pace of change that has been unleashed by technological advances. The glimmers of optimism appear in works such as Carl Sagan's *Pale Blue Dot* (1995) or George Land and Beth Jarman's *Breakpoint and Beyond* (1992). Sagan believed that the ability to view the earth from afar as a beautiful, fragile, life-sustaining world without obvious borders among peoples is the key to building worldwide consensus for protecting the earth. Land and Jarman are among those who believe that the understandings of "new sciences," such as quantum physics, both have contributed to the rapid pace of change and offer ways to deal with the pessimists' concerns. New scientists, they argue, have found the keys to how natural systems sustain and renew themselves, and human beings can use this knowledge to renew civilization.

The seers who look toward the next century with foreboding resonate with Heraclitus' aphorism, "Nothing endures but change." They might add that the nature of change itself also changes—that is, its pace has accelerated tremendously. The more optimistic seers, interestingly, resonate more with Alphonse Karr's reminder that the more things change, the more they remain the same. At the end of the millenium, this group is saying that human beings have always been inextricably tied to their natural habitat and that the natural order (which includes evolutionary processes) has always underlain everything that happens on earth and even beyond.

SUMMARY

The founders of Amnesty International and IWRAW exercised leadership in context by aligning their efforts to remedy global public problems with certain political, social, economic, and technological "givens" while taking advantage of political, social, economic, and technological changes. As other leaders begin to work on a transnational public problem, they should seek answers to the following:

- What political systems will affect efforts to solve this problem, and how are those systems changing in the post-Cold War environment?

- What important social forces and systems are at work here? Above all, what cultural differences, social hierarchies, demographic trends, and connections to the natural environment are important?

- What economic forces and systems are important? How does global economic integration affect this problem?

- What technological developments are affecting the social, economic, and political systems identified in the previous questions?

- How is this problem connected to, or affected by, the end of the current millenium?

Leadership in context is one of the two logical starting places for leadership in the global commons. The other is personal leadership, the focus of the next chapter.

CHAPTER 3

Personal Leadership

We ask ourselves, who am I to be brilliant, gorgeous, talented and fabulous? Actually, who are you not to be? You are a child of God.
—Nelson Mandela

Every being cries out to be read differently.
—Simone Weil

There always remains a mystery in each country, in each human being.
—Octavio Paz

Drawing on personal strengths and overcoming personal weaknesses is the heart of personal leadership in the global commons. Probably the best way to start this process is by identifying your deepest passions, cares, or concerns and then listening for the call to public action in the global context. As noted earlier, Peter Benenson and his associates launched Amnesty International because of their passion for human freedom; Arvonne Fraser and Rebecca Cook were passionate champions of women's rights. Each of these people heeded the call to stand up for human rights around the world.

An ethical public passion is a vital asset or strength for anyone seeking to exercise leadership in the global commons. Such passion energizes leaders and helps them endure long struggles to accomplish far-reaching change. It supplies leaders with strong moral authority to counter other types of authority. Aspiring leaders also need to draw on many additional personal strengths, either their own or others'. Moreover, wise leaders recognize or compensate for their own and others' weaknesses so that these weaknesses do not sabotage their leadership work. Thus, leaders should assess their own strengths and weaknesses as well as those of potential collaborators and likely opponents.

Leaders should identify the commonalities that draw potential collaborators together and those personal differences that can foster creativity and goal accomplishment if honored rather than disregarded. In addition, they should identify commonalities among likely collaborators and opponents, even when their differences seem most salient. The commonalities can be the bridge that facilitates communication between the two camps.

Let us consider key personal strengths and weaknesses—for example, education, skills, and connections—that the founders of Amnesty International and IWRAW brought to their leadership work. Then we can turn to methods that can help aspiring leaders to identify their passions, other strengths and weaknesses, and commonalities and differences.

THE FOUNDERS OF AMNESTY INTERNATIONAL

Amnesty International was enduringly shaped by the personal strengths and weaknesses of its founding group. At the group's center was *Peter Benenson,* who was Amnesty president or secretary during the first 5 years. Amnesty cofounders referred to him as charismatic. They said he was "bursting with ideas" (Crane, 1985), a "genius" (Sargent, 1985), "impulsive and warm-hearted" (Sargent, 1985), and, despite health problems, "irrepressible" (Archer, 1986) and "energetic" (Baker, 1983). One colleague (Sargent, 1985) called him the "kindest possible man," yet some cofounders conceded that he could be nearly impossible to work with. These people illuminated what might be called Benenson's shadow side—his tendency to be too demanding, disorganized, and resistant to delegation. One colleague called him "a law unto himself" (Sargent, 1985).

As a schoolboy at Eton in the 1930s, Benenson demonstrated considerable idealism. Like many other young English people at the time, he was politicized by the Spanish Civil War. He even "adopted" an orphaned Basque baby through a program helping victims of the war. Later, as the persecution of Jews in Nazi Germany intensified, he turned his attention to helping Jewish children.

After graduating from Oxford University, he served in the Army during World War II. Once the war was over, he studied law and he set up his own chambers in 1953. He was a strong supporter of the Labour Party and ran unsuccessfully for Parliament.

In the 1940s, Benenson volunteered to serve as observer for Britain's Trade Union Congress at a trial of Spanish Syndicalists in Barcelona. Subsequently, he became deeply involved in efforts to ensure fair trials for defendants whose political views clashed with those endorsed by their governments. This work brought him into contact with other British lawyers interested in civil liberties, and in the mid-1950s, he organized a lawyers' group called Justice, which he hoped would continue the fair trial work and gather suggestions for legal reform.

Benenson's family of origin was well connected but troubled. Both parents were Jewish; the father was a British army officer, and his mother was from Russia. The match was unhappy, and the family's economic fortunes were insecure. His mother became a reformer of employment practices in a British retailing chain and a committed Zionist. Although Benenson's background was Jewish, as a young man he was agnostic; he converted to Catholicism in 1958. He saw his Amnesty work as very much in keeping with Catholic traditions. He claimed as his hero Dietrich Bonhoeffer, a man who lived (and died) by his religious convictions.

Benenson, who was 39 at the time of Amnesty's founding, brought several special skills to his Amnesty work. They included journalistic writing, networking (among former Eton and Oxford classmates, Labour Party acquaintances, lawyers in Britain and elsewhere, and family members), and the ability to speak or understand several languages. He already was knowledgeable about, and actively promoting, the human rights that would be central to Amnesty's mission. He also was inspired by the model of the American Civil Liberties Union.

Eric Baker was a strong partner with Benenson in running Amnesty's affairs in the earliest years, but more of a behind-the-scenes figure. A Quaker from a working-class background, he shared Benenson's moral commitment to helping others. With his wife Joyce, he had been in charge of an educational center in India; later, he was general secretary of the National Peace Council in London. He met Benenson because of their mutual concern about conditions in Cyprus.

Amnesty coworkers describe Baker as tremendously disciplined in organizing his time, as "quiet, a rather diffident man, solid in his faith" (Crane, 1985) and as "a thoroughly good, honest-hearted Quaker" (Sargent, 1985). At the same time, he developed a reputation for having an authoritarian style during the years he headed the British national section of Amnesty.

In addition to these two men, several others served as close advisers and/or fellow organizers in the early years. They included

- *Louis Blom-Cooper,* a lawyer and Labour Party supporter

- *Sean MacBride,* a lawyer and former Irish republican militant who had served in the Irish government and had become, by the time of Amnesty's founding, a European statesman

- *Neville Vincent,* a retired lawyer, interested in penal reform, who was acquainted with Benenson through Labour Party politics

- *Norman Marsh,* a committed supporter of the League of Nations as a student at Oxford who became a lawyer and later was head of the International Commission of Jurists. During the founding of Amnesty, he was director of the British Institute for International and Comparative Law

- *Peter Archer,* a lawyer and member of Justice

- *Tom Sargent,* a Labour Party activist who helped organize Justice and served as its executive secretary for many years

- *Duncan Guthrie,* who served as Amnesty's first treasurer and had previous fundraising experience with another voluntary group

In addition, a small group of women were at the heart of the organization, mainly volunteering their time in the nitty-gritty work of organizing the membership, doing research on prisoners of conscience, and producing publications. Among them were

- *Peggy Crane,* a Labour Party official and freelance journalist

- *Christel Marsh,* who had fled from Germany as a young woman, fearing that she would be persecuted by the Gestapo, which had already arrested her once. She was married to Norman Marsh and was a longtime volunteer worker for Oxfam and other organizations

- *Marlys Deeds,* whose brother had been brought out of Germany in the 1930s as a result of Peter Benenson's work. She was a teacher and volunteer before joining Amnesty. Her husband Leonard Deeds was part of Amnesty's policy-making group in the early years

Two other women played vital supporting roles. *Margaret Benenson,* Peter's wife, paid considerable attention to the social side of Amnesty affairs—for example, organizing dinners at which influential people might be recruited for Amnesty's work. Like her husband, she was a longtime Labour Party activist; she had also been elected to a local council seat in London. *Joyce Baker,* Eric's wife, also backed her husband's causes. She was a teacher and, like her husband, a committed Quaker. Both women managed child care and other household tasks that freed their husbands for devotion to Amnesty work.

Some of the people who launched Amnesty were specifically committed to guaranteeing justice for political prisoners; others were more generally interested in fighting injustice, and Amnesty provided a means of acting on this interest. Amnesty's founders were well educated and strongly connected to the political and legal establishment in England. Several had international experience, and a number had strong religious convictions that undergirded their desire to right worldly wrongs. As founders of what they envisioned as a global movement, their main weakness was their lack of knowledge about the world outside Europe.

Many of Amnesty's founders had also demonstrated courage to challenge powerful institutions and side with those who were unjustly treated. They had the courage to start untried ventures and persist in their efforts. They and those who joined them in Amnesty have needed such courage to proceed when the success of their efforts is never assured. Courage has been especially required for those who undertake missions to confront directly the officials who are ordering or condoning abuses.

IWRAW'S FOUNDERS

In addition to Arvonne Fraser and Rebecca Cook, five other women and one man—Lois Brunott, Jane Connors, Norma Forde, Stephen Isaacs, Silvia Pimentel, and Isabel Plata—provided the critical energy and commitment for launching IWRAW. Fraser and Isaacs served as the organization's codirectors in the early years. They were assisted by Marsha Freeman, who joined the IWRAW staff shortly after it began. Together, these founders represented considerable experience in the global women's movement, international law, and organizational development—experience that contributed immensely to the success of IWRAW.

Arvonne Fraser is often described as outspoken, strong-willed, tough, energetic, charismatic, efficient, and sincere. She is noted for her wide grin and the ease with which she combines the roles of politician, mother, grandmother, feminist, and administrator. Now in her late 60s, she grew up on a Minnesota farm, the oldest of five children. Her father was a political activist, and her mother, who had wanted to be a doctor, "became a schoolteacher and turned her ambitions to her children" (Waldemar, 1983, p. 12).

Fraser became active in Democratic politics while she was a student at the University of Minnesota during the 1940s. During the 1950s, she developed a reputation as a premier political organizer for the party's candidates. In the early 1960s, she moved to Washington, D.C., and began serving as an administrative aide to her husband, Don Fraser, who had been elected to Congress. Through her constituent work, she became more aware of women's economic plight. She also was affected by the beginnings of the contemporary women's movement and became very active in efforts to increase women's political participation and economic security.

She traces her involvement with international women's issues to the years when her husband, who was on the House Foreign Affairs Committee, invited her to accompany him on his official travels. Instead of going along on the usual State Department-organized shopping tours for congressional spouses, she asked that the department set up meetings for her with people in the women's movement. In 1974, she was appointed as a member of the U.S. delegation to the UN Commission on the Status of Women, and in 1975 she attended the International Women's Year Conference in Mexico City as an advisor to the U.S. delegation. In 1976, President Carter appointed her to head the new office of Women and Development in the U.S. Agency for International Development, and she continued in that position until 1981. She returned to Minnesota and began the Women, Public Policy and Development Project at the Humphrey Institute, which she continued to direct after IWRAW's founding.

Along with great accomplishments, Fraser had had great personal tragedy. One daughter was struck and killed by a car, and a second, remorseful over her sister's death, committed suicide.

Rebecca Cook was staff attorney for the Development Law and Policy Program at Columbia University at the time of IWRAW's founding. She had previously worked for International Planned Parenthood. Marsha Freeman described her as "truly an academic" and "personally very committed to women" (interview by author, March 5, 1993).

Lois Brunott, of the Netherlands, had been active in the Dutch feminist movement and had worked for a Dutch development agency. At the time of IWRAW's founding, she was studying for a PhD in law at the University of Maastricht. Fraser said that Brunott's important contributions to IWRAW's work included her knowledge of European and Southeast Asian law, her connections with European institutions and human rights scholars, her "appreciation of theoretical and practical aspects" of IWRAW's work, and her "great sense of humor" (interview by author, May 29, 1996).

Jane Connors was a member of the law faculty at the School of Oriental and African Studies in London and was active in the British women's movement. When asked why she had become active in the women's human rights movement (in my questionnaire; see Appendix B of this book), she commented, "I have always been involved in women's rights. I attended a single-sex school, studied law at [Australian National University], and first started actively working in this area in 1980." Fraser described her as "extremely bright and energetic, learned, and committed" (interview by author, October 15, 1996).

Norma Forde was a member of the law faculty at the University of the West Indies and was most involved in the early planning meetings for IWRAW. Soon after the Nairobi conference, she was elected to the Committee on the Elimination of Discrimination Against Women (CEDAW).

Marsha Freeman was a Minnesota lawyer who had been active in women's professional groups and involved in women's issues. In addition to her law degree, she had a PhD in English.

Stephen Isaacs, a lawyer, was director of the Development Law and Policy Program at Columbia University. He had previously been a consultant for the U.S. Agency for International Development and was knowledgeable about foreign aid, international development, health, and population issues. Fraser said that as IWRAW codirector he demonstrated an aptitude for "being tough about money" and organizing meetings that brought people together from around the world and kept them focused on women's legal rights (interview by author, October 15, 1996).

Silvia Pimentel, a lawyer, was a veteran Brazilian feminist and political activist and a founding member of the National Council of Women in Brazil. "She is so passionate about women's rights," commented Fraser. "She is very charismatic, energetic, outspoken, tremendously well organized. She always has a million things to do" (interview by author, November 10, 1992).

Isabel Plata, a Colombian lawyer, worked in Profamilia, Colombia's major family planning organization. In addition to her law degree, she had a master's degree from Southern Methodist University. Fraser described her as "pragmatic, intelligent, creative, open, willing to disagree. . . . She is a democrat with a small d, yet she is very sophisticated and an internationalist." Partly because she has studied in the United States and speaks English very well, "she is a thoughtful bridge between North and South America" (interview by author, November 6, 1992).

Like Amnesty's founders, the founders of IWRAW had elite status. They were in the middle or upper classes of their societies. They were highly educated, and almost all were lawyers. As a group, they had extensive experience in the global women's movement at the local to global level. Thus, they brought to IWRAW rich organizational affiliations, comparable to those that Peter Benenson and his colleagues brought to Amnesty.

IWRAW's eight women founders seem to have developed a passion for women's rights because of their own experience of being discriminated against, their direct involvement with poor or abused women, or their sense of gender solidarity and power. Fraser, for example, became acutely aware of U.S. women's second-class status when she handled constituent requests in her husband's congressional office. As she tried to help women constituents obtain government benefits or services, she realized that women were being treated unfairly. Jane Connors' commitment to women's rights was rooted in her education at schools exclusively for young women.

IWRAW's founders also had demonstrated the courage to endure the ridicule and resistance of those who opposed women's rights. For example, championing family planning in a Catholic-dominated country such as Colombia, as Isabel Plata had done, was highly courageous.

ADDITIONAL RESOURCES AND GUIDANCE FOR PERSONAL LEADERSHIP IN THE GLOBAL COMMONS

Most of the people involved in establishing Amnesty International and IWRAW had considerable personal assets, such as international experience and political connections, for leadership in the global commons. This section will explore how we, at any stage of leadership development, can assess and expand our personal capacities for exercising leadership in the global commons. The Greek aphorism "Know thyself" is a sure guide, but the goal is not self-knowledge that simply enables us to be strong individuals. The goal is self-knowledge as a path for understanding the human condition and relating to other people.

A starting place for personal leadership is recognizing and assessing our public policy passions and considering how those passions call us to action in the global commons. Next, we can do formal and informal assessments of our strengths and weaknesses for exercising leadership around our policy passions. Finally, we can consider how these strengths and weaknesses are sources of commonality and difference. That is, how do they connect us to some people and separate us from others?

Discovering Passions

By the time they founded Amnesty International and IWRAW, most of the men and women introduced in the previous two sections had clearly identified their public policy passions and responded to the call to leadership arising from the gap between the social conditions they desired and the current reality. Many of us, however, may still need to discover or recover our passions in order to know what leadership work is calling us. I will suggest two simple exercises for clarifying personal passions, concerns, and cares. Both exercises require some means of recording your reflections. Thus, you will need a journal, notebook, computer, tape recorder, or video camera. And you will need distraction-free time to focus on the exercises. (Other helpful exercises can be found in the section on "personal mastery" in *The Fifth Discipline Fieldbook,* by Senge, Kleiner, Roberts, Ross, & Smith, 1994.)

Cares Exercise. Begin by answering the question, "What do I care about in my family, occupational, and community life?" The more specific your answers can be, the better. You also can begin generally and move to specifics. In the family category, you might jot down "a satisfying partnership with a loving spouse" and then develop a picture of what you mean by "satisfying partnership." In the occupational category, you might answer "work that makes the world a better place" and elaborate from there, depending on your profession or skills. For example, if you are a journalist drawn to environmental reporting, your elaboration might include "Use my reporting skills and access to information to wake up my fellow citizens to environmental destruction." Turning to community, you might say, "a peaceful neighborhood," a "world without war," "decent schools for children," "equal opportunities," or "an end to poverty" and then explain what, for example, a peaceful neighborhood or equal opportunity means to you.

So far, I have suggested only selfless or otherwise admirable responses to the question about cares. What if an answer is blatantly self-serving, destructive, or just morally ambiguous? No matter what the answer is, you should assess the ethical implications of what you want. Most of us have a set of moral precepts, grounded in philosophy or religion, for making such an assessment. I also recommend an assessment based on the main ethical categories identified by Robert Terry in *Authentic Leadership* (1993) and consisting of the following questions about your passion:

- Does it affirm human existence and development, as well as ecological diversity and survival?

- Does it help ensure that everyone has the necessities of living and is allowed to fulfill his or her potential?

- Does it affirm fairness, especially in the distribution of resources?

- Does it affirm every member's participation in the decisions that shape a group or society?

- Does it affirm care, respect, and forgiveness toward oneself and others?

- Does it promote personal responsibility and promote a thriving future for the earth and its inhabitants?

The process of answering these questions can help you understand the moral basis of your cares. It also can help you revise or discard cares that will not survive ethical scrutiny.

For the cares that pass ethical muster, ask: What is the extent of my commitment to acting on these cares? Is there a gap between what I really care about and how I spend my time? Your answers to these questions may reveal that the passions you identified are truly central to your life. Or they may alert you to a disparity between your espoused values and your behavior and lead you to reexamine what you espouse or how you behave. It is possible that the way you are spending your time, or how you are longing to spend your time, will reveal hidden passions.

Personal Credo. Another way of getting in touch with one's cares, concerns, and interests is a variation on an exercise recommended by Kouzes and Posner (1993). Simply draft a page-long memo outlining your personal credo. The memo should trumpet, "This I believe." It is your guide for living, what you think is worth doing, how people should relate to each other, and what gives you joy. The memo can be directed to coworkers, your family, yourself, or other audiences.

Like the cares exercise, this one may highlight a discrepancy between your values and your behavior. It also may prompt personal reexamination and reordering of your priorities.

Commitment and Calling. Whether you do the cares exercise or draft your personal credo, you are likely to benefit from sharing the results with someone you trust—a friend, family member, colleague, or mentor. This step can make your cares or your credo more real; telling about your concerns and values is an act of commitment to them. Engaging someone else in dialogue about your passions also may give you new insights. In case you feel that some of your passions are too personal for sharing, you can talk about them in general terms or reserve them for solitary reflection.

Next comes another question: How do these passions summon you to leadership? With this question, we make the transition from personal to public policy passions. For example, a woman's personal desire to be treated as a full-fledged human being in her family, workplace, or community can awaken her to the necessity and potential of working with other people to remove the barriers that thwart women's development. My own passions for doing worthwhile work and for giving my children a secure future have called me to use my writing and teaching skills to help other people be leaders.

Finally, we should ask: How do our passions summon us to leadership in the global commons? The global connection may be obvious or obscure. A man in Rwanda may deeply desire peace for his village. He knows, however, that international weapons suppliers (including foreign governments) are keeping local paramilitary groups well armed. He cannot place direct pressure on those suppliers, but transnational peace and human rights groups can mobilize global public opinion against them and help persuade governments to change their policies. The Rwandan man can easily see the logic of working, covertly if necessary, with the global human rights community to achieve his desires.

The global connection may be less obvious for a woman who simply wants to be paid as well as the men who do the same job she does. As she becomes involved in efforts to reform her particular workplace, however, she may realize that a reform campaign could draw on women's organizations from the local to global levels. She may extend her own activism to these other organizations. Arvonne Fraser was concerned about helping women who came to her husband's office with various problems; that concern led her to broader analysis of U.S. women's economic condition, which in turn fueled her campaigns to reform the U.S. Social Security system and other economic arrangements. Her involvement in the U.S. women's movement and her travels helped her see connections between the fight for women's rights in the United States and other places in the world. Isabel Plata's primary cause has been giving Colombian women access to family planning and legal services, but she also contributed to the international women's movement.

Sometimes the call to leadership seems to arise less from a clear sense of one's passions than from an immediate need for action. Perhaps you have never given water pollution much attention, but if an oil spill happens on the coast near your home, you may feel called to rally your neighbors to combat the spill's harmful effects and may even join global efforts to prevent oil spills. In such a case, your response to the need reveals a passion you could hardly have suspected.

Soulwork. Until now, I have concentrated on the energizing and liberating effect of identifying our passions. The process can also be frightening and frustrating. What if I care about one thing and build my life around something else? What if I really care about a cause that is unpopular, dangerous, and financially draining? What if my devotion to a cause is undermining my health or taking a toll on those around me (as was true of Peter Benenson's devotion to Amnesty)? The converse situation is being unable to identify any real passion at all. What do I do when I try to get in touch with my passions and find only shallow concerns or none at all? What if my passions are obviously destructive? Spirituality, or what I call "soulwork," can help us deal with fear arising from passions, a paucity of passion, and even unsavory passions.

What do I mean by *soul*? Like Bolman and Deal (1995), I think of it as an internal force sustaining meaning and hope, as one's deep center. This internal center is connected to the creative spirit of the universe that is called by different names in different religions. This personal core is a place where concerns of the ego, certainly one's ephemeral passions, disappear. Yet, as Bolman and Deal (1995) said, it also is the place we experience the "rapture of being alive" (p. 57). It is both temporal and eternal (Moore, 1992). The soul is the well of wisdom, love, courage, and compassion that is essential to leadership. Soulwork is the path to the integrity of character and commitment to service championed by so many contemporary proponents of leadership (e.g., Covey, 1991; Kouzes & Posner, 1993; Luke, 1994).

The purpose of soulwork is to find and stay in touch with this deep center, or inner core, and thus to be in touch with the creative spirit that sustains the world and our own creative and imaginative power. Though soulwork can be thought of as a spiritual journey, it is not about separating from the mundane, material world. As Moore (1992) and Carse (1995) suggested, it is seeking the mysterious in the ordinary. It is experiencing our unity or connection with the humblest object, as well as the most dazzling. It is not about leaving the earth but about knowing deeply the cycles of earthly life. It is about releasing our desire to laugh and cry about the human condition.

Recognizing that people are attached to many different spiritual traditions or none at all, I hesitate to suggest a "correct" spiritual path for anyone. There are, however, several essential practices recommended by sages from a variety of traditions: undertaking the spiritual quest or journey, engaging in reflection, confronting paradox and shadow, and "killing the Buddha."

As Baldwin (1990) stated, everyone is on a *spiritual journey.* The challenge is to realize it. Terry (1993) believes that this awareness is triggered by "some limit or possibility" (p. 60), such as major illness, death, birth, failure, great triumph, or neurosis, that makes us question the meaning of life. At such times, much of what we take for granted is stripped away, or we lose interest in it; we can more easily feel the stirrings of our own souls. In response, we may embark on outward or inward quests—that is, our personal heroic work (see Campbell, 1949; Murdock, 1990; Pearson, 1986).

Engaging in *reflection* is the requisite discipline for the spiritual journey. Reflection, basically, is taking the time to consider what we are learning about our true selves from our inner and outer explorations. Many spiritual advisers recommend going on retreats (one of Peter Benenson's practices) or spending time in natural settings where we can more easily sense nature's rhythms. We may benefit from joining retreats offered by our religious traditions; we may spend several days or much longer with Catholic sisters, Buddhist monks, or a medicine man or woman. We may simply spend a few days alone at the seashore or in the mountains. We may begin or end every day with a period of prayer or meditation.

Keeping a journal can also help. In a journal, we can record our questions, spiritual struggles, our dreams, our insights, and our new commitments. Many guides to journal keeping are available. Baldwin's *Life's Companion: Journal Writing as a Spiritual Quest* (1990) is my favorite for compiling a written journal.

So far I have emphasized solitude as an aid to reflection. Contact with other people can also help. In conversation, perhaps about a journal entry, we may extend our insights; our souls may emerge in a flash, like a trout coming swiftly to the pond's surface in pursuit of a fly. Moore (1992) noted, "Soul is revealed in attachment, love, and community, as well as in retreat on behalf of inner communing and intimacy" (p. xi).

Spirituality is full of *paradox,* calling us, for example, to face the coexistence and fundamental connection of life and death, and to see the humor in absurd events. A central paradox of the spiritual journey is that with all its connotations of action, the journey succeeds only if the person making it rests—that is, takes the time for reflection and relaxing into meditation. Lao-tzu asks:

> Do you have the patience to wait
> till your mud settles and the water is clear?
> Can you remain unmoving
> till the right action arises by itself?
> (Mitchell, 1988, No. 15)

When the water is clear, we also may see some things we do not like. We may see our own obsessions, harmful attachments, and fears protruding from the muck. We may see, for example, an overweening desire to succeed or save the world; we may see our devices for warding off death, failure, and vulnerability— devices such as a tough attitude, drug dependency, overcrowded schedules, or abusive behavior. The muck is likely to include all those objectionable things I can so easily see in other people and so seldom see in myself. Jesus had powerful imagery for this: "Why beholdest thou the mote that is in thy brother's eye, but considerest not the beam that is in thine own eye?" (Matt. 7:3).

The beams in our own eyes usually are hidden in *shadow* unless we find ourselves in trouble. Maybe someone challenges our tough attitudes, maybe we get picked up for drunk driving, maybe our overcrowded schedules get completely out of hand. We get a glimpse of what is in shadow, and we can choose—either to fortify our defenses or to pursue self-knowledge.

This is not an appeal for perfection. Getting rid of our obsessions can become a new obsession. Simply examining an obsession may cause it to lose its power and magnitude and to shrink at least to mote size. As we realize that it was a means of covering up or denying our own mortality, weakness, or need for love, we may accept those things and move on to the business of crafting our best gifts to offer humankind (Becker, 1973). The parable *Pigs Eat Wolves* by Zen master Charles Bates (1991) is a playful guide for confronting both paradox and shadow.

Carse (1995) also warned us against becoming so devoted to a spiritual discipline or ritual that it becomes an end in itself and subverts our spiritual journeys. He cited the admonition "If you meet the Buddha on the road, kill him" to remind us that our preconceived ideas and methods may need to be jettisoned as we advance.

Releasing Charisma

An especially soulful leader, Nelson Mandela (1994), has suggested that the fear most hidden in shadow is not what we might expect. Consider this passage from his 1994 speech at his inauguration as president of South Africa:

> Our deepest fear is not that we are inadequate. Our deepest fear is that we are powerful beyond measure. It is our light, not our darkness, that most frightens us. We ask ourselves, who am I to be brilliant, gorgeous, talented and fabulous? Actually, who are you *not* to be? You are a child of God. Your playing small doesn't serve the world. There is nothing enlightened about shrinking so that other people won't feel insecure around you. We are born to manifest the glory of God that is within us. It's not just in some of us; it's in everyone. And as we let our own light shine, we unconsciously give other people permission to do the same. As we are liberated from our own fear, our presence automatically liberates others.

Basically, Nelson Mandela is saying that each of us has a touch of charisma, or divine grace. We release it by letting go of our fear of it.

Assessing Other Strengths and Weaknesses

We already have considered a crucial personal asset for leadership in the global commons: a commitment to some policy passion, accompanied by an awareness of its global implications and by soulwork to clarify and sustain the passion and probe personal shadows. For the person who has made this commitment—whether or not the policy passion is well defined—the question now becomes, "What is my capacity for exercising leadership around this passion?" More specifically: What is my preferred style of learning and lead-ing? What competencies do I have? What stimulates and hampers my courage? Am I sufficiently optimistic? Who will support or oppose my leadership work? How successful am I in achieving balance? How is my leadership affected by my gender, ethnicity, nationality class, sexual orientation, religion, age, and physical ability? Simply answering these questions can boost one's leadership capacity because the answers often reveal many previously unrecognized strengths. They also reveal where people called to leadership need additional training, supports, or new approaches.

There are many approaches and methods for assessing and developing one's capacity to inspire and mobilize other people to pursue a worthy goal. I will describe three that have been well received in leadership programs I have conducted for midcareer learners from throughout the world. Then I will suggest several questions for further assessment.

Myers-Briggs Type Indicator (MBTI). Based on a psychological framework derived from Jungian theory (see Myers, 1980), this instrument helps its users identify their preferred ways of taking in and evaluating information, relating to self and others, and organizing time. The framework emphasizes four major psychological scales: sensing-intuiting, thinking-feeling, extraversion-introversion, and judging-perceiving. The MBTI consists of numerous questions designed to reveal where a respondent falls on each scale. My own responses, for example, alert me to several strengths. I have an ability to mediate between those who base their decisions on analysis and logic and those who place concern for others at the core of their decision making. I have a strong capacity to discern patterns, to see the big picture. I am energized and stimulated by being with groups of people, and I am fairly attentive to schedules and deadlines. The test alerts me to related weaknesses. For example, I resist making decisions mainly on the basis of logic and analysis and can become so concerned about the impact of my decisions on people that I become very burdened by the decision-making process and my sense of responsibility for others.

The MBTI has been used for everything from choosing a career to choosing a mate. Its main usefulness for leadership development is identifying one's preferred styles of learning and leading.

Leadership Highs and Lows. The leadership highs and lows exercise (see directions in Appendix C) provides a picture or graph of one's leadership experiences over time. Using a time line, you chart your successes and failures, the "peaks" and the "pits," from the time you first became involved in leadership work. The starting point might be your elementary or high school days, young adulthood, or even midlife.

Once your leadership experiences are recorded, you can add major personal events to the chart and indicate whether and to what extent they were personal highs or lows. Using the completed chart, identify common themes connecting the highs, common themes connecting the lows, and relationships between events in your personal life and your leadership.

Either alone or in conversation with someone else, explore what this exercise tells you about your leadership. For example, you might realize that you have been most successful when you were working with a strong team, or when you had significant authority, or when you were able to start something new. You might realize that your successes have grown in some way from your responses to the failures. You might see that triumphs in your personal life have helped you deal with leadership failures or, conversely, that you have compensated for personal problems through public accomplishments.

It may be especially helpful to spend time analyzing the lows. Leadership consultant and colleague Lonnie Helgeson believes that the most important question for people who want to improve their leadership is: Where do I habitually run into difficulties in my dealings with other people? Answering this question as honestly and thoroughly as possible is yet another way of revealing one's shadow side, of understanding how one's greatest strength can all too easily become a decided weakness.

Stories of Courage. Telling stories about our courageous actions can help us realize, first of all, that we are courageous. It also can deepen our understanding of what prompts and sustains courage. This storytelling is beneficial as a group exercise. The act of telling one's story may require courage; one person's story may trigger another's; audience feedback can give the teller additional perspectives on the story.

Here is the exercise I recommend. In advance, ask participants to think about a time they were courageous. Ask someone in the group to prepare to tell a traditional or mythological story of courage. My favorite is the Russian tale of Vasalisa, told by Clarissa Pinkola Estés in *Women Who Run With the Wolves* (1992). Religious and cultural traditions are full of such stories; for this exercise, the important thing is to choose one that appeals to the teller and can be told in 10 minutes or less.

Open the exercise with the telling of the traditional or mythological story and invite group dialogue about the sources, practice, and effects of courage in the story. Next, invite each participant to tell his or her story of courage. Give the group a chance to respond after each presentation. Conclude with group comments on common themes in the stories and new learning about courage. Following the exercise, each participant can write a journal entry or "memo to self" assessing his or her capacity for courage based on previous experiences and available supports.

Here is an illustration of the insights this exercise can generate. An English-speaking journalist from Cameroon participating in this exercise told the story of her battle to gain admission to a university journalism program despite discrimination against English-speaking applicants. She was harassed and her family threatened, but she persisted and finally triumphed. As she discussed her story with the others participating in the exercise, her listeners realized that her very personal fight was an exercise in leadership because of the example and opportunity that it provided other English-speaking applicants who followed her.

As noted earlier, soulwork also fosters courage. Terry (1993) recommended several additional methods of promoting this vital element of leadership. They include writing "exit cards" (i.e., permission to leave a situation) and participating in "boundary experiences," such as outdoor challenges.

Further Capacity Assessment and Development

The insights about leadership strengths and weaknesses generated by the MBTI and the leadership highs and lows exercise can be augmented by answering questions about learning, optimism, authority, personal supports and affiliations, commitment to balance, and status in social hierarchies. The questions will be posed as a means of self-assessment. They can be rephrased and used for gathering other people's insights about one's leadership strengths and weaknesses, thus obtaining a much fuller assessment.

Many modern leadership gurus—for example, Warren Bennis (1989), Stephen Covey (1991), and James Kouzes and Barry Posner (1993)—argue that a fundamental competency for leaders is *continual learning.* With an attitude of curiosity and openness to new information, leaders use formal and informal education to gain the knowledge and skills vital to their leadership work. As an example, formal legal training contributed to the leadership of many Amnesty and IWRAW founders. Arvonne Fraser's experience organizing political campaigns gave her training in fundraising and political strategizing that was probably more valuable for her IWRAW work than all of her college courses put together. Much of the formidable political skill that Sean MacBride brought to Amnesty was the result of his involvement in Irish revolutionary politics from birth onward. Many of the IWRAW leaders received formal education in foreign countries; Amnesty and IWRAW founders received some cross-cultural training through their foreign travel.

It is important to focus on emotional as well as logical intelligence (Goleman, 1995). Leaders must learn to recognize and appropriately express their own emotions, exercise emotional self-discipline, and understand and respond to the views and feelings of diverse others.

Remember too that one's education can be a hindrance. Formal legal training may have prepared many IWRAW leaders to perform well in the courtroom, but it separated them from the poor women they sought to serve. Peter Benenson gained valuable training and connections from being active in Labour politics, but the Labour connection was a liability in his efforts to ensure Amnesty was strictly nonpartisan.

Leaders also must be willing to learn about themselves. As Kets de Vries (1993) pointed out, leaders, especially those with considerable power, all too easily succumb to exaggerated self-confidence, pride, and arrogance unless they cultivate loving self-criticism and tolerance of frank feedback from others.

A useful method of continual learning is what Terry (1993) called "bumping." Any situation in which our preconceptions bump against something that doesn't fit, that brings us up short, is an opportunity for learning. Terry urged us to explore these "bumps" in order to move out of ethnocentrism and expand our knowledge of the world.

For assessing your own leadership capacity, ask: How does my formal and informal training (especially in cross-cultural communication) help or hinder me in exercising leadership around my policy passion? Do I seek and accept frank feedback from others?

Without a certain amount of *optimism,* leaders cannot hope to inspire others to undertake the risky business of combatting the status quo. Leaders need optimism tempered with reality—the "flexible optimism" endorsed by Kouzes and Posner (1993) or the "pragmatic idealism" recommended by Collins and Porras (1994). The MBTI, the leadership highs and lows exercise, or the courage exercise can help us develop a realistic (and often surprising) view of our own strengths and thus increase our optimism about what we can do. Seligman (1991) offered additional advice for assessing and developing realistic optimism.

For assessing your leadership capacity, ask: Do I have and convey a generally positive outlook and a realistic optimism about the possibility of people working successfully together on their common concerns?

Heifetz (1994) identified *authority* as a crucial asset for leaders as they attempt to engage citizens in tackling important problems. Authority can come from many sources, including one's position in a family, a craft, a profession, an organization, or a community. Moral authority is especially important. As exemplified by Nelson Mandela, moral authority is rooted in soulwork and demonstrated integrity, or trustworthiness—that is, consistency between one's espoused moral values and behavior. Conversely, moral authority is destroyed by evidence that someone is not living up to accepted moral standards. Leaders may restore their lost moral authority by engaging in public acts of repentance and atonement.

For assessing your own leadership capacity, ask: What sources and amounts of personal authority can I apply to my leadership work?

Leaders need *supportive spouses, other family members, friends, colleagues, and mentors* to bolster their spirits, share their burdens, augment their resources, serve as role models, and offer reality checks. Jane Connors, for example, noted that her husband, by handling most of the domestic work in her household, frees her to work for women's rights. Arvonne Fraser's parents encouraged her to go to college and support herself.

Although working directly with a mentor is most helpful, we can be mentored by the example of people we know mainly through stories, books, movies, and such. We may think of these people as our heroes or heroines. Dietrich Bonhoeffer was such a person for Peter Benenson. Isabel Plata cited Madame Curie, Rigoberta Menchu Tum, Emma Goldman, Simone de Beauvoir, and Virginia Woolf as her heroines.

For assessing your own leadership capacity ask: Who among my family, friends, and colleagues can be counted on to support or oppose me in this work? Who can mentor me? Are there people whose example I can follow even if I can't work with them directly?

Many of today's leadership analysts—for example, Stephen Covey (1991), Sally Helgeson (1990), and Ronald Heifetz (1994)—urge leaders to *balance* their devotion to jobs or public causes with attention to family, spiritual life, or other forms of renewal and recreation. These other engagements actually help leaders find energy, insight, and courage to sustain their public work. Janet Kelly Moen (1995), who studied women leaders in Norway, emphasized that balancing public work and family demands is a necessity for most women leaders, bringing difficulties along with the advantages.

Of course, striving for balance can become burdensome, especially if we seek some perfect time allocation for all these categories. Playfulness is needed, as suggested by an Irish friend of mine, whose motto is "Moderation in all things, including moderation."

For assessing your own leadership capacity, ask: What engagements and attachments do I have to balance my involvement with public work? How do they help and hinder my leadership?

Our place in the various *social hierarchies,* or structures of power difference, dramatically affects our ability to inspire and mobilize other people. Thus, it is important to locate ourselves in at least the major hierarchies—gender, class or caste, ethnicity, nationality, religion, sexual orientation, physical ability, and age—in order to clarify the leadership assets and liabilities associated with our positions.

It might seem that the assets would be concentrated at the top of the hierarchies. Certainly, being in a society's dominant gender or class or ethnic group would give an aspiring leader some advantage in trying to influence decision makers in those groups. Higher status might also provide protection. Arvonne Fraser recalled a story that Farida Shaheed, a Pakistani sociologist and IWRAW activist, told her. Farida Shaheed was trying to persuade another Pakistani woman to join a demonstration. The woman told her, "I can't join this. I'll probably get arrested, wind up in jail, get raped, and my family will hate me. If you do it, you probably won't be arrested, and your family will support you" (interview by author, December 1992).

Being part of an oppressed group can also cause us to internalize negative stereotypes that dominant groups have affixed to our group. These internalized stereotypes can be a definite liability in our leadership work unless we uproot them by claiming the strengths of our group, acknowledging the pain the stereotypes have caused us, and confronting the sexism, racism, or other oppressive systems that nurture the stereotypes. (Writers in Anzaldúa's *Making Face, Making Soul/Haciendo Caras,* 1990, have especially powerful insights about casting off the negative stereotypes attached to us because of our gender, ethnicity, class, or sexual orientation.)

Being at the top of social hierarchies also has its liabilities. Certainly, the middle- to upper-class status of Amnesty and IWRAW founders had its advantages, but it was a barrier to their connecting with poor people. It also is important to recognize some fluidity and complexity in these categories: For example, one's class may change over time, and one's age certainly does. Arvonne Fraser was from a farming background but became a part of the white-collar middle class. By the time she helped found IWRAW, she was at home with the economic and political elites in her country, but she could turn to her farming roots to connect with women living in rural areas around the world.

For assessing your own leadership capacity, ask: How is my gender an asset and a liability in this leadership work? (Repeat this question, substituting *ethnicity, nationality, class or caste, religion, sexual orientation, age,* and *physical ability* for *gender.*)

Understanding Commonality and Difference

So far, this chapter has focused on self-understanding. Leaders in the global commons also need to understand other people, especially those they hope to lead. Such understanding flows from recognizing the inherent tension, in all human relationships, between commonality and difference.

All human beings have much in common. We are natal, mortal, sentient meaning makers dependent on other human beings and the earth's resources. At the same time, as philosopher Simone Weil reminded us, we have many differences stemming from our life experiences and our biological and social heritage. Each of us has more in common with some groups than with others by virtue of our upbringing, occupation, gender, ethnicity, education, or some other characteristic or experience. Moreover, each person is unique, a singular product of his or her genetic endowment and socialization.

How do we figure out what we have in common with others and where we differ? How can we appreciate the differences, even as we recognize our inability to fathom what Octavio Paz calls the mystery in each human being?

Moreover, how do we understand each other across the especially powerful divides of gender, class, ethnicity, and the like? When these divides are rationales for the domination of one group by another, this understanding is especially difficult. It is often harder for people in a dominant group to gain insights about people from the group being dominated. The assumptions and preferred methods of the dominant group are everywhere in evidence. The less powerful group may actively resist being understood by outsiders because they fear that such understanding will be used to keep them down.

I will suggest several methods for understanding commonalities and differences while remembering the powerful limitations on such understanding. Time is the main necessary resource in all the methods, except travel to other countries, which can be very expensive.

The Passions and Highs and Lows Exercises. The previously discussed exercises for discovering passions and assessing leadership capacity can highlight commonalities and differences. For example, two people who talk together after the passions exercise may find that they share a particular public passion but that the source of the passion is different. A woman who engages in soulwork and assesses her strengths and weaknesses may see that she has some of the qualities she admires in her heroes as well as some of the qualities she deplores in others. This kind of self-knowledge, Gordon Allport (1954) suggested, is likely to make a person more tolerant of others.

As I share my Myers-Briggs scores with a partner, I may find that we are both strong on feeling but that one of us is a sensor and the other an intuitor. Two women might do the highs and lows exercise and find that becoming mothers temporarily set back their leadership work. But one of them may have a chronic illness that permanently altered her leadership calling and opportunities.

Two men who do the highs and lows exercise may have had leadership successes in very different realms but may feel an immediate bond because both have been deeply wounded by the loss of a parent. When a group of men and women talk together about acts of courage, they may discover that the men are afraid of things the women face fearlessly and that the women are afraid of things the men hardly notice. Or their stereotypes may be dispelled by learning that a woman is afraid of relationships and a man afraid of public speaking.

Respectful Conversation. One of the most obvious ways to understand other people is through extended, respectful conversation with them. "Active listening," which I will describe more fully in the next chapter, is important in all cases. When there are strong power differences among the conversation partners, the setting should be one in which the less powerful feel safe. For example, the conversation might be on their turf. More time might be allocated to the less powerful; it probably will be helpful if the more powerful explain at the outset their motives for engaging in the conversation.

People with less power may grow very tired of educating the more powerful. Women may grow tired of explaining women's perspectives to men. A black South African may feel less than eager to educate Afrikaners about black Africans' views. It is important, for this reason alone, to supplement conversation with the other methods described here.

Insights Into Prejudice and Stereotypes. Psychologists explain that human beings often negatively stereotype people they see as *other*—that is, part of an unfamiliar group. Negative stereotypes are rooted in humans' need to simplify information and feel secure and satisfied with our groups. Sometimes stereotypes have a more positive cast—for example, the idea among many European Americans that Asian Americans are high achievers in school. (Further exploration of the psychological roots of stereotyping can be found in Allport, 1954, and Stephan, 1985.)

Social historian Barbara Fields (1992) argued that prejudice against a particular group is often consciously exacerbated by those who seek to exploit the group. Indeed, she argued that the very concept of race as we know it in the United States today grew out of European settlers' need to rationalize enslavement of Africans.

Intercultural Education. Formal, interactive instructional programs called intercultural sensitizers can help us break down stereotypes about people from other cultural or ethnic groups. These programs can help us learn how to interpret correctly the behavior of people from a different culture. (Psychologist Rosita Albert, 1983, elaborated on the use of intercultural sensitizers in her chapter in the *Handbook of Intercultural Training.*)

Even informal role-playing or perspective-taking exercises can help us understand other groups. For example, if you are an intuitor, try responding to a situation or a problem in the way you think a sensor would. If you are a middle-class person, try calculating how you would survive on a poor person's income.

To some extent, intercultural sensitizers help participants move from rigid and negatively inaccurate stereotypes to flexible, more accurate stereotypes. We must remember that any individual is more complex than a Myers-Briggs profile, that no individual purely reflects the habits of his or her culture, and that some people are aberrations in their own cultures.

Intercultural Cooperation. Organizing or joining an intercultural group working on a common project can help break down one's stereotypes about the groups represented. It is important, however, to create conditions that favor cooperation within the group. For example, group members should be of roughly equal status and competence. The convenor or the group should establish norms that support cooperation. Stephan (1985, p. 643) presented additional means of fostering cooperation in intercultural groups.

Travel. Spending extended time on other people's turf can help us understand them better. If that turf is in a distant country, this method can be quite expensive, but the payoff in multilevel learning will be considerable. Short of (and in addition to) literally traveling to foreign places, those who want to increase their understanding of other cultures and other worlds can host foreign visitors and draw insights from personal essays, novels, firsthand accounts, films, or other creative forms.

SUMMARY

The prime task of personal leadership in the global commons is discovering one's passions, listening to the call for leadership, and exploring possible global connections. Public passions are clarified, sustained, and moderated by soul-work. A second task of personal leadership in the global commons is assessing and developing one's capacity for exercising leadership around a chosen passion. Important facets of personal leadership capacity are one's style of learning and leading, continuous education, courage, optimism, supports, balance, and position in social hierarchies. Self-understanding opens the door for a third task of personal leadership: understanding commonalities and differences among various people to be affected by one's leadership work.

This chapter has described many methods for accomplishing these tasks. The next chapter will examine how leaders can build on understanding themselves and diverse others to assemble strong teams.

CHAPTER 4

Team Leadership

Can you love people and lead them without imposing your will?
—Lao-tzu

A big part of love is caring enough to find out what really matters to others.
—Lee Bolman and Terrence Deal

The imagery of effective teams is varied. We could think of a team of Clydesdales—well-trained and disciplined animals harnessed together, performing their assigned task. We could think of a soccer team—again well trained and disciplined, task focused, but with more individuality, more artistry. Different members play different positions and contribute different skills. New opponents and new conditions bring fresh challenges that require team members to engage in ongoing problem solving and mutual adjustment. We could think of a group of improvisational actors, perhaps in the streets of Calcutta or in London's Covent Garden, who use their discipline, individual skill, and most of all their close attunement to each other and the audience to create new entertainment each time they perform.

Teams that come together to undertake the hard work of policy change in the global commons are probably most like the acting troupe. Team members must be disciplined and must contribute individual skills to their common task. They thrive in an atmosphere of trust and empathy based on close attunement to each other and a wider audience of people connected with the problems that concern them. Most importantly, they must develop strong relationships that help them generate and carry out responses to the policy passion that energizes them. Drawing on discipline, skill, attunement, and strong relationships, they are continually improvising to accommodate unpredictable developments outside and inside the team. To build this kind of team, leaders must pay attention to three dimensions—group cohesion, individual satisfaction, and task achievement (Johnson & Johnson, 1994). All three dimensions will be enhanced by skillful recruitment, communication, empowerment, and leadership development of all team members.

Let us consider each of these aspects of team leadership using examples from Amnesty International and IWRAW. The founders of Amnesty International and IWRAW built teams that effectively translated their passion for global human rights into concrete initiatives for beneficial change. Neither the Amnesty nor IWRAW teams practiced all aspects of good team leadership, but they adopted enough of them to accomplish their main mission.

RECRUITMENT

In assembling teams to tackle a global problem, leaders should use their understanding of self and others to recruit people who share their passion, provide needed skills and other assets, and are able to work cooperatively. Team members should be diverse enough to foster creativity and widespread acceptance of team-adopted solutions.

Amnesty International

Peter Benenson put together two main teams to plan and implement Appeal for Amnesty. There was a predominantly male policy or advisory group and a predominantly female office team, with Benenson playing the central role in each. (This is not to say that these groups would have identified themselves as a team. I view them as teams because of their strong commitment to a common task.) In assembling these teams, Benenson turned to people whose previous professional and volunteer work revealed a passion for civil liberties and international justice. He recruited people whose skills complemented his own. For example, Eric Baker, Neville Vincent, and Christel Marsh had operational or administrative skills that he lacked. One Amnesty colleague noted that Vincent also contributed a "frantic sense of humor" that helped release the tension of working with so many tragic cases.

As is normal for small voluntary operations, the policy team actually did organizing and administrative work as well. Despite Benenson's centrality, the policy team was more a group of equals, each contributing key ideas or special skills, from fund-raising to financial management. Members of the office team, while also bringing needed skills to Amnesty's work, relied more on directions from Benenson; they were inspired by him yet found him sometimes impossibly demanding.

In both teams, Benenson's most important contribution seems to have been articulating a clear purpose for the teams and serving as a role model, someone giving his all for the cause. Besides Benenson, Baker and Vincent played strong leadership roles in the policy team. After Sean MacBride became chair of Amnesty's International Executive Committee in 1962, he was an important partner with Benenson in making policy and undertaking highly visible international missions.

The policy and office teams interacted with and overlapped the local adoption groups, mainly in England, that Amnesty's founders organized to work for individual prisoners of conscience. These local teams often contributed policy ideas to the central teams. By 1963 there were 260 adoption groups, and by 1965 there were 400.

The early Amnesty teams generated creative ideas for dramatizing and advancing the Amnesty cause. They developed a strong visual symbol—a candle surrounded by barbed wire—for their campaign. They recruited celebrities to participate in their first Human Rights Day ceremony in 1961. They adapted methods used in other humanitarian campaigns to their own ends.

IWRAW

IWRAW's founders also established two main teams—a policy team called the core network and a staff team. Arvonne Fraser, Marsha Freeman, Stephen Isaacs, and Rebecca Cook served on both teams. For the core network, they sought people from around the world who, in Fraser's words, were "doing things" on behalf of women's rights and who were inspirational and likely to be inspired by interacting with other core network members. One way of describing the core, Fraser said, is "those who have worked the hardest lately and usually longest in implementing the [Women's] Convention" (interview by author, November 6, 1992). Members of the staff team provided skills such as legal analysis, report writing, and publications production. As in Amnesty, core network members who were not on the staff also performed staff functions—for example, report writing and legal analysis.

The mainly female core network members were united by several similarities. The women were all veterans of women's rights battles. All the members had college educations, all spoke English, most were trained in a profession, and many were lawyers. They were unified around a clear general purpose: to be a catalyst for implementation of the Convention on the Elimination of All Forms of Discrimination against Women.

At the same time, the group embodied the cultural, national, and ethnic diversity that could help them develop problem definitions and solutions that fit the diverse world they are trying to lead. The range in their ages, from the 30s through the 60s, also enabled the group to more easily identify with several generations of women and blend the perspectives of seasoned veterans and energetic newcomers.

COMMUNICATION

Good communication among team members is necessary for aligning and coordinating members' actions, building mutual understanding and trust, and fostering creativity and commitment. If more than one team is working together on a common project, leaders must establish reliable communication channels among the teams.

Amnesty International

In Amnesty, effective communication was fostered, at least in the policy team, through regular meetings in or near Peter Benenson's law chambers. Although the office team held meetings, one member commented that office team members felt they did not really know what was going on. Yet Benenson communicated so strongly that the team's mission was important and urgent that team members worked intensely on the tasks for which they were responsible. Even so, the atmosphere of ambiguity, coupled with a sense of urgency, contributed to high levels of stress and burnout among office team members.

IWRAW

The staff leaders—Arvonne Fraser, Stephen Isaacs, Marsha Freeman, and Rebecca Cook—had the greatest responsibility for building the strong, creative relationships that promote teamwork. They understood the importance of communication in this effort. In addition to organizing an annual core network meeting, they communicated with the other, far-flung network members through a continuous flurry of international mailings, faxes, and telephone calls. My examination of files in the Minnesota IWRAW office revealed that letters from the two Minnesota women, as well as those to them from other core network members, had a comradely, supportive tone; often they included very personal notes about the writer's family life, successes, or personal tragedies. The letters contained requests for information and assistance, or they provided requested information, funding prospects, or promises of aid.

EMPOWERMENT

The word *empowerment* has been so popularized and so abused, that anyone can be rightly cautious about promoting it once again. Yet it can be salvaged for purposes of team leadership by being defined as *helping each group member claim and develop his or her power in service of the group's mission.* To encourage other team members to claim their power, leaders help them to

- Mutually clarify the team's mission, goals, decision-making rules, and norms
- Secure necessary resources for accomplishing the mission

Good communication is vital for each of these efforts.

Mission, Goals, Decision-Making Rules, and Norms

Teams have differing degrees of latitude in defining their mission. When Peter Benenson and his team of policy advisers had their initial meetings to plan the Amnesty appeal, and when Arvonne Fraser, Rebecca Cook, Jane Connors, Norma Forde, Silvia Pimentel, and Isabel Plata met in Nairobi, each team had fairly free rein to decide on its mission. Other teams are assigned their missions by outside authorities. Even those teams, however, usually have plenty of room for defining and expanding their mission and agreeing on goals.

Along with clarifying mission and goals, team members should agree at the outset on how they will make decisions and establish norms that promote team effectiveness. All groups that stay together for an extended period develop norms—that is, rules for customary behavior. These rules usually are implicit and may contribute to effective teamwork or undermine it. An example of a norm promoting teamwork is "openness to everyone's point of view." An example of the opposite type is "avoidance of conflict at all costs."

Amnesty International. The Amnesty teams' mission was stated in Benenson's 1961 *Observer* article announcing the Appeal for Amnesty. He enumerated the following aims for the appeal:

1. To work impartially for the release of those imprisoned for their opinions

2. To seek for them a fair and public trial

3. To enlarge the Right of Asylum to help political refugees find work

4. To urge effective international machinery to guarantee freedom of opinion (p. 21)

The teams' immediate goal was to enlist citizens in England and other countries in support of these aims.

Both Amnesty teams were permeated by Benenson's charismatic decision-making style. Sometimes he consulted other team members before making important decisions; on other occasions he made major decisions, such as hiring office administrators, unilaterally. Moreover, he refused to delegate decision-making authority to these administrators once he hired them. Benenson's charisma overwhelmed any disenchantment with his decision-making style. Occasionally, he was overruled by other powerful members of the policy team. Finally, Amnesty's International Executive Committee, established at the 1962 international meeting in Luxembourg, forced him to go through with his threatened resignation over an internal crisis.

The teams developed norms, such as idea sharing and working hard for intangible rewards, that promoted their effectiveness. They also developed a norm of deferring to Benenson, which made the teams overreliant on a single leader's strengths and nearly incapable of overcoming his weaknesses.

IWRAW. The overt mission of the IWRAW teams was to promote the Women's Convention and ensure that it actually was being implemented in the countries that had signed it. A less overt mission was simply to keep the spirit of the International Decade for Women alive after the concluding Nairobi conference. The founders' immediate goal in the wake of the Nairobi conference was to flesh out the concept of a global women's rights network and raise enough money to launch the network. As the staff team put together grant proposals and early IWRAW publications, they emphasized several objectives:

- Forming a worldwide network that would educate women and men about the Women's Convention

- Promoting legal and policy changes in members' countries in accordance with convention principles

- Monitoring compliance with the convention

The core network developed a consensual policy-making process. The members of the core network bring their ideas for a work plan to the annual meetings, where together they work out what should be done. Arvonne Fraser elaborated on the process: "Everyone picks some things to do. What gets done depends on who can raise money and has the time for it, how circumstances change, and what opportunities arise" (interview by author, March 5, 1993).

Important norms in the IWRAW core network are mutual respect and appreciation of differences. Fraser commented that to bridge divides, "We deal in universals and analogies. It is an interesting intellectual, subjective, and emotional experience. . . . Deep down, we're all people" (interview by author, March 5, 1993). Marsha Freeman added that the group is held together by both shared values and shared respect: "I am not going to tell my colleague from Malaysia how things should be done. She is not going to tell me I'm just a Western imperialist trying to foist my values on her" (interview by author, March 25, 1993).

Resources

Leaders help their teams secure a variety of tangible and intangible resources. The most important are money, time, information, and skills.

Amnesty International. Finding adequate funds for Amnesty teams' activities was often a problem. Peter Benenson and other members of the Amnesty policy team funded some of Amnesty's work out of their own pockets. The adoption groups raised money through local fundraising activities, and the central office received some contributions from individuals responding to the *Observer* article or to subsequent publicity about the Amnesty campaign. Benenson also provided office space for the staff. Team members gave hours and hours of volunteer time to Amnesty's work, and they recruited other volunteers, including celebrities who donated their drawing power to Amnesty's public events. (In the early years, only a few staff members were paid, and their salaries were meager.) As noted previously, team members had numerous skills and connections that were useful in accomplishing their mission. Benenson also turned to outsiders, such as a public relations firm, to supplement the skills of team members.

IWRAW. As codirectors of IWRAW, Arvonne Fraser and Stephen Isaacs devoted much of their time to raising funds from foundations and individual donors for IWRAW core network meetings, educational activities, and staffing expenses. Unlike their Amnesty counterparts, most of IWRAW's staff were paid, and their wages were comparable to those of other university employees with similar responsibilities. Core network members also gave significant amounts of volunteer time to IWRAW's work. Members of both teams supplied vital skills and connections for promoting the Women's Convention.

LEADERSHIP DEVELOPMENT

Development of leadership skills could be included under empowerment, but it deserves separate consideration because it is important for teams regardless of the task they are pursuing. Developing the leadership skills of all team members has several advantages. One or two team leaders cannot hope to inspire and mobilize all the various constituencies represented by team members. The initial leaders also may be unable to lead all the subgroups that a team forms to deal with different aspects of its work. Beyond that, the initial leaders may want some relief from being responsible for all the tasks of good communication and empowerment described above. Sharing leadership widely within the team contributes to a more egalitarian atmosphere, allows people to contribute their expertise in a particular leadership skill such as conflict management without being responsible for all areas of team leadership, and enables everyone to sometimes be in a follower role—for example, by contributing freely to a dialogue rather than facilitating it.

Amnesty International

Developing the leadership capacity of team members does not seem to have been a conscious goal for the two Amnesty teams. Leadership development probably was not an issue for the policy group because most had had opportunities to direct programs or become powerful in electoral politics. As for the office team, Benenson's lack of interest in delegating authority made it difficult for staff members to develop full-fledged leadership. The formation of adoption groups provided leadership opportunities for those who joined the Amnesty campaign because the groups had considerable leeway to organize themselves.

IWRAW

Arvonne Fraser was especially committed to sharing leadership and developing the leadership skills of core network members. She was the driving force for organizing and raising money for three summer workshops that helped members become more effective leaders.

ADDITIONAL RESOURCES AND GUIDANCE FOR TEAM LEADERSHIP IN THE GLOBAL COMMONS

Those who seek to build effective teams—either freestanding or within organizations—to work on global public problems can draw on a plethora of communication, empowerment, and leadership development methods. The methods I will recommend promote shared leadership and full participation of all team members. Some groups, because of one member's personal power, members' culture or past experience with groups, or the task to be performed, will be more comfortable with one strong central leader, such as Peter Benenson, who provides directive, mainly task-oriented leadership. In that case, the methods I recommend may be introduced as helpful tools when the group gets stuck or finds itself in crisis or in need of more creativity. In general, I recommend trying as much participation as the team can accept. Average citizens around the world are seeking more power in their workplaces and in the political realm; it is just possible that leaders will find team members more ready than the leaders are for full-fledged participation.

The methods presented here should enable those who are already gifted or skilled in some aspects of team leadership to improve, especially in their areas of weakness. Those who have little experience with good team leadership can also use these methods to develop a basic team-building repertoire. Finally, these methods should be useful to those seeking to train others to be more effective team leaders. The methods must be tailored to any actual group; indeed, an important team leadership skill is matching method to group.

Let us begin our exploration of team-building methods by focusing on recruitment, or team membership. Then we will turn to communication, empowerment, and leadership development methods. Finally, we will consider how skillful use of these methods creates an atmosphere of trust and spirit that enables a team to accomplish great things.

Recruitment

If you want to recruit a small band of people who will be the core of a transnational initiative to solve a public problem such as human rights violations, you obviously will turn to people who share at least your general purpose of creating a more just and humane world. Like the founders of Amnesty International and IWRAW, you will seek especially those who are already knowledgeable and concerned about the problem and have vital contacts, affiliations, skills, and other resources to contribute to the initiative.

In addition to this commonsense approach, you can use a *stakeholder* approach to think more comprehensively about who should be on the team. By *stakeholders,* I mean the people who are connected to the public problem in some important way—who either are directly affected or have a responsibility to do something about the problem. Identifying and analyzing stakeholders allow leaders to assemble a team diverse enough to generate optimal solutions that will be acceptable to the various groups asked to adopt them.

The first step is identifying the groups that have a stake in the outcome of efforts to solve the problem. You can begin by simply brainstorming such groups and then prioritizing them by importance. Two questions help with prioritizing:

• Which groups should benefit from solving the problem?

• Which groups have critical ability to implement or thwart proposed solutions?

Using this analysis, leaders can then identify particular people who would represent important stakeholders *and* share the goal of solving the public problem. It is especially important to recruit representatives who have access to existing organizational networks that can disseminate information about the team's work and help recruit additional supporters.

For the founders of IWRAW, key stakeholders were women in each country of the world (or at least every major region), poor women, girls, rural women, urban women, global and country-based organizations serving women, political decision makers in each country and on UN bodies, and internationally minded philanthropic organizations. As they put together their core network, IWRAW's founders welcomed women from all regions of the world, and although the core network members themselves were mostly well-educated, middle-class, urban women, many were deeply involved in serving and empowering poor women, girls, and rural women in their own countries. Most of the network members were leading women-focused projects, campaigns, or organizations at home. Some held decision-making positions in national government agencies or commissions. One member, Hadja Soumare, of Mali, had served on the UN committee overseeing implementation of the Women's Convention.

The size of a team should be large enough to represent important stakeholder groups and incorporate needed talents. At the same time it should be manageable. The optimal size is from seven to nine people (Delbecq, Van de Ven, & Gustafson, 1975). Larger teams can function well if members have clearly assigned roles and opportunities to form subgroups.

Sometimes leaders have little choice about the composition of their teams. Perhaps the team has been appointed by a political authority, or members volunteer without being recruited. Even in these situations, leaders should seek to drop team members who are not committed to the team's purpose and to add people who bring needed skills or connections.

Teams hoping to begin a project, organization, or social movement can start small and expand, but team leaders who hope to eventually include members from less powerful groups should be sure that representatives from these groups are included as early as possible. Otherwise, the team and its agenda will take on the coloration of the powerful group, and those initially excluded will be reluctant to join. The Amnesty policy team, for example, was very nearly an Englishman's club, despite the fact that the team hoped to launch a global movement. This homogeneity fostered team cohesion but hampered the group's ability to develop strategies that would appeal to people from a wide range of other countries.

Communication

Whether recruiting team members or helping them work together, leaders must foster communication that helps team members build respectful, supportive, and creative relationships. Such communication requires that leaders emphasize listening more than talking, dialogue as well as discussion, and conflict management rather than conflict suppression. Some methods descriptions that follow will include specific guidance about physical arrangements; no matter what methods they are using, team leaders must always pay attention to the physical setting, because as Hall (1959) has emphasized, the way space is organized communicates strong messages about underlying assumptions about correct behavior. If you hope to promote a participatory team environment, you will be best served by physical arrangements, such as seating everyone in a circle, that communicate the importance of each team member and his or her views.

Listening. The art of listening has lately received considerable attention from popular leadership authors. Covey (1991) urged leaders to seek first to understand rather than be understood. Kouzes and Posner (1993) and De Pree (1992) promoted listening as a means of appreciating or staying in touch with followers.

What, specifically, should leaders listen for? They should listen carefully for team members' feelings and ideas about the three main aspects of team life: the individual members' needs, the group's cohesion, and the task to be accomplished. This requires more than opening one's ears. Leaders need to ask questions or volunteer information that invites team members to speak up about each aspect. If the communication is in person, leaders can also offer verbal and nonverbal cues and follow-up questions that indicate real interest in team members' responses and encourage them to keep talking. Throughout, leaders of diverse teams need to keep in mind that what they hear and what is being said is affected by their own and the other members' culture, group affiliations, attitudes, ways of processing information, and even the physical environment (see Gudykunst & Kim, 1984). For example, it may be easier for people from a women's culture, or Middle Eastern or African culture, to seek out, hear, and appreciate information about families and social obligations. For these people, the difficulty may be that attention to these personal concerns begins to dominate and divert needed attention from the team's collaboration on a task.

Leaders may need to preface their listening efforts with at least some explanation of why they are so interested in the other members' point of view. Team members also are likely at some point to expect leaders to divulge more of their own views. Leaders should communicate that their interest is genuine by structuring the physical setting for conversation. For example, they may go to a team member's office, rather than having the person come to them, or they may hold the conversation around a coffee table instead of sitting behind their desks.

Once a team comes together, I recommend that the conveners use a "listening" rather than "telling" approach to developing shared awareness of good team leadership practices. Here is an exercise I have used for this purpose:

1. A convener asks team members to respond to the following: "Think about a time you have been part of an effective team. What made it effective?" To promote everyone's participation, the convener asks team members to jot down their thoughts.

2. The convener invites the members to take turns sharing their thoughts with the whole group. The convener or one of the members can record the main ideas that emerge.

3. The convener presents at least the main team-building ideas at the heart of this chapter:

    • Communication practices should promote full participation, constructive conflict, group cohesion, and creative problem solving.

    • To empower team members, leaders help members clarify the team's mission, goals, decision-making rules, and norms; secure necessary resources; and evaluate their work.

    • Leaders should seek to build the leadership capacity of all team members.

4. Team members comment on the connections between their own responses and the ideas presented by the convener.

This exercise has several benefits. It respects and recognizes the existing knowledge and expertise in the group, it connects the group to ideas from others who have studied team leadership, and it begins the work of perspective taking that is a central aim of the next communication method.

Dialogue. A formal dialogue process can help all team members view a problem from each other's perspective and enhance their creativity. As psychologist and veteran facilitator Edgar Schein (1993) noted, such a structured conversation is vital for teams in which members feel anxious or distrustful of each other or have run into other difficulties working together. Without perspective taking through dialogue, members' differences too easily become personalized conflicts that stifle creativity and commitment. The process described below is derived from the work of David Bohm (1994), a British theorist who believed that groups could use dialogue, in the Greek sense of developing shared meaning through words, to examine the assumptions and implicit rules in their ordinary communications.

To begin the dialogue process in a team, Schein recommended bringing team members together in an introductory meeting. Everyone sits in a circle, and the facilitator asks the group to think about experiences of good communication and then talk about the experiences with a neighbor. Next, the facilitator asks the group, "What made these experiences good communication?" As people respond, the facilitator records their answers on a flipchart and then invites each team member to react to the recorded answers. After everyone has had a chance to react, the facilitator lets the conversation flow naturally, intervening as needed to clarify or elucidate what the group is revealing about communication problems.

This introductory dialogue allows the group to begin developing a common language and shared understandings that help the group to become a cohesive team working cooperatively on its tasks. It allows the facilitator to introduce important concepts such as suspension of judgment, dialogue versus discussion, and containment.

In the path of dialogue, as described by Schein (1993) and Senge (1990), participants practice *suspension:* That is, if another team member disagrees with them, they do not react immediately to defend their view. Instead, they suspend judgment and reaction and wait to see what clarification will emerge as the other person talks further. During suspension, they try to be aware of what is going on and how their past experience shapes their assumptions about what they are hearing. If they do not practice suspension, and instead disagree and elaborate their own position, they are headed down the path of discussion, dialectic, and debate, in which conflict is resolved by "logic and beating down" (Schein, 1993, p. 46). When groups are not already cohesive, the path of discussion only exacerbates its difficulties.

Dialogue is a *containment* process—that is, it contains conflict rather than suppressing it or allowing it to degenerate into a win-lose battle. To foster this containment, the facilitator draws on his or her own authority and team members' commitment to work together. Thus, Arvonne Fraser, when leading contentious IWRAW core network meetings, was able to hold people in the room together and help them listen to each other because of her authority as a veteran women's rights activist and as director of the organization. She avoided win-lose outcomes.

After a team has participated in one or more preliminary dialogues and grasped its basic concepts, it can use dialogue to focus on vital questions about the team's mission and how to achieve team goals. Once dialogue has helped the team develop shared understanding of the questions and alternative answers, team members can advocate particular courses of action and seek consensus on what to do.

Managing Conflict. Teams will experience internal conflict because their members are human. My colleague Thomas Fiutak emphasizes that the challenge for teams is to abjure false peace, in which conflict is smoothed over and submerged, yet to avoid destructive combat. Team leaders seek a middle territory in which conflicting views contribute to group learning and wise problem solving. Dialogue is one method of managing rather than suppressing conflict in teams. Many other methods can also enrich or deepen the perspective taking and collaboration fostered by dialogue. Some of these methods are especially helpful when people who need to work as a team have such deep conflict or mistrust of each other that they cannot or will not engage readily in dialogue.

The ethical persuasion method developed by Rusk (1993) can be used by two team members to deal with a conflict between themselves or can be used by the entire team. For example, consider the following scenario. Two Amnesty members find themselves on the opposite side of the 1964 debate over whether Nelson Mandela should be accorded prisoner of conscience status. Before they know it, the one championing Mandela has accused the other of being a smug, middle-class supporter of the status quo. The second person then denounces his or her attacker as a mindless advocate of violence. If one of the participants cools down enough to use ethical persuasion, he or she might go to the other and suggest they try the process.

The person initiating the process gives the floor to the other person first. He or she elicits the other's thoughts, feelings, and desires about the conflict and tries not to defend him- or herself or disagree. When the other is finished, the initiator tries to repeat in his or her own words what the other has said. He or she asks the other to correct inaccuracies and then restates the other's views until the other agrees that he or she has it right. The initiator then reverses roles with the partner so that the initiator can use the same process to present his or her viewpoint. This respectful examination of each other's perspective opens the door to developing solutions. The two Amnesty members might come out of the process still disagreeing about whether Nelson Mandela should have prisoner of conscience status, but they might now understand that each is deeply committed to protecting freedom of expression. They might be amenable to a compromise similar to the one Amnesty actually adopted—that is, doing what the organization could to support Mandela short of reinstating his prisoner of conscience status.

Probably the most difficult conflicts in teams are those that occur when people from the most powerful social groups try to collaborate with people from other groups. The most powerful often have difficulty understanding that their take-charge attitudes, their culture, and their style of communication not only are not shared by others on the team but are resented and rejected.

When women and men, for example, work together in a group, they are likely to need special training in understanding each other's communication styles and sharing power. For example, linguist Deborah Tannen (1990) found that U.S. women typically view conversation as a means of building relationship, whereas U.S. men typically view it as a chance to exert their independence and compete. Thus, U.S. men tend to be more accustomed to following the discussion, dialectic, and debate path described by Schein, whereas women gravitate to the dialogue path. On a team, male and female members need to be relationship builders *and* independent thinkers. Therefore, members who have been intent mainly on winning debates should try active listening, whereas those who are adept in active listening should develop skill in championing their ideas.

Teams seeking to avoid replicating hierarchical, oppressive, and exclusive relations prevalent in the outside world should establish norms of mutual respect and appreciation, mindfulness of stereotypes and generalizations about groups, and a commitment to inclusive discourse. The group also can set aside time to hear how discrimination and oppression have affected team members and to develop strategies for equalizing relations in the team. Such strategies include giving leadership responsibilities to those from less powerful groups, tactfully challenging stereotypical comments, and ensuring that the less powerful have at least equal opportunity to voice ideas, feelings, and concerns. At least some team meetings should be held on the less powerful members' territory. Attention to language also is important. Ideally, all team members will be at least minimally fluent in the language used for the team's work. When necessary, leaders should ensure that translation is provided for any team member who is not fluent in that language.

The team that includes people from social groups with disparate power may want to use a formal reconciliation process such as that developed by the National Coalition Building Institute in Washington, D.C. (see Brown & Mazza, 1992). In this process, team members

- Explore their own negative stereotypes and positive feelings about social groups, including their own

- Identify mistreatments of their group that they want stopped

- Share personal experiences of oppression

- Practice using humor, careful listening, and respectful questions to interrupt bigoted comments

- Engage in joint problem solving to deal with controversial issues

Brown and Mazza recommended maintaining a hopeful, upbeat, even raucous atmosphere throughout.

Common Themes. We have considered several communication methods that foster a team's cohesion and creativity. I could list many more, such as the sacred circle or council, which is resonant with many cultural traditions and is beautifully described by Baldwin in *Calling the Circle* (1994); the concept-mapping process developed by Bryson, Ackermann, Eden, and Finn (1995, pp. 262-271); empathic projection techniques developed by my colleague Michael Miner (1993); the "fishbowl" and other team learning methods recommended by Senge et al. (1994); the creativity techniques presented in *Lateral Thinking* (de Bono, 1970) and *A Whack on the Side of the Head* (von Oech, 1983); and the conflict resolution strategies developed by Thomas Fiutak at the University of Minnesota and those in *Getting Together: Building a Relationship That Gets to Yes* by Fisher and Brown (1988). Leaders of diverse teams can experiment with, mix, and modify these methods as needed. What is important about all of the methods is that they promote equality and connection; honor thoughts, opinions, and feelings; foster mindfulness of one's own mental processes and group dynamics; and increase group learning. To work well, the methods require patience, honest engagement, and a desire to work together.

Depending on their cultural backgrounds, people are likely to be more comfortable with some aspects of these methods than with others. For example, Japanese culture instills a wariness about revealing personal feelings to anyone other than family and close friends. People from cultural backgrounds such as this may need considerable experience with the team before they feel close enough to express their feelings. To take a contrasting example, a Japanese team member is likely to be much more skilled than a European member in staying mindful of what surrounds the verbal messages exchanged in a team.

Several of the methods require a facilitator. This leadership role can be passed around in the team, or a skilled outsider can do the job. The advantage of using the outsider, in addition to benefiting from his or her skills, is that everyone on the team will be able to participate fully in the process. No matter who serves as facilitator, he or she has the central and crucial responsibility for maintaining the consistently constructive and lightheartedly serious atmosphere that promotes cooperative relationships. He or she needs always to occupy the ample ground between neutrality and control of the group.

Because the purpose of communication is mutual understanding, team leaders should encourage all team members to make their messages as clear and accessible as possible. For example, everyone should avoid using jargon that is not part of the team's common language. Written communication should be concise and vivid.

A final observation about communication: Team members need to be in frequent, if not continuous, contact with each other—a point that the founders of Amnesty and IWRAW understood. In addition, team members should schedule regular face-to-face meetings. No technology for transmitting sounds and images across distances can substitute for the rich interaction among people who are fully present to each other. Especially when the team is from diverse cultural backgrounds, such in-person meetings should be planned with sensitivity to members' holy days and dietary practices.

Empowerment

The communication methods noted above help empower team members because they emphasize the importance of all members' opinions and expertise and promote learning for each team member. These methods have general usefulness, but they definitely should be employed as team leaders enlist team members in clarifying what the team will do, how it will operate, and how it will obtain necessary resources. A clear mission is the group's touchstone, a focal point for members' passions and energies, and their reason for being together as a team. Goals, decision-making rules, and norms are the framework for aligning members' actions with the mission.

Mission, Goals, Decision-Making Rules, and Norms. When teams begin cordially and their members have at least a general shared sense of why they are coming together, they can proceed directly to defining their *mission*. They can use the dialogue method to answer the question, "What is our mission?" or "What do we want to accomplish?" (To expand the team's thinking about its mission, a leader may precede the dialogue with a brainstorming exercise— using, for example, the "snow card" technique described in Appendix D.) Once consensus has emerged about at least a provisional mission, the team can set some *goals* for carrying out the mission (and, if team members seek more precision, can establish objectives as well).

Plans for carrying out the team's mission do not have to be elaborate, but they should be recorded, at least in outline form, to reinforce group memory and keep people accountable. A basic plan includes desired outcomes, strategies for obtaining them, an action calendar, designation of responsibilities, and a means of assessing the plan's effectiveness and revising the plan if necessary.

Teams that come together with obvious disagreement about their mission or with strong potential for divisiveness may benefit from postponing mission talk until they have an initial dialogue about their different viewpoints or engage in reconciliation. In addition, people from future-oriented cultures may be more comfortable with mission talk than people from past-oriented cultures or present-oriented cultures. In the United States, where citizens are used to "missions to the moon" and to many other places, where political leaders speak of the "next frontier," and where there is a dominant sense that the future ought to be better than the present, team members can readily see themselves on a mission moving toward a better future. The mission question may need to be asked differently to engage team members from cultures that place the greatest value on living rightly in the present or cultures that adhere strongly to past traditions. For people who focus on the present, the question might be: "What should this group be doing?" For people who focus on the past, the question might be: "What should this team do to build on the best of our society's traditions?"

Along with clarifying their mission and goals, team members should agree at the outset on how they will make *decisions*. Consensus decision making has the most advantages: The resulting decisions will be based on more information and be more accepted by team members, and the team's problem-solving capacity will be enhanced (see Fisher & Ury, 1981; Johnson & Johnson, 1994). The chief disadvantage of consensus is the time required—for dialogue, information gathering, and proposal revision—to gain every member's endorsement of a particular choice. The team can use several methods to retain the benefits of consensus without becoming mired in process. For example, the team may agree to make the most important decisions, such as what the mission should be, by full consensus—that is, endorsement by all. Other decisions could be made by modified consensus—that is, after thorough dialogue, most team members endorse a decision and the others agree that they can live with it, even if it is not their first choice. The team also may empower individuals or a small group to make decisions that must be made quickly or really do not require the full group's attention.

Teams can be strengthened by explicitly identifying, early in their existence, the *norms* that members agree should govern their behavior. Through exercises such as snow-carding and dialogue, team members can propose norms and evaluate them. A possible approach is to have team members do two snow card exercises, one beginning with the question "What are my hopes for how team members will work together?" and the other with "What do I hope we do *not* do in our work together?" After the individual answers are pooled and categorized, the group can talk about what they mean and decide which ones to adopt as group policy. These agreed-on norms can then be written down so that the team can refer to them and newcomers can be "indoctrinated." They can even be placed on a poster in the team's regular meeting place. One team member can be designated at each meeting to assess how closely the team is abiding by its agreed-on norms. Over time, the team may find it needs to revise the norms in response to changing conditions or new insights.

The benefits of engaging in an explicit norming process are several. Everyone participates directly in norm setting, and the group takes more control over its destiny and modus operandi. Moreover, the considered judgment of the group should transform an individual's desire for unhelpful norms, such as "no conflict," into more helpful ones, such as "creative rather than destructive conflict."

Resources. A team's plan for carrying out its mission should identify necessary resources—that is, money, time, information, and skills—and strategies for obtaining them. These resources can come from inside and outside the team.

Raising *money* from team members may be relatively easy if the team members are well-paid professionals, as many of Amnesty's founders were. Such team members are convinced already that the money will go to a good cause. To raise money and other contributions from outsiders, team members must convince individuals, corporate donors, government agencies, or foundations that the team's work is important, that it will not happen without the requested resources, and that there will be some benefit to the giver as well as society. For additional guidance about raising money, see *Nonprofit Organizations in a Market Economy* (Hamminck, 1993) and *Achieving Excellence in Fundraising* (Roseau & Associates, 1992).

Team members should consider what *time* commitment from whom is needed to accomplish their task. Should some people be paid for their time, and how much? Can the group persuade more outsiders to volunteer their time? How does the group ensure that volunteers' time is well spent? How does the group avoid asking people to spend so much time on the team's work that they are overstressed and burned out? Leaders should remember especially that volunteers should be recognized for their work. For both volunteer and paid team members, the most important compensation for their time may well be intangible. For example, in the early Amnesty teams, the main rewards were a feeling of being needed and doing something important and the opportunity to work with a charismatic person—namely, Peter Benenson.

Much of the *information* needed by a team already exists in the minds, files, and connections of team members. This information can be pooled and evaluated in brainstorming, dialogue, and planning sessions. The group also can decide what additional information gathering is needed and who will do it. For example, when the Amnesty policy team planned a public event to promote Appeal for Amnesty, they could draw on their own experience in organizing political events and fundraising activities for charitable causes. Benenson also turned to outsiders, such as a public relations firm, for advice.

A team also should decide what *skills* it needs to carry out its tasks. Team members will have some of the skills already, and they can obtain the others by turning to outsiders or undergoing additional training themselves. The advantage of training team members is that the capacity of the team itself is enhanced. For example, a team can hire someone to write funding proposals, but sending a team member to a workshop on fund-raising adds to the team's skill repertoire and probably increases the team member's satisfaction.

Team leaders cultivate team members' resources by varying the amount of direction and support they give each team member according to the team member's competence and commitment (Hersey & Blanchard, 1988). As a team member's skills grow, leaders should give him or her less direction; as the team member's commitment grows, he or she will need less emotional and social support from the leaders. This coaching and motivation process is facilitated by two-way feedback between the leader and team member. It is especially important for the person who is giving verbal feedback to praise as well as criticize; focus on behaviors, not personal qualities; share information and ideas rather than advice; be specific; time the feedback well and gear it to the person's needs; and encourage the person to offer his or her own feedback (Hunsaker & Hunsaker, 1986).

Team members need to remember that leaders and followers empower each other. It is especially important for committed and courageous followers to remind leaders who are abusing their powers, mistreating followers, or otherwise letting their "shadow side" run amok that leaders do not exist without followers.

Leadership Development

Team leaders have several options for helping other team members develop leadership skills. They may select one or more team members to groom as their successors, they may organize leadership training sessions for younger or less seasoned team members, or they may rotate responsibilities for chairing meetings or subgroups. (Arvonne Fraser used all of these approaches.) Or they can confer with the team, emphasize the benefits of leadership development for all, and let the team decide on its own leadership development program—what skills will be emphasized and who will participate.

Once several people in a team are prepared to exercise leadership, the team needs some mechanism for allocating leadership responsibilities. It may authorize an executive director or committee to decide. Or the team itself may assign responsibilities and set up a schedule for rotating them.

Trust and Spirit

Together, the methods presented here foster an atmosphere of trust and spirit. Trust enables a team to be more than the sum of its parts, whereas distrust and mutual suspicion cause a team to be less than the sum of its parts. Team spirit is the enlivening of a team by a sense of high purpose, mutual connection, and efficacy, even when resources are scarce and outside recognition is slow in coming.

Teams with high levels of trust and spirit are prepared to create "improvisational jazz," in which team members with the common purpose of creating great projects contribute their strengths and play off each other's contributions, shared history, and the materials at hand. Each member can trust the others to leave him or her a lot of space but to bail him or her out when necessary. (For more on improvisational jazz as a metaphor for leadership, see Terry, 1993, pp. 178-179.)

Trust. The source of trust is the knowledge that we can count on each other for support (whether sympathy or expertise) and that the other team member will reliably carry out his or her responsibilities without constant direction and supervision. Trust allows team members to improvise successfully—that is, to use the materials and knowledge at hand to cope creatively with new situations. Trust allows each team member to be more effective because his or her own skills are released and strengthened by the connection with other members who have complementary skills.

An atmosphere of trust in a team is fostered by open dialogue in which information and perspectives are generously shared, by cooperation, and by expression of mutual support and appreciation (see Kouzes & Posner, 1987). Trust builds in a group over time, as we learn what we can expect from each other (especially when the going gets tough), practice cooperation, forgive each other's shortcomings, and at times function as one.

Spirit. Leaders promote team spirit by reminding the group of the importance of its work, working side by side with team members, displaying humor, mining lessons from losses, highlighting what outside recognition there is, and otherwise celebrating individual and group achievement. One method of fostering team spirit is to ask the team to choose an exemplary team from history or contemporary society that can serve as its model. It might be the Three Musketeers, a quilting bee, or the Jamaican Olympic bobsled team.

SUMMARY

Leaders seeking to build diverse teams to effectively tackle public problems that spill across national boundaries should foster communication that unifies team members while drawing out their diverse perspectives. To develop and focus the group's power, leaders also should help team members to clarify the team's mission, goals, decision-making rules, and norms and to secure necessary resources for accomplishing the mission. Finally, leaders should help other team members develop their leadership skills. All of these efforts should be aimed at building the trust and spirit that will sustain the team over the long haul.

Leaders in the global commons need the base of strong teams to build effective and humane organizations, the focus of organizational leadership. Let us now turn to the complex tasks of organizational and interorganizational leadership.

CHAPTER 5

Organizational Leadership

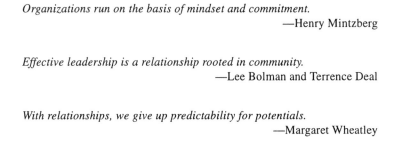

Organizations run on the basis of mindset and commitment.
—Henry Mintzberg

Effective leadership is a relationship rooted in community.
—Lee Bolman and Terrence Deal

With relationships, we give up predictability for potentials.
—Margaret Wheatley

In addition to building committed teams, leaders in the global commons nurture effective and humane organizations and interorganizational networks that can bring the energies of many people to bear on resolving global public problems. Indeed, one of the tasks of an initial team, such as the founding group of Amnesty International or of IWRAW, is to decide whether the team should create a new organization or whether existing organizations are sufficient and need only change their priorities, tactics, or affiliations. The greatest need may be for an umbrella organization or interorganizational network that can pull together existing related organizations and encourage the growth of new ones.

Whether leaders are starting new organizations or trying to reform old ones, they should

- Pay attention to organizational purpose
- Align organizational design with purpose
- Adapt to organizational and environmental contingencies
- Build community inside and outside organizations

Let us explore each of these tasks further, using examples from Amnesty International and IWRAW. Following this exploration, I will suggest several resources that can help leaders carry out these tasks.

ORGANIZATIONAL PURPOSE

Like the members of an effective team, the members of an organization need a clear sense of their mutual purpose, or mission. The mission inspires and coordinates their action. To those outside as well as inside the organization, the mission is the organization's raison d'être, its declaration of core values.

As long as an organization is small and its leadership charismatic, it may not need a formal mission statement. Leaders who want to build transnational organizations and avoid reliance on charisma, however, should help their organizations develop brief, written mission statements that can be widely disseminated and easily condensed into a slogan or a few words. Leaders also should help people in the organization agree on a process for revisiting or revising the mission in response to experience and changing conditions.

Amnesty International

Even before Amnesty International was officially inaugurated with adoption of its constitution in Belgium at the 1962 international gathering of Amnesty activists, Peter Benenson and other founders had clearly articulated the core of the new organization's mission—that is, the protection of human beings' free expression of political and religious views. The focus was on people imprisoned for their beliefs, or "prisoners of conscience." Indeed, the title of the campaign that spawned the organization was "Appeal for Amnesty" for these prisoners.

IWRAW

As Arvonne Fraser, Rebecca Cook, and others put together grant proposals and early IWRAW publications, they identified IWRAW's core mission as promoting the Women's Convention. Early IWRAW publications included this succinct statement: "IWRAW is a collaborative project to facilitate and monitor law and policy reform under the United Nations Convention on the Elimination of All Forms of Discrimination against Women." The very name *International Women's Rights Action Watch* also communicated the mission of achieving women's rights throughout the world.

ORGANIZATIONAL DESIGN

Organizational leaders intentionally design governance and administrative systems and organizational culture to accomplish the organization's purpose. Conversely, organizational leaders must guard against creating governance and administrative systems and a culture that actively undermine the mission. For example, an organization that promotes human rights will hardly be credible if it has no process for allowing employees, volunteers, and members a voice in its governance. Amnesty's founders and IWRAW's founders set up contrasting systems and developed distinctive cultures. In each case, the organizational design has been crucial in helping the organization carry out its mission. IWRAW's more flexible structure is more easily adaptable to varying conditions and approaches to advancing women's rights around the world.

Governance and Administrative Systems

An organization that seeks to mobilize and serve diverse constituencies in the effort to tackle a global public problem needs participatory, transparent governance systems that allow constituents to affect and understand policy making without paralyzing the organization. As Lakey, Lakey, Napier, and Robinson (1995) noted,

> Most people do a better job when they get more satisfaction from their work. They get more satisfaction when they see how their own efforts connect with the work of others, when they have input in decision making and when they have some control over their work. (p. 69)

An organization's formal governance and administrative systems also supply cues for how other organizations relate to it. These systems must include reliable means of generating organizational resources and managing internal conflict. Formal and informal administrative systems should help constituents carry out the organization's day-to-day work as humanely and effectively as possible.

Amnesty International. To carry out Amnesty's mission, early leaders drew on experiences in other voluntary initiatives (especially those organized by Peter Benenson) to select strategies and set up an organizational structure. The adoption groups were adaptations of Benenson's youthful work on behalf of Spanish orphans and young Germans. The attempt to achieve ideological balance—by having each group adopt one prisoner from the communist bloc, one from the "West," and one from the "Third World"—echoed the multipartisan design of Justice, which drew lawyers from all three of Britain's major political parties. Amnesty's international missions were simply a continuation of those undertaken by Justice members. The initial Appeal for Amnesty campaign was modeled on the World Refugee Year, an intensive and successful UN-sponsored appeal aimed at finding homes and providing rehabilitation for over a million refugees in Europe, Palestine, China, and Hong Kong.

Amnesty's founders also strove to continually expand the numbers of adoption groups and national sections. They visited other countries to promote the organization, they organized a speakers' group to carry the Amnesty message to other British organizations, they advertised, and they courted publicity for their cause.

Amnesty's initial central structure was minimal: an advisory committee, officers, and mainly volunteer office staff, headquartered in Benenson's law chambers. In the first 2 years, numerous local adoption groups and a handful of national Amnesty sections were formed, mainly in Europe.

The concept of an international voluntary organization comprising national sections, which in turn comprised the local groups, emerged at the first international meeting in 1961. Those attending the 1962 international meeting adopted, at Sean MacBride's insistence, a constitution formalizing the organization's structure.

Amnesty's governing body was the annual International Assembly, attended by representatives of the national sections. The assembly (later named the International Council Meeting) elected members of the International Executive Committee (IEC), which oversaw implementation of policies between annual meetings. (The national sections were grouped by language, and each group nominated a member of the committee.) MacBride became the first IEC chair, and Benenson was designated secretary.

Participants in the 1963 International Assembly decided to reorganize Amnesty's central office, which was responsible for both international and British operations. Henceforward, part of the office became the International Secretariat (IS), responsible for international matters, and the remainder became the British section office.

Amnesty's official structure provided a means—the International Assembly—for the organization's members to be involved in its governance, and it divided responsibilities for policy making and administration. The International Assembly was to make overall policy, the IEC, was to oversee policy implementation, and the IS was to assist Amnesty sections and local groups in the actual implementation. In practice, decision-making roles were more blurred. The IEC and the IS exercised considerable influence over the annual meeting agenda, and IEC members involved themselves in day-to-day operations of the secretariat.

Amnesty's founders also began the practice of consulting people in national sections well in advance of a major policy decision that would come before the annual meeting. Although the process was time consuming, it allowed far-flung Amnesty members to express their views on proposals to be presented at the annual meeting.

Formalizing Amnesty's governance structure was an easy task compared to establishing effective administrative systems in the central office. As in many fledgling volunteer organizations, Amnesty's founders struggled to establish reliable systems for handling information, responding to members or supporters, and raising money. Benenson's multiple roles as a chief administrator, policy maker, and international missionary for Amnesty were especially problematic in this struggle. Administration was not his forte, and even if it had been, he hardly had enough time for it, given his dedication to the policy-making and missionary roles. As an attempted solution, Benenson agreed to cease being the organization's chief administrator. He hired a man from outside the organization to fill his former position, but he never delegated much real power to him, and he ultimately replaced him with another man, who suffered the same fate as his predecessor. Even though Benenson's work for Amnesty increasingly took a toll on his health, he continued to hold on to his central role in all aspects of the organization.

One crucial administrative innovation was setting up a research department, initially headed by Christel Marsh, to collect information on prisoners of conscience. "We worked out everything by trial and error," she recalled (Marsh, 1984). She and other volunteers collected information by any means they could think of: reading newspapers, monitoring the overseas broadcasts of the BBC, contacting other organizations or groups with knowledge of human rights violations, sending Amnesty delegations to investigate reported abuses. They developed case sheets on individual prisoners, produced on pink paper for cases being investigated for possible adoption and on white paper for prisoners actually adopted.

Amnesty's founders had more difficulty with designing organizational systems that generated adequate financial resources for accomplishing its mission. As noted in the previous chapter, the costs for operating the central office and organizing international missions and conferences in the early years were paid by Benenson, other members of the policy-making team, donations from supporters, and proceeds from adoption group fundraisers. Amnesty also set up a prisoner of conscience fund that allowed British donors to receive tax relief on their contributions. With this financial patchwork, Amnesty found its resources constantly outstripped by its ambitions, and financial crisis was common.

IWRAW. IWRAW's founders settled on a variety of methods for carrying out IWRAW's mission. First, they wanted to make the Women's Convention more accessible by producing a shorter version using popular language. They planned a global newsletter that would gather and disseminate information about progress or setbacks in achieving women's rights. They planned to issue reports and develop a bibliography of materials about the convention. They decided to begin informing lawyers and family planning, human rights, and other professional groups about the convention.

They also decided that IWRAW would try to improve the quality of reporting to the Committee on the Elimination of Discrimination against Women (CEDAW), which monitors implementation of the convention. They would encourage governments that had ratified the convention to make thorough reports on implementation in their countries, and they planned to assist nongovernmental groups in those countries in preparing their own reports to CEDAW.

The founders decided to hold an annual IWRAW meeting in conjunction with the annual CEDAW session to foster collaboration with the committee.

IWRAW's founders decided that a loose, decentralized network would be the best design for an organization that sought to adapt its efforts to different conditions around the world and take advantage of what people were accomplishing already in grassroots organizations, national and nongovernmental organizations, and in official commissions or other bodies. Arvonne Fraser compared IWRAW to a cobweb, an organizational form that often has been connected to women's leadership (see Helgeson, 1990). She also said, "It's like the rippling out when you throw a stone. We have to trust we've got a ripple effect" (interview by author, March 5, 1993).

Fraser added, "I have found that creating a network is very different from creating a [traditional] organization. This experience has reinforced for me that my success is based on treating people as peers and using a nonhierarchical approach, [yet] understanding that hierarchy may be needed sometimes" (interview by author, March 5, 1993). In trying to persuade traditionally minded donors that a network is an effective organizational approach, she sometimes reminds them that World War II was ultimately won by a network.

IWRAW's founders welcomed individuals and organizations around the world to join the network. They recruited an advisory board and decided that policy making, planning, and project evaluation would be handled by core network members in sessions at the annual meeting, which also would include educational seminars for scholars and activists interested in women's rights. They agreed that staff functions would be split between the Women, Public Policy and Development Project, directed by Fraser at the University of Minnesota, and the Development Law and Policy Program, directed by Stephen Isaacs at Columbia University. Because their programs were part of universities, the two directors had limited leeway for designing IWRAW's administrative systems—its budgeting and personnel practices had to conform to university requirements.

The leaders who made up the core network decided which projects IWRAW as an organization would pursue, but they did not try to set guidelines for projects undertaken by IWRAW members. Instead theirs was a let-a-thousand-flowers-bloom approach. They celebrated, and often channeled resources toward, whatever projects sprang up that advanced women's rights.

IWRAW is essentially a shared-power arrangement that reflects the complexity of global society. It is not a global representative democracy, like Amnesty; the core network operates democratically, but IWRAW does not attempt to regulate the governance of participating organizations or recruit large numbers of individuals to act in its name.

The potential for conflict in IWRAW is reduced by this willingness to let participants advance women's rights in their own way. Conflicting views about what IWRAW itself should do are resolved in the core network meetings, even without procedural rules. Arvonne Fraser explained, "Networks don't have

Robert's Rules of Order which respect differences and get everybody talking. We try to deal with each other based on human rights principles" (interview by author, March 5, 1993).

IWRAW's founders used two main mechanisms for generating funds. Fraser and Isaacs sought funding from foundations and individual donors, and sub-scribers to the IWRAW newsletter paid an annual fee. In approaching potential donors, Fraser kept in mind lessons she had learned from years of political fund-raising. For example, she recognized that she needed to say clearly what she wanted to do and why, and she recognized that donors often need to be educated about the cause they are being asked to fund. Accordingly, she invited donors to the network's annual meetings so that they could better understand what the organization was all about.

Organizational Culture

Governance and administrative systems shape and are shaped by an organi-zation's culture—that is, the organization's distinctive rituals and symbols, its espoused values, and its fundamental shared assumptions. As Schein (1992) emphasized, an organization's founders powerfully influence the enduring culture of the organization. Ideally, the founders will nurture a culture of integrity (see Jeavons, 1994; Wallace & White, 1988), in which ethical princi-ples are emphasized; in which behavior, espoused values, and fundamental assumptions match up; and in which everyone has a sense of personal respon-sibility for ethical practice.

Amnesty International. Amnesty's founders attempted to establish a shared organizational culture by distributing regular magazines, bulletins, guides, and handbooks to its members and by sponsoring special events such as Human Rights Day rallies and Prisoner of Conscience Week. These activities reinforced the vital shared assumption that the members' work mattered—that the work was urgently needed and that the organization's various pressure tactics were paying off. The events and publications highlighted specific human rights violations and cited the large numbers of political prisoners who had been released or treated better after having been adopted by Amnesty. The events were, in effect, organizational celebrations, often presenting former prisoners of conscience who paid tribute to Amnesty's work, and thereby directly rein-forcing a culture of dedication to the Amnesty cause.

Amnesty's founders had a fundamental faith in the moral authority and efficacy of law. International law was their touchstone in attempting to influ-ence governments and public opinion alike. The founders assumed that officials even in oppressive regimes could be influenced to abide by international law if they were confronted with Amnesty delegations, postcard or letter campaigns, or censure from other governments acting on their own or through the United Nations.

In keeping with Amnesty's commitment to freedom of expression and belief, Amnesty founders also acted on the fundamental assumption that everyone in the organization should participate in discussing and selecting policies and strategies. Various democratic rituals, such as the annual international meeting, were manifestations of this assumption.

In the central office, certain shared assumptions no doubt contributed to stress and high turnover. During the early years, the office seemed to operate on the assumption that staff and volunteers could be expected to give their all to the organization for minimal tangible rewards. Personal and organizational lives were often merged. A strongly connected assumption was that Peter Benenson had special standing as the zealous originator of the Amnesty campaign. His charisma both motivated people to dive wholeheartedly into Amnesty work and blunted criticism of his modus operandi.

Peggy Crane (1985) commented on the central office culture, with its exciting mix of fervor for a cause, devotion to Benenson, and operational chaos. When she came to the office in October 1961, "There were people everywhere, . . . masses of people coming in and out, and everywhere congestion. . . . Peter brought with him a great feeling that he was producing some real goodness [whether] political or whatever. And this was all marvelous in the situation. Everybody was feeling marvelous and good." She recalled that Benenson had "all these exquisite women rushing after him, two or three young girls looked after him, typed, ran errands." He expected everyone to work "all hours" and was clearly disappointed in those who would not.

Amnesty's founders were partially successful in establishing an organizational culture of integrity, in which ethical principles were emphasized in word and deed. Benenson and MacBride, for example, continually emphasized the need to apply the principles contained in Amnesty's mission to all countries, regardless of their political systems. Their declarations were reinforced by the requirement that adoption groups adopt one prisoner from the "West," one from communist countries, and one from the nonaligned world. Probably the greatest, most publicized blow to Amnesty's integrity was Benenson's agreement to secretly channel funds from the British government to help British subjects illegally imprisoned by the Rhodesian government in 1966 (see Power, 1981, pp. 27-29). When the agreement became the subject of debates in Parliament and news articles, Amnesty leaders' efforts to establish a reputation of impartiality toward all countries was severely undermined.

Another critical decision in the early years reinforced Amnesty's commitment to nonviolence, which had been emphasized in Benenson's (1961) *Observer* article. For example, Amnesty members and staff engaged in considerable debate in 1964 over whether Nelson Mandela should be designated a prisoner of conscience when South African authorities imprisoned him on charges of sabotage. (He had been adopted by Amnesty in 1962, when he was jailed for his antiapartheid organizing efforts.) The International Assembly reaffirmed the policy of adopting only political prisoners who did not advocate violence, but it also broadened its mission to include humane prison conditions and sentencing practices.

In some crucial areas, the founders gave scant attention to organizational integrity. For example, they failed to establish adequate policies and administrative systems for raising and tracking money, and they condoned or failed to change practices promoting staff and volunteer burnout.

Amnesty's founders established a culture in which men were dominant—as positional leaders and even as prisoners. The culture also had a distinctly British flavor that was manifest in Amnesty's systems and methods. It would be future leaders who gradually instigated changes to make Amnesty's culture more inclusive of women and a rich array of nationalities and ethnic backgrounds.

IWRAW. The most influential shared assumption in IWRAW, expressed in its publications and events, seems to have been that women are men's equals and entitled to the full panoply of human rights. This assumption is manifest at IWRAW meetings where men are present. The men, who are strongly outnumbered, participate in large group conversations and small problem-solving sessions, but the women do not defer to them. Meetings are held in commodious surroundings, a practice signaling that women deserve to be treated well.

Another important assumption is that a loose, weblike structure is best for coordinating the efforts of diverse and dispersed groups of people in pursuit of common goals. Hierarchical structures are suspect because they so frequently have been tools of male domination. As a result, IWRAW has no book of organizational procedures, no elected officers, and no membership requirements other than signing up and paying for a newsletter subscription.

IWRAW's founders, like their Amnesty counterparts, assume that international law has moral authority and impact. They too believe that it is possible to influence powerful officials—in this case, by explaining the merits of signing the Women's Convention or by offering assistance in implementing the convention or meeting its reporting requirements. Some IWRAW core network members have even obtained government positions that give them more ability to influence government policy and actions.

IWRAW, like Amnesty, operates on democratic assumptions—for example, that everyone has a right to express his or her views and participate in decisions affecting him or her. Everyone who participates in an IWRAW meeting or seminar is given opportunities to be heard; IWRAW's main policies and strategies are decided by a consensus of the core network. At the same time, partly because of its belief in loose structure, IWRAW does not try to enforce democratic governance beyond the core network—that is, it does not require that members of the core network be elected representatives of their organizations.

IWRAW's early leaders also operated on a shared assumption that multiple aspects of people's lives are important. They were concerned with women as workers, mothers, family members, and citizens. They focused on girls and older women. Thus, they highlighted in turn provisions of the Women's Convention pertaining to different aspects of women's lives.

As in Amnesty, IWRAW leaders have nurtured the shared assumption that the organization's work is important and that time is of the essence. The IWRAW newsletters include very specific accounts of current abuse directed at women and reports on the efforts of IWRAW and other groups to combat the abuse. The newsletters cheer successes of these efforts and deplore setbacks, and they rally readers to prepare for upcoming events.

Although Arvonne Fraser has played the most central role in IWRAW's early history and certainly has a touch of charisma, the organization's culture has focused much less on her personality than Amnesty focused on Peter Benenson. She has been greatly respected but not idolized.

A lot of IWRAW's energy is concentrated on preparatory meetings and drafting of reports and position papers for imminent international human rights gatherings or meetings of the UN committee that oversees the Women's Convention. Early leaders in IWRAW talked about the difficulty of finding enough time for this work and other women's projects. Yet there seems to have been less expectation in IWRAW, compared to Amnesty, that members and staff would give their all to the organization, perhaps because IWRAW's founders also operated on the feminist assumption that people need to attend to their personal and family lives as well as their occupational and civic lives.

IWRAW's culture resonates with the assumption that sisterhood is powerful. The talk and attire at meetings, the words in publications communicate this message: Our connections as women overcome differences of occupation, class, ethnicity, and nationality. You can wear a sari or a business suit, expensive jewelry or blue jeans. You can be petty and demanding as well as large-hearted and sacrificing. No matter—you are included if you are dedicated to women's advancement.

IWRAW's woman-centered culture has attracted many women and a few supportive men from around the world to participate enthusiastically in its meetings, seminars, and communications network. The assumption that centralized control is unnecessary allows IWRAW leaders and members to spend relatively little energy on questions of organizational structure and procedures.

IWRAW's founders generally succeeded in establishing a culture of integrity within IWRAW. They continually emphasized their commitment to helping all the world's women claim their rights and allocated resources to help women in poorer regions participate more fully in the network and develop their leadership. The strongest question about IWRAW's integrity is whether the relatively elite group of women who constitute its core network can truly represent the interests of the many poor and undereducated women around the world.

ORGANIZATIONAL AND ENVIRONMENTAL CONTINGENCIES

If organizations are to survive for more than a few years, their leaders must help them adapt to internal and external changes. Leaders monitor these changes and help their organizations revise their design and sometimes even their mission accordingly. Let us consider how leaders in Amnesty and IWRAW helped their organizations evolve.

Amnesty International

Amnesty's governance structure facilitated careful modification of its mission in response to new information from the external environment. Amnesty's founders also readily adopted new ideas to attract a more diverse membership. They had more difficulty in managing the growing differences surrounding Peter Benenson's role in the organization. By early 1967, these differences had escalated into an internal and external controversy that engulfed and nearly foundered the organization 5 years after its founding.

Modifying the Mission. The aims enumerated in Benenson's 1961 *Observer* article were gradually modified to deal with practices other than imprisonment that effectively deprived people of free expression. For example, in 1965, Amnesty called on the United Nations to abolish capital punishment for "peacetime political offenses" (Amnesty International, 1976, p. 5). The next year, participants in the annual international meeting called for several initiatives to end torture. In response to the growing U.S. draft-resistance movement, they also decided to extend the prisoner of conscience designation to those who refused to take part in specific wars as well as all wars—a decision that positioned Amnesty well to build U.S. membership. In 1968, participants in the international meeting adopted a new organizational "mandate" that incorporated Article 5 (prohibiting torture and cruel, inhuman, or degrading treatment) and Article 9 (prohibiting arbitrary arrest, detention, or exile) in addition to Articles 18 and 19 of the Universal Declaration of Human Rights. Egon Larsen (1978) reported that the inclusion of torture in Amnesty's mandate resulted from leadership by people in the Swedish section, who were especially outraged by the many cases of torture revealed by an Amnesty investigation of abuses by the ruling military junta in Greece.

Appealing to a More Diverse Membership. As Amnesty expanded beyond its British base, organizational leaders attempted to broaden the organization's methods to appeal to a more diverse membership. Amnesty founders had initially emphasized adoption groups and letter writing as the main means by which members would work for individual prisoners of conscience. The efforts by Benenson and others to establish Amnesty sections in Europe led them to add the option of sending postcards, which seemed more acceptable to potential members in France and Italy. To appeal to North Americans, whom they deemed more individualistic than Europeans, Amnesty activists developed a "kit scheme" that allowed individual members to work on behalf of prisoners of conscience without joining adoption groups.

Managing Controversy, Moving Beyond the Founding Father. The crisis that almost destroyed Amnesty was connected to an Amnesty investigation in 1966 into allegations that British soldiers had tortured prisoners arrested during a state of emergency in the former British colony of Aden. The investigation was conducted by a representative of the Swedish Amnesty section, who wrote a report charging British officials with violating the Universal Declaration of Human Rights. The central Amnesty office did not release the report. Instead, according to Robert Swann (then head of the office), the report was used to pressure the British Foreign Office to end the violations. Benenson, however, suspected that Amnesty staff had actually submitted to Foreign Office pressure in withholding the report. He subsequently visited Aden to check on the report's allegations himself and released the report on his own. The British press, according to Power (1981, p. 25), reacted with outrage, accusing the report's author of bias.

As for Benenson, he became even more suspicious of Amnesty colleagues. As Power (1981) described it:

> The atmosphere at Amnesty became supercharged. [Benenson] began to suspect that Swann and many of his colleagues were part of a British intelligence conspiracy to subvert Amnesty. To his way of thinking, the only way the organization could survive was by moving its headquarters from Britain to a neutral country such as Sweden or Switzerland. But he could not convince anybody else at Amnesty. (p. 26)

Benenson at one point resigned from Amnesty, then reconsidered, and finally talked Sean MacBride into appointing an impartial investigator into the whole matter. Before the investigation was complete, however, Benenson's attention was drawn to reports that the U.S. Central Intelligence Committee was secretly channeling money to the International Commission of Jurists, of which MacBride was secretary. Although MacBride emphatically denied knowing about the funding and severed his ties to the commission, Benenson now suspected him too. Around the same time, Benenson's own probity came under attack when British news media revealed that he had secretly accepted British government funds to help people imprisoned in Rhodesia.

By this time, Amnesty officials, staff, national sections, and adoption groups were all caught up in the controversy. The organization was at a distinct crisis point. Finally, the IEC met in March 1967, reconfirmed Benenson's resignation, and appointed Eric Baker, then chair of the British section, to take over direction of the IS. Benenson then withdrew from Amnesty affairs and turned his attention to restoring his health. The crisis weakened the organization and damaged its public image, but enough of the founders remained dedicated to Amnesty that it survived. (Eventually, Benenson also reestablished cordial relations with the organization, but he was never again very involved in its work.)

The hiring of Martin Ennals as secretary general in 1968 brought stronger management to the IS. He came to Amnesty after many years of working for UNESCO, the (British) National Council of Civil Liberties (where he was general secretary from 1959 to 1966), and the (British) National Committee for Commonwealth Immigrants. Power (1981) described him as a "dogged persistent administrator" with "strong political motivations that lent a certain cutting edge to Amnesty" (p. 31).

By the end of its first decade, Amnesty had rebounded from the controversy that almost destroyed it and was once again expanding. Ennals remained as secretary general and MacBride as chair of the IEC.

In the years to come, people in Amnesty would continue the careful expansion of the organization's mission and the development of new strategies for responding to human rights abuses and for recruiting and retaining new members. They sought to make central governance and administrative systems responsive to member and staff needs and to the goal of making Amnesty a truly global, or multicultural, organization.

In the 1990s, Amnesty's leaders could point to impressive achievements, but they also had to respond to formidable challenges. They had to help the organization adapt to a major shift in its external environment—the end of the Cold War. This shift has exacerbated the chaos and complexity of international political systems, and armed conflicts have increased, especially in regions formerly under Soviet Union control. In this environment, it is harder to hold anyone accountable for human rights abuses. Also Amnesty now finds itself a relatively bureaucratic, slow-moving organization competing for members with the growing host of human rights organizations that have flourished in recent years, partly because of Amnesty's success. To respond to these challenges, Amnesty policy makers and Secretary General Pierre Sané have undertaken a strategic planning process and reorganization of the IS.

IWRAW

The weblike organizational structure adopted by IWRAW's founders enabled it to easily adapt to internal and external changes in the second half of IWRAW's first decade. The process, as described by Marsha Freeman, is organic:

> A series of connections may grow out in this direction, while another series of connections may lapse and then people come back in when they feel the need. . . .

The beauty of the network is there is no program that says you have to do it this way or you don't belong. This makes for chaos in some people's minds. I happen to think it's extremely creative, because you cannot tell people how to do things. They will do things only in the way that is best for them to accomplish it, and they have to make their own mistakes. And they also think of things that are very creative that you couldn't tell them. (interview by author, March 25, 1993)

Working within this fluid structure, IWRAW's leaders helped the network modify its mission, respond to opportunities, and cope with leadership succession.

Modifying the Mission. Stephen Isaacs laid the groundwork for broadening IWRAW's mission beyond the championing of women's rights as enumerated in the Women's Convention to a campaign for recognition and promotion of women's rights as human rights. He saw the importance of connecting women's rights to the already strong international human rights movement that Amnesty activists had been so instrumental in building. Arvonne Fraser joined him in 1987 in hosting a meeting to explore women's rights as human rights. By 1993, when the World Conference on Human Rights convened in Vienna, Fraser and Freeman were among the leading voices there promoting the recasting of human rights from a women's perspective.

IWRAW's overarching mission now is clearly the advancement of women's human rights generally, even as the organization maintains its core competency— expertise about the Women's Convention and the work of CEDAW. Freeman would like to see IWRAW become "the women's human rights center in the world" (interview by author, December 20, 1995). She wants IWRAW to generate "a steady flow of information" on the rights women have under various international treaties as well as guidance for claiming those rights.

Responding to Opportunities. In response mainly to funders' priorities, Fraser, Freeman, Shanthi Dairiam (core network member from Malaysia), and others in the early 1990s began developing regional IWRAW networks for Asia and Africa. The philanthropic organizations interested in advancing women's rights globally wanted to channel more of their money directly to areas where women had the fewest financial resources.

IWRAW also responded wholeheartedly to the opportunities presented by two major UN-sponsored conferences, the 1993 World Conference on Human Rights in Vienna and the Fourth World Conference on Women in Beijing 2 years later. At the human rights conference, Fraser and Freeman conducted a workshop at the NGO forum held in conjunction with the World Conference on Human Rights. By this time, Fraser also was serving as head of the U.S. delegation to the UN Commission on the Status of Women and as such was a delegate to the conference itself. She and Freeman helped build the precedent-setting consensus at the NGO forum and conference itself that "women's rights are human rights." Almost as soon as the Vienna conference was over, IWRAW focused on Beijing. The core network members committed themselves to giving a human rights flavor to the preliminary documents that would be a part of the Beijing conference. They devoted the IWRAW core network meeting in January 1994 to educating themselves about the official and unofficial preparations for Beijing, drafting position papers, and strategizing. They planned to be strong participants in the UN-sponsored regional preparatory meetings.

In preparatory meetings with UN staff, government representatives, and other voluntary organizations, as well as at the conference itself, IWRAW's goal was to ensure that the Action Plan adopted by government representatives at the official conference would emphasize women's rights, in contrast to the plan adopted in Nairobi, which emphasized women's need for development. IWRAW members and their allies largely realized this goal by working hard to develop specific language for incorporation into official documents and then lobbying official delegations to adopt the language.

From the beginning, IWRAW took advantage of modern computer and communications technology to stay in touch with people around the world. By the time of preparations for the Beijing conference, IWRAW staff, along with other U.S. women's rights advocates, were bringing computers and disks to preparatory meetings to generate their preferred versions of the documents being debated at the meetings. Thanks to the Internet, IWRAW had a preliminary copy of the Action Plan adopted at Beijing soon after the conference adjourned, instead of waiting months for the United Nations to distribute the official document.

Since the Beijing conference, IWRAW has had the Action Plan to reinforce its efforts to promote and monitor implementation of the Women's Convention. In addition, it is benefiting from the heightened global women's activism stimulated by the conference and now being channeled into follow-up activities.

Coping With Leadership Succession. IWRAW also has had to deal with leadership succession, but its methods of doing so are unlike Amnesty's. As noted previously, the amorphous and democratic organization of the core network allows people to come and go; it allows people who have provided strong leadership in the network to become less influential or drop out entirely while others become more central. The leadership training that Fraser organized for core network members ensures that more than a handful of the members have leadership skills.

The most critical leadership transition for IWRAW was Arvonne Fraser's appointment as head of the U.S. delegation to the UN Commission on the Status of Women in 1992. Even before the appointment, she had anticipated moving on to a senior advisor status or "the next stage of work" (Fraser, letter to Isabel Plata, August 28, 1990), once IWRAW was well established. Marsha Freeman prepared to succeed her; in 1994 she became IWRAW director, and another staff member, Sharon Ladin, became deputy director.

INTERNAL AND EXTERNAL COMMUNITY

Essentially, organizations are a series of human relations, embracing varying degrees of intimacy and separation, depending on societal and organizational cultures and personal proclivities. Moreover, the members of organizations and the organizations themselves are usually part of many external relationships.

For organizations to be effective and humane, internal relationships should be mainly supportive and synergistic, rather than antagonistic and enervating. The organization's external relationships are more complicated. The leaders of an organization interested in solving public problems that involve many other groups and organizations need to view their organization as part of an organizational field that includes potential allies, partial supporters, opponents, and neutral parties. Organizational leaders will want to build supportive, synergistic relationships with allies and partial supporters, woo neutral parties, and struggle respectfully with opponents.

The metaphor of inclusive community is particularly apt for describing the human interconnections in effective, humane organizations. Inclusive communities (equivalent to what Drath and Palus, 1994, called "communities of practice") comprise relationships among diverse people, who have some common interests and goals and a sense of mutual responsibility. Community is built as people inspired by a shared mission work together, in a democratic atmosphere, to define problems and resolve them.

The metaphor of community also applies beyond the organization. Organizational leaders should strive to build larger communities (including opponents, if possible) that are built on a commitment to democratic governance and problem solving.

Amnesty International

Amnesty's founders created an organizational design that connected positional leaders, staff, and members to each other in local groups, national sections, international meetings, missions, and research efforts. They referred often to the sum of these relationships as the "prisoner of conscience movement." The design also allowed volunteers, staff, and top managers and officials alike to contribute their ideas about what the organization should do and how it should do it, and the design allowed them collectively to decide on a course of action.

On the other hand, the design did not include systematic concern for staff well-being. Stress is an occupational hazard for people working with the life-and-death cases and wrenching issues that were and are part of everyday operations at Amnesty. In the first decade, the IS did not have strong internal systems for helping staff and volunteers cope with this stress. Moreover, the stress was exacerbated by the constant struggle to accomplish ambitious goals with minimal resources and to establish effective administrative systems in an atmosphere highly influenced by Peter Benenson's charismatic personality.

Amnesty's founders built extensive relationships with other organizations. They attempted to persuade UN bodies to strengthen human rights enforcement and by 1965 had obtained consultative status at the United Nations as well as at the Council of Europe. Amnesty representatives also cooperated with the International Committee of the Red Cross in the mid-1960s to establish the right to investigate alleged cases of torture. Larsen (1978) reported that by 1965 Amnesty had good relations with the International Red Cross and the International Commission of Jurists "as well as with organizations representing the trade unions, the students, the churches, the war veterans of many countries, and the various Human Rights associations in America; there were even promising contacts with lawyers' organizations in Eastern Europe" (p. 30).

IWRAW

Although IWRAW is not as closely knit as Amnesty, the organization's leaders have built internal community in several ways. IWRAW's newsletter has been its main means of helping people in the extended network feel connected with each other. The newsletter reminds readers that others in the network are gathering information about violations of women's rights and are organizing projects to stop these abuses and educate fellow citizens about women's rights. The newsletter also allows readers to share information that may be helpful to each other's problem-solving efforts. And it conveys the message of global sisterhood—that what happens to women anywhere is a concern of women everywhere.

The annual core network meetings also contribute to community building as diverse women come together to learn more about each other, find partners for new ventures, and collaboratively develop strategies for advancing women's rights in international forums, arenas, and courts. Marsha Freeman has put special emphasis on building supportive relationships with core network members. When she can, she travels to their turf and works with them directly on their projects. Freeman noted that establishing a strong personal relationship is a necessity for good professional relations in Asian countries but added that it is important in other countries as well—especially to overcome the understandable distrust that may arise when powerful U.S. groups try to work with people outside the industrialized "West" (interview by author, December 20, 1995).

The decision of IWRAW's leaders to play a strong role in shaping the Beijing conference also contributed to internal community. For 2 years before the conference, people in IWRAW's network shared in the enormous project of preparing for it, and many attended the conference, which was a vast celebration of women's strength and connections amidst diversity.

IWRAW's leaders also have built relationships with organizations outside the network. They have emphasized cooperation with CEDAW from the beginning. They also have worked with other human rights organizations to assist women who are suing government officials over violations of rights contained in the Women's Convention. They have collaborated with other women's organizations in shaping proceedings at the Beijing conference and promoting implementation of the Platform for Action adopted at the conference. Freeman has welcomed opportunities to supply information for the UN Center for Human Rights.

ADDITIONAL RESOURCES AND GUIDANCE FOR ORGANIZATIONAL LEADERSHIP IN THE GLOBAL COMMONS

There is a wealth of resources and tools for those who, like the founders of Amnesty International and IWRAW, want to build successful transnational citizen organizations. I will describe several of these resources and tools that should be especially helpful for those trying to provide organizational leadership in the global commons. They will be grouped under four main headings: strategic planning, cultural analysis and change, other methods of change and innovation, and community building.

Strategic Planning

In my experience, the most useful overall organizational leadership tool is strategic planning. It can help people in organizations clarify organizational mission, assess design, cope with internal and external change, and build community. It can be useful at varying stages of an organization's development. I will outline a strategic planning process developed by John Bryson (1995) specifically for public and nonprofit organizations and used successfully by many types of organizations throughout the world. What is crucial, however, is not a particular process. What counts is that organizational leaders think and act strategically—that they engage in a "disciplined effort to produce fundamental decisions and actions that shape and guide what an organization is, what it does, and why it does it" (Bryson, 1995, p. 4).

The Bryson process comprises 10 steps:

1. Developing an agreement to initiate a strategic planning process

2. Identifying organizational mandates

3. Clarifying organizational mission and values

4. Assessing the organization's external and internal environments

5. Identifying the strategic issues facing the organization

6. Formulating strategies to manage these issues

7. Reviewing and adopting the strategic plan or plans

8. Establishing an effective organizational vision

9. Developing an effective implementation process

10. Reassessing strategies and the strategic planning process

Organizational goals may be developed at several points in the process. Preexisting organizational goals may prompt the initial agreement, or goals may emerge from examination of the organization's mandates. Goal setting can be an approach to identifying strategic issues; goals may be developed to guide strategy formulation and implementation. Goals should be set high enough to encourage extraordinary achievement (in the spirit of the "Big Hairy Audacious Goals" recommended by Collins and Porras, 1994), but not so high that people are reluctant to even try to reach them.

Developing an Initial Agreement. Organizational leaders seeking to begin a strategic planning process should identify key decision makers (including themselves) outside and inside the organization who must support the effort if it is to succeed. They should also identify potential members of teams that will oversee and conduct the process. Often, two teams will suffice—one providing coordination and oversight and the other doing the planning. The oversight team may be an existing organizational policy-making group, such as IWRAW's core network or Amnesty's IEC. In small organizations, one team may handle both functions. The teams should include at least some of the key decision makers and other people representing the main parts of the organization.

Once the decision makers and potential team members are identified, the initiators should work out an agreement with them on the purpose of the strategic planning process, steps in the process, form and timing of reports, composition and functions of the oversight and planning teams, commitment of necessary resources, and limitations on the process. An important function of the planning team should be to ensure that organizational members understand and support the process—possibly by directly involving them in the strategic planning activities.

Organizational consultant Robert Jacobs emphasized the desirability of involving the entire organization in "strategic change" efforts. See his book *Real Time Strategic Change* (1994) and *Discovering Common Ground* by Marvin Weisbord et al. (1992) for methods of involving large numbers of people in organizational change efforts. One of these methods, the future search, will be outlined in Chapter 6.

Identifying Organizational Mandates. Organizational planners should examine their own constitutions and bylaws, the organization's contractual obligations, and legal requirements to identify what the organization *must* do. In addition to identifying mandates from these formal sources, planners should consider informal mandates, those that may be important but not officially recorded. For example, a major organizational donor may not impose formal restrictions on his or her donation, but everyone in the organization knows that the donor's informal requests about the money's use must be honored.

In addition to clarifying what an organization's mandates require it to do, the planners should consider what the mandates *allow*. Usually, organizations have considerable room to maneuver within or beyond the mandates, and planners should delineate this territory of opportunity.

Clarifying Mission and Values. The founders of an organization have a more or less clearly defined mission that led them to start the organization in the first place. Clarifying that mission and the values it embraces is key to attracting organizational members, relating to other organizations, and generally deciding what the organization should do.

At the outset, leaders seeking to build an organization that prompts collective action to tackle a complex public problem should recognize that the organization will be part of a multiorganizational field—that is, it will coexist with a host of other organizations that are potential allies, partial supporters, neutral parties, and opponents (see Klandermans, 1992), all dependent on various constituencies. Analyzing that multiorganizational field is the groundwork for clarifying organizational mission and values.

To develop a picture of the most crucial elements of an organization's field, organizational planners conduct a stakeholder analysis. They initially ask, "Which people, groups, and organizations can place a claim on our organization's attention, resources, and output or are affected by that output?" (It is important to include internal and external stakeholders.) Once these stakeholders have been identified, the next question is: "What criteria do (or will) each of these stakeholders use to judge our organization's performance?" The third question is: "How well are we (or will we be) able to perform according to those criteria, from the stakeholders' point of view?"

Additional questions are:

• How does or will each stakeholder influence our organization?

• What does our organization need from stakeholders?

• Which stakeholders are most important to our organization's success?

Building on the stakeholder analysis, organizational planners can proceed to clarify mission and values by asking the following questions:

• Who are we, or what is our core identity? What makes us unique?

• In general, what are the basic social or political needs or problems that prompt our existence?

- In general, what do we do to recognize, anticipate, and respond to these needs or problems?

- How should we respond to our key stakeholders?

- What are our philosophy, values, and culture?

Each participant in the planning process should answer the questions using precise and inspiring language; through dialogue and discussion, the group can then decide what should be included in the mission statement. A small group can be assigned the task of actually drafting the statement, incorporating when possible the best language from the individual answers to the mission questions. The statement should be brief (no longer than a page) and should present the essence of the organization in compelling, memorable words. The draft mission statement should be submitted to the larger group for review and adoption. The entire statement, or at least one to two key sentences, should be made a prominent part of the organization's publications and pronouncements and should be displayed in the physical spaces inhabited by the organization.

The mission is, in effect, the organization's covenant, or what business theorists Michael Treacy and Fred Wiersema (1995) would call the organization's "value-proposition." The mission promises stakeholders who support the organization that it will perform certain highly valuable work.

Assessing External and Internal Environments. Once they have a clear sense of their mission, organizational planners ask:

- What are the relevant opportunities and threats in the external environment that will affect our ability to carry out our mission?

- What internal strengths and weaknesses do we have for carrying out our mission?

In answering the first question, planners should look at forces and trends in political, economic, social, technological, educational, and physical environments, especially in relation to key external stakeholders. In answering the second question, planners should attend to

- The organization's resources (people, skills, governance and administrative systems, core values, culture, ties to other organizations)

- Strategies

- Performance (especially from the standpoint of key stakeholders)

They should seek especially to identify core competencies, the organization's "strongest abilities and most effective actions and strategies" (Bryson, 1995, p. 30).

Snow cards or some other method can be used to pool the planners' answers to each question. The pooled answers to both questions constitute an organizational "SWOT" analysis—a picture of the organization's strengths, weaknesses, opportunities, and threats. Using this analysis, planners can identify and respond to the strategic issues, or critical challenges, that they face.

Identifying Strategic Issues. Organizations must confront their strategic issues and the conflicts surrounding them if they are to survive. The conflicts connected to strategic issues "may involve ends (what), means (how), philosophy (why), location (where), timing (when), and persons favored or disadvantaged by different ways of resolving the issue (who)" (Bryson, 1995, p. 31). Identification of strategic issues includes

- Posing the issue as a succinct question that the organization actually can do something about

- Listing the aspects of the organization's mandates, mission, strengths, weaknesses, opportunities, and threats that make the issue critical

- Noting the consequences of failing to address the issue

The final step can help organizational planners decide which strategic issues need attention first. An important strategic issue for an organization working on a transnational public problem might be: "How do we divide our time and other resources between service that directly alleviates the problem and advocacy aimed at long-term solutions to the problem?" or "Which decisions and functions should be centralized and which decentralized?"

Formulating Strategies. To resolve or manage strategic issues, organizational planners must formulate and implement strategies that deal with the issue in ways that advance the organization's mission. To formulate strategies, planners

- Identify practical alternatives, dreams, or visions for resolving the strategic issues

- Note the barriers to achieving these alternatives, dreams, or visions

- Develop proposals for achieving the alternatives, dreams, or visions directly or for overcoming the barriers noted in the previous step

- Identify actions that must be taken in the next 2 to 3 years to implement the proposals

- Develop a work program for the next 6 months to a year that incorporates or lays groundwork for these actions

Planners should encourage organizational members to consider diverse possibilities as they formulate strategies. People can draw on their own experiences and on research into strategies adopted in other organizations, including business. The customer service strategies of excellent businesses may be especially instructive as planners develop strategies for serving stakeholders.

Reviewing and Adopting the Strategic Plan. Unless the entire organization is involved in formulating the strategies, planners will need to present them to the organization's decision makers for review and approval. It will be easier to obtain this approval if the decision makers have been directly involved in the planning process or at least have been kept informed about it. It is also important to make sure that people from distinctive intraorganizational cultures are included in the planning process because these groups may have the most creative ideas for resolving strategic issues.

Establishing an Effective Organizational Vision. Before moving to implementation of adopted strategies, organizational planners develop a vision of what the organization will look like as it successfully implements the strategies and achieves its mission. Typical elements include the mission, strategies, criteria for judging performance, important decision rules, and ethical standards. Ideas for creating compelling visions will be elaborated in the next chapter, on visionary leadership. A small group may produce an initial version of the vision that is then reviewed by everyone in the organization, or a representative group, and is modified to reflect their suggestions. The final vision can be communicated through a written statement, a video production, or other media.

The vision presents the organization's desired future and the means of reaching it. When it is highly inspiring and widely accepted in the organization, it provides powerful impetus for implementation of the strategies it depicts. The best visions succeed in bringing the future into the present.

Developing an Effective Implementation Process. Organizations, especially small ones, may be able simply to proceed with the action program that they develop as part of strategy formulation. But the more complex an organization or interorganizational network becomes, the more planners will need to develop more detailed and long-term implementation plans. Such plans include

- Roles and responsibilities of policy-making groups, organizational units and teams, and individuals

- Specific objectives and expected results and milestones or benchmarks

- Specific action steps and relevant details

- Schedules

- Resource requirements and sources

- A communication process

- Review, monitoring, and midcourse correction procedures

- Accountability procedures

Innovative approaches to organizational management—for example, total quality improvement initiatives (Cohen & Brand, 1993) or process reengineering
(Hammer & Champy, 1993)—can be incorporated in the implementation plan.

Reassessing Strategies and Process. Once strategies have been implemented
and given enough time to produce results, organizational planners should
reassess them. The strategies may need to be discontinued or altered because
the strategic issue that prompted them has been resolved or changed drastically.
Planners also should evaluate the strategic planning process itself. They should
identify what worked well, what did not, and what improvements should be
made in the next round of strategic planning.

Strategic Planning and Community Building. A well-designed, participatory
strategic planning process builds community as people in an organization
identify and resolve problems together. The process builds their awareness of
each other's perspectives and delineates common ground. In other words, each
stage is an opportunity for drawing forth conflicting views and goals and
allowing the group to reframe, modify, or choose among them, rather than
suppressing them. Personal antagonisms or past injustices and misunderstand-
ings may hamper the effort if ignored; alternatively, strategic planning can
provide a safe environment for people to get at the issues behind old conflicts
and move beyond them.

Strategic Planning and Strategic Plans. Organizational planners may put the
results of their strategic planning process into a formal document, or strategic
plan. Such a formal document, however, is not nearly as important as doing the
planning and implementing the resultant strategies. If compiling a formal plan
diverts attention and resources from strategic thinking and acting, don't do it.
The leaders of IWRAW, for example, have engaged the core network in strategic
thinking and acting by keeping members focused on their overarching mission
and prompting them to develop strategies that take advantage of opportunities,
counter threats to women's human rights, build on IWRAW's strengths, and
recognize its limitations. The grant applications prepared by Arvonne Fraser,
Marsha Freeman, and others are the closest the organization comes to formal
strategic plans. Amnesty International, on the other hand, began a formal
strategic planning process in the early 1990s to help it deal with dramatic
changes in its environment and move into its next phase of organizational life.

As the IWRAW and Amnesty examples suggest, organizational leaders
should adapt strategic planning to their organizations' needs and culture (see
Bryson, 1995, pp. 37-42). For example, steps might be sequenced differently
(such as doing a SWOT analysis before completing a mission statement),
skipped, or repeated in the light of new information.

Cultural Analysis and Change

Cultural analysis can and should be included in strategic planning, but I want to give it special attention because an organization's culture is its strongest cohesive force and often its biggest impediment to change. As noted earlier, a group's culture includes artifacts, espoused values, and shared assumptions. Most important are the shared assumptions, which guide group members' actions without much overt thought or deliberation.

Establishing and managing organizational culture is an especially vital task for the founders of transnational citizen organizations such as Amnesty International and IWRAW. The organization's founders should attempt to establish an organizational culture that supports the organizational mission, especially its transnational aspect. A vital underlying assumption should be that the organization's internal and external stakeholders are highly important to the organization's survival and success (Bryson, 1995, p. 27). This assumption is the foundation of an organizational culture of service to stakeholders.

According to organizational psychologist Edgar Schein (1992), the founders create and enforce organizational culture through

- What they regularly pay attention to, measure, and control

- How they react to critical incidents and crises

- How they allocate scarce resources

- Role modeling, teaching, and coaching

- How they allocate rewards and status

- How they recruit, select, promote, retire, and excommunicate organizational members

Leaders in transnational citizen organizations should aim for an inclusive culture from the outset. For example, they should gear recruitment to cultural groups they want to participate in the organization's campaigns. Thus, they might offer family as well as individual memberships to connect better to cultures that emphasize the family as the basic social unit. They might seek endorsement from elders in societies that revere elders. If they are trying to recruit people from societies where government oppression or neglect has hampered development of a strong tradition of nonprofit, voluntary, or nongovernmental organizations, they may need to join efforts to circumvent or alter government policies toward such organizations. Leaders of transnational citizen organizations may need to subvert or find creative ways around cultural practices that would prevent certain groups from joining the organization. If they wish to reach people who speak different languages, they will need to translate organizational information into these languages, as both Amnesty and IWRAW have done. They will need to be sensitive to cultural differences in decision making, conflict resolution, and propensity for sharing leadership (Triandis &

Albert, 1987). They may also need to allocate resources to multicultural education for staff and members.

Founding leaders also should establish a culture of organizational integrity that supports ethical practice. To do this, leaders

- Make a public commitment to ethical principles

- Emphasize mission and stewardship

- Emphasize personal responsibility

- Help people in the organization analyze the ethical implications of their work and make plans for resolving ethical conflicts

- Make hard decisions supporting ethical principles

- Reward ethical behavior

- Model ethical behavior (Wallace & White, 1988)

Once an organizational culture is established, changing it is likely to be very difficult even if it has become highly dysfunctional. Strategies for change will depend on whether the organization is still young, at midlife, or mature (Schein, 1992, pp. 297-333). In general, however, organizational leaders that want to prepare their organizations to adapt to a rapidly changing external environment should try to establish what Schein called a "learning culture," in which organizational members embrace change. They do not rest on past laurels; they experiment and see failed experiments as learning opportunities and steps toward success.

A learning culture is grounded in the following assumptions:

- The environment is manageable (though not controllable).

- People should be practical problem solvers and learners.

- Truth is arrived at, or approximated, through a pragmatic discovery process.

- Both individuals and the group are important.

- A midterm focus is best—when *midterm* means long enough to "test whether or not a proposed solution is working but not so much time that one persists with a proposed solution that is clearly not working" (Schein, 1992, p. 369).

- Communication should flow along many channels.

- Both diversity and unity are important.

- Attention to both tasks and relationships is important.

- The world is complex and interconnected.

These assumptions are closely attuned to the theme of this book: that diverse people can come together across national boundaries to solve (or manage) complex public problems.

Many forces tend to undermine a learning culture as a transnational citizen organization grows larger and more bureaucratic. Open communication flow, which always is problematic in an organization that spans national boundaries, may be thwarted by divisions into different offices and departments. Many people are connected more by policies and procedures rather than by personal relationships. The outlook of the most powerful group in the organization supersedes all others. Leaders of transnational citizen organizations can avoid or mitigate such problems through many strategies—for example, by limiting growth, by using decentralized structures as IWRAW has done, by undertaking participatory strategic planning, by convening future search conferences (described in the next chapter), or by using teams within and across organizational units or categories. They can disseminate vivid stories that carry the message that people in this organization are intrepid problem solvers (see Taylor & Novelli, 1991). Special care must be taken to fully include people from diverse backgrounds and conditions within the organization. Indeed, one of the problems that a cross-departmental team may take on is how to celebrate diversity and ensure that people from different social groups feel included and powerful in the organization. As a beginning, the team itself should reflect the organization's diversity. The team may decide to tackle intergroup stereotypes and prejudice using techniques such as those recommended in the previous chapter. It may recommend strategies to attract people from minority groups and help them play increasingly powerful roles in the organization. Recruitment strategies include publishing job announcements in the media that reach these groups or establishing contacts with schools and programs that serve them. Organizational analyst Ann Morrison (1992) suggested additional strategies for retaining and promoting members of minority groups who join the organization—for example, by giving a highly qualified minority group member the same challenging assignments, support, and rewards for achievement that any other highly qualified person in the organization would receive.

It is also important to recognize that some assumptions of a learning culture may not fit the basic assumptions of particular ethnic, religious, or national cultures. For example, people from the United States may give so much importance to individual entrepreneurialism that they cringe at the thought of group consultation and decision making. People can alter their assumptions through various educational processes: The introduction of a new technology (such as quality circles) may do it, storytelling and role playing may work, and pilot projects and research may help. The crucial thing, as Edgar Schein and management analyst James O'Toole (1995) noted, is always to start where people are, to help them see how beneficial change can evolve from their previous assumptions. For example, the committed individualist might develop a stronger understanding that an entrepreneur builds on knowledge generated by others and must work with others to find how his or her great ideas mesh with their needs and aspirations.

Other Methods of Change and Innovation

Thinking about an organization as an enterprise of collective learning, or a self-renewing system, can help an organization adapt to internal and external contingencies. Helpful resources for developing a learning organization include *The Fifth Discipline Fieldbook* (Senge et al., 1994), *Leadership and the New Science* (Wheatley, 1992), *Leading Change* (O'Toole, 1995), and *Out of Control: The Rise of Neo-Biological Civilization* (Kelly, 1994). Leaders in learning organizations invest in the organization's human capital by developing the skills and capabilities of organizational members in support of a mission that everyone cares about and by nurturing a learning culture. They push authority and accountability down and spread it throughout the organization. They provide "venture capital" for experimentation and tolerate and even celebrate small mistakes resulting from experimentation (Light, 1995). They ensure that work groups have supervisory encouragement, training, and other resources needed to function well. When work groups are made up of competent and committed people, organizational leaders help them become "self-directed teams" by making sure they have meaningful work and by outlining and honoring the boundaries of their decision-making authority (Terry, 1996). Organizational leaders might use a tool such as the KEYS instrument (Center for Creative Leadership, 1995) to assess the organization's climate for creativity. They remember that change cannot be imposed and pay special attention to convincing the most powerful people in the organization that needed changes can help them accomplish their goals.

Leaders in learning organizations promote multiframe thinking—that is, they view their organizations through several lenses to diagnose problems and foster creative, sustainable solutions. Terry (1993) recommended looking at organizations through his human action framework, consisting of seven dimensions that increase in complexity as one moves up the list from existence to fulfillment:

- Fulfillment

- Meaning

- Mission

- Power

- Structure

- Resources

- Existence

In advising organizational leaders, he listens to how people in the organization talk about organizational problems. For example, if they continually complain about not having enough money or people with the right skills, they are using the resources lens. If they emphasize the need to refigure departments or change reporting channels, they are using the structure lens. If they complain of not knowing where they are going, they are using the mission lens.

Terry has found that the natural tendency of people in organizations is to solve problems at a level below the one where the problem presents itself, when the real problem and the most promising path to solution lie at the level above. For example, when people in an organization say they need more power and authority to do their jobs well, the real problem may be that the top executives in the organization do not believe that others in the organization understand and support the organizational mission well enough to have additional decision-making power. In this situation, organizational leaders may be easily attracted to structural solutions, such as organizing cross-functional teams or putting together a task force to study decentralization, when their time might more productively be spent on building a sense of shared mission in the organization.

Bolman and Deal (1991), Morgan (1986), and Quinn (1988) offered comparable lists of frames or lenses for thinking about and shaping organizational life. Bolman and Deal urged leaders to emphasize especially the "symbolic" lens, analogous to Robert Terry's "meaning" and "fulfillment" lens. Using the symbolic lens, leaders can think of organizational life as theatrical performance acting out the organization's core values and beliefs, replete with metaphor, humor, and play. Leaders also need to recognize that organizational dimensions may differ in importance, depending on stages of organizational development (see Quinn, 1988). For example, in an organization's early stage, leaders can give less attention to structure and resources, while galvanizing followers around existence and mission.

Community Building

To build internal community, leaders focus on creating shared mission and establishing democratic systems and culture and consistently remind followers in words and actions that "we're in this together." One important way that leaders care about others in the organization is by listening to them and following up on what they say. They pay attention to what people care about, what they need to do their jobs well, and what will help them grow. They help identify the assets of the community (see Kretzmann & McKnight, 1993) and help people share information and resources across internal boundaries. They reach out to the people on the periphery of the organization and make them more central. All of these activities nurture the leadership capacity of people in the organization (Drath & Palus, 1994).

Organizational leaders also establish internal leadership development programs geared to the type of organization and people's place and role in the organization. Appropriate leadership development for people in a bureaucratic organization will differ from that for people in a grassroots organization. To be helpful, leadership development programs must be attuned to the different responsibilities and opportunities attached to positions such as executive director or member of a volunteer board of directors. Tom Shaver (1995) offered helpful guidance, based on his study of organizations in the United States and "less industrialized countries," for leadership development in grassroots organizations. Brown and Covey (1987) offered advice for leaders of citizen-organized "private development agencies," designed to promote self-help among disadvantaged people in the United States and other countries. U.S. authors have generated tomes of leadership advice for boards of directors and executive officers of nonprofit groups (e.g., Herman & Associates, 1994; Lakey et al., 1995; Wood, 1995). Advice also abounds for leading and managing volunteers (e.g., Brudney, 1994; Lakey et al., 1995). Harder to come by is guidance geared to people trying to lead from the middle or bottom of organizations. Leadership development for people in these positions should include recognition that they have proportionately less positional authority in the organization compared to an executive director or senior managers. To exercise leadership, they need to make up for what they lack in positional authority by forging alliances with others at their level and winning over those above or below them in the organization. They may unionize, as Amnesty's IS staff did in 1972. They may form strong ties to powerful constituents outside the organization. Even more than the people at the top, people at the middle and bottom need what Robert Terry calls "exit cards" if they are to exert leadership. That is, they should develop viable alternatives to staying in the organization so that they can reduce the danger associated with challenging the status quo.

To nurture the relationships that sustain external communities, leaders remind people inside and outside their own organizations that "we're all in this together" when it comes to our neighborhood, our village, our nation, a several-nation region, or the whole world. The well-being of any one of us is best secured by a commitment to the well-being of all. We do not have to like each other, but at the very least, we can agree to argue respectfully. We may be able to collaborate in areas of agreement while going separate ways in other areas. We should celebrate progress in tackling mutual problems and honor individual community builders. We must resist efforts to wipe out or undermine the development of citizen organizations and networks.

Leaders attempting to build communities that embrace several organizations must become skilled in interorganizational collaboration, which can take many forms, from informal networking to issue-focused coalition building. Organizational consultants Michael Winer and Karen Ray (1994) and professor Jeffrey Luke (1998) offer detailed guidance for collaboration efforts.

A crucial challenge for leaders who hope to build and sustain interorganizational collaboration is negotiating the demands and expectations of their own constituencies and those of the other network participants. A leader must remember that an important reason for participating in interorganizational collaboration is to advance the mission of the organization he or she is representing, yet he or she must recognize that some part of that mission may be a low priority or even unacceptable to other participating organizations. Leaders of formal interorganizational networks such as IWRAW will need to negotiate a new mission that includes at least part of all the participating organizations' mission.

SUMMARY

The founders of Amnesty International and IWRAW built lasting transnational citizen organizations by helping their organizations develop clear and compelling missions and establishing governance and administrative systems and culture that enabled the organizations to make significant progress in carrying out their missions. The organizations have adapted to external and internal change by carefully refining their missions, building core competencies, modifying internal structures and strategies, taking advantage of modern telecommunications technology, engaging in formal and informal strategic planning, and providing for leadership succession. They fostered internal community by promoting democratic governance and problem solving and by honoring or celebrating individual and collective contributions. They fostered external community by collaborating with other organizations and building relationships with neutral and even opposing parties.

   In addition to describing organizational leadership within Amnesty and IWRAW, this chapter has presented resources and tools that can help leaders build strong transnational citizen organizations. The next chapter will consider how leaders in the global commons help create and build support for compelling visions that can animate their organizations, social movements, and global society.

CHAPTER 6

Visionary Leadership

The advent of a world in which human beings shall enjoy freedom of speech and belief and freedom from fear and want has been proclaimed as the highest aspiration of the common people.
—Universal Declaration of Human Rights

Leaders in the global commons create and communicate widely shared visions that inspire and unify many people beyond their own organizations. They respond to citizens' desire for meaning—for understanding and improving their worlds. Specifically, visionary leaders in the global commons

- Seize opportunities to be interpreters and direction givers in areas of uncertainty and difficulty

- Reveal and name real needs and real conditions

- Help followers frame and reframe public problems that spill beyond national boundaries

- Champion new, improved ideas for dealing with these problems

- Offer compelling visions of the future

- Pay careful attention to the design and use of formal and informal forums

Let us examine these tasks more thoroughly, drawing illustrations from Amnesty International and IWRAW. Then we can explore helpful resources and tools for exercising visionary leadership in the global commons.

INTERPRETATION AND DIRECTION GIVING

Building on their understanding of the social, political, economic, and technological context, visionary leaders offer explanations for changes in the context.
They connect these changes to the public problem that concerns them and
indicate generally what might be done to counter or take advantage of the
change.

Amnesty International

Amnesty's founders understood that the British and global political environment had changed tremendously by 1960. European nations were entering a
postcolonial era; totalitarian regimes had been defeated in Germany and Italy
but were strengthening their position in the Iberian Peninsula, Russia, and
Eastern Europe; and a fledgling United Nations offered some promise that civil
and political rights sustaining North American and European democracies could
be extended to the rest of the world. Peter Benenson and his colleagues urged
fellow citizens to stay concerned about what was happening in other countries
around the world and to pledge themselves to assisting anyone anywhere who
was imprisoned because of his or her beliefs. They held up the UN Declaration
of Human Rights as authorization for this course of action.

IWRAW

As a result of the UN Decade for Women, a global consensus had formed
around the rhetoric that all women should have the opportunity for full development. That consensus was embedded in an international treaty, the Women's
Convention. At the Nairobi conference concluding the UN Decade, a crucial
question was: What should the women's organizations that had worked so hard
to shape the convention and the action plan ("Forward Looking Strategies")
emerging from the Nairobi conference do next? Should they leave the monitoring of the convention to the Commission on the Elimination of Discrimination
Against Women (CEDAW) and simply work on some part of the action plan?
IWRAW's founders concluded that a concerted transnational citizen initiative
(focusing on the Women's Convention) was needed to maintain the momentum
of the UN Decade.

REVEALING REAL NEEDS AND CONDITIONS

Visionary leaders help constituents see real conditions and needs that were
previously obscured or easily ignored. They gather evidence and present it in
attention-getting ways that highlight the discrepancy between how things are
and people's deepest and best sense of how they should be. They suggest how
constituents could remedy the needs they identify.

Amnesty International

Amnesty's founders and their successors have understood that the best way to make human rights violations real is to put names and faces on men, women, and children imprisoned, tortured, murdered, or driven from their communities because of their politics or faith. Moreover, they have identified specific repressive governments and paramilitary organizations who have persecuted these people. Finally, they have shown people around the world how they might take effective action to help particular prisoners or to combat torture, "disappearances," and the like.

IWRAW

In their newsletter and their reports, IWRAW core network members and staff have used statistics and individual cases to highlight injustices perpetrated against women, whether female slavery, denial of parental rights, rape as a war tactic, government censorship, female infanticide, discrimination in the workplace, or some other violation. The newsletters and reports also indicate how supporters of women's rights can fight and already are fighting back against these abuses, often using provisions of the Women's Convention or other international human rights treaties.

PROBLEM FRAMING

Usually, visionary leaders explain how a public problem, or societal need, fits into certain interpretive schemes or frames already available to constituents. Sometimes visionary leaders actually propose new interpretive schemes that can be used to frame public problems. Thus, the founders of Amnesty International relied on the universal human rights interpretive scheme to summon up a repertoire of values and sanctioned actions that would help people categorize the problems that concerned them and consider a limited range of solutions. The universal human rights interpretive scheme itself had been developed most effectively by the framers of the Universal Declaration of Human Rights.

Visionary leaders also forge new links between interpretive schemes. IWRAW's leaders have linked the women's rights interpretive scheme (popularized by the global women's movement during the 1970s and 1980s) to the human rights interpretive scheme. That is, IWRAW leaders argue that "women's rights are human rights" and therefore that human rights programs and campaigns should include special attention to women's experience.

Amnesty International

As a result of visionary leadership by its founders and others in the organization, Amnesty has declared that the persecution of people for their political and religious views or because of their ethnicity, gender, sexual orientation, or place of residence is an issue of human rights and responsibilities. The rights framing allows the movement to use the Universal Declaration of Human Rights as legitimation and also as a primary tool for pressuring governments because the declaration is aimed at governments and because governments are the signatories of the conventions aimed at enforcing it.

Interestingly, although Peter Benenson contributed to the human rights framing of Amnesty's work by tying it to articles of the Universal Declaration, he wanted the organization to cast itself mainly as a civil liberties crusader. His view was overridden by those who were attracted to the broader and more compelling human rights scheme. At the same time, there has been considerable additional debate within Amnesty over the linking of free expression of political and religious views to other human rights. Some Amnesty members have argued that Amnesty should be more directly involved in what are commonly called economic, social, and cultural rights. They argue that those rights are at least as important as the right of free expression and that their fulfillment actually helps establish the conditions for free expression. As Thomas Hammarberg noted in the 1977 annual report, Amnesty's official policy, while recognizing that all human rights are important, has been to maintain its emphasis on civil rights in order to "achieve practical results" (Amnesty International, 1977, p. 12). Amnesty has strongly resisted arguments that civil rights should be overruled by certain cultural traditions or set aside even temporarily to promote economic or social development. Currently, Amnesty seems to be highlighting the interrelationship of the different types of human rights more strongly than it has in the past. For example, Pierre Sané (1994) wrote, "Empowerment of communities [around the world] can only be achieved if the spaces of freedom from fear and freedom from want are enlarged at the same time" (p. 42).

Although they tended to emphasize the human rights frame, Amnesty's founders less overtly defined the imprisonment of people for expressing their opinions and beliefs as a human family problem. In other words, these men believed, in Judeo-Christian terms, that they were their brothers' keepers and that their brothers were all mankind.

IWRAW

By invoking the women's rights interpretive scheme on behalf of women everywhere, IWRAW's founders were sending the message that all women have the right to full human development. Discriminating against women workers, beating women, restricting their access to education, depriving them of family planning services—anything that deprived women of their right to full human development—was a violation of their rights and therefore unjust. IWRAW's founders were situating themselves within a tradition, aligning themselves with heroic figures who had fought for women's suffrage, literacy, reproductive freedom, and the like around the world. They were raising the banner of global sisterhood.

By linking the women's rights scheme to the universal human rights scheme, IWRAW's leaders claimed the added legitimacy of the UN human rights treaties and summoned UN bodies and human rights organizations such as Amnesty to include women in their human rights visions. This linkage also offered a counter to arguments that respect for different cultural practices should override women's rights. The core tenet of the Universal Declaration of Human Rights is that everyone has certain rights regardless of the accepted practices of the society or community in which he or she lives. That tenet is still debated at international human rights gatherings, but it was strongly reaffirmed by the majority of delegates to the 1993 World Conference on Human Rights in Vienna.

IWRAW's leaders also interpret culture as evolving rather than static. The report of IWRAW's fifth annual conference stated:

> Tradition and custom, by their nature are not writ in stone. The essence of custom is its reflection of community norms and behavior, which change over time. As communities adapt to changing economic, social, and political conditions, their customary ways—from forms of dress to forms of government—change as well. Invoking custom and tradition as a set of rigid, unchanging historical rules is a disservice to custom and a disservice to community. And invoking custom only to control women, by insisting that they bear the burden of maintaining customs to which the rest of the community is not bound, is patently discriminatory and a profound denial of their human rights. (IWRAW, 1990, p. 4)

IWRAW core network member Farida Shaheed exemplifies this approach in her work with Women Living Under Muslim Laws (WLUML). She emphasizes that WLUML is not anti-Muslim but rather is striving for a more enlightened interpretation of the Koran, laws, and practices.

IWRAW's interpretation of culture puts it at odds with fundamentalist interpretations. Indeed, Arvonne Fraser believes that fundamentalism, which she defines as "religious fundamentalism turned political," is the "biggest obstacle against change" in women's condition. "People are going to have to figure out that we have to respect diversity, and fundamentalism doesn't" (interview by author, March 5, 1993).

IDEAS FOR DEALING WITH PUBLIC PROBLEMS

The framing of a public problem will determine the range of solutions to be considered for solving it. Visionary leaders help constituents identify what solutions within that range are most promising. They encourage consideration of solutions already available, needed modifications of those solutions, and completely new approaches.

Amnesty International

Having emphasized government responsibility for protecting the rights of their citizens, Amnesty's founders focused on a certain range of solutions for pressuring governments to carry out their responsibility. Later, it became clear that the idea that governments were mainly responsible for human rights protection was inadequate, and Amnesty began to develop tactics that could reduce abuses by opposition groups and paramilitary organizations, which were often outside formal government control.

Amnesty's founders argued that international organizations do not have the clout to enforce human rights laws and that governments will not enforce them without a lot of pressure from the world's citizens. Therefore, the general solution to human rights violations is individual responsibility. Every individual is responsible for upholding human rights, and by banding together with others in Amnesty, individuals can be effective. In Amnesty's 1978 annual report, Martin Ennals quoted Amnesty's acceptance speech on receiving the UN Human Rights Award: "Human rights cannot be left to governments, legislators, and jurists. They are the concern and the responsibility of the man and woman in the street, of the labourer, the farmer, the office clerk, the student" (Amnesty International, 1978, p. 1). Through the years, Amnesty founders and their successors have developed more specific solutions, or tactics—some of them adapted from other groups and campaigns and some of them invented—to accomplish the general solution of citizen pressure on governments and other groups.

IWRAW

Because IWRAW's leaders defined discrimination against women as a global problem, they were naturally interested in using and strengthening the Women's Convention, the only international treaty that bound signatory governments to eliminate many kinds of discrimination against women and girls. Thus, the solutions they initially adopted included working closely with the UN body responsible for overseeing the convention, helping signatory governments put together their reports on implementing the convention's provisions, pressuring other governments to sign the convention, and educating women and men around the world about the convention. As IWRAW's core network put more emphasis on the human rights scheme, they became more interested in efforts to prod UN human rights bodies to include attention to women's rights in their deliberations.

Because of their concern with the full development of women everywhere, IWRAW's leaders have sought change in entire systems of laws, rules, and customs. From IWRAW's inception, Arvonne Fraser argued that small, short-term projects by themselves will never be enough unless they are pursued as part of a comprehensive, long-term strategy.

One important solution adopted by IWRAW's leaders, after considerable debate, has been women's leadership development. For some in the core network, leadership had such strong associations with elitism and male authority that they wanted nothing to do with it. On the other hand, some of IWRAW's core network members—for example, the African women—were eager to talk about and claim leadership, while also defining it for themselves.

Fraser, who sees leadership as a process of working outside and inside established political systems and governing structures, was a strong advocate of developing women's leadership as a tool for achieving women's rights. In a letter to core network member Isabel Plata, she wrote, " I really intend to push women into leadership or this world will never change. I don't really care if people like me or not for it—at least I'll feel better in that something is accomplished" (Fraser, 1991b). She found it somewhat difficult to understand "how fearful women are of leadership and leaders, . . . because I've been reinforced in politics and leadership all my life." Nevertheless, she recognized that powerful social forces have conveyed the message that leadership is not for women. In a letter to core network member Miren Busto, she wrote, "My sense is that the socialization against women being leaders or decision makers is very, very deep both within women and about them" (Fraser, 1991a).

Despite their recognition that many men have actively discriminated against or abused women or at least have gone along with such practices, IWRAW's leaders believe an important strategy for combatting these practices is working with men who support the women's rights vision. Core network members also have recognized that some women resist or actively oppose the vision they are promoting.

COMPELLING VISIONS OF THE FUTURE

Visionary leaders weave together their understandings of context, social needs, the interpretation of problems, and promising solutions into visions that help followers develop a sense of what they have in common with each other and the larger world. These visions are stories drawing on past experiences, present opportunities, fundamental values, and cultural traditions. They show how values can be realized in the future through leaders' and followers' behavior.

Amnesty International

Here is the opening paragraph of Peter Benenson's (1961) newspaper article that launched the Appeal for Amnesty:

> Open your newspaper any day of the week and you will find a report from somewhere in the world of someone being imprisoned, tortured or executed because his opinions or religion are unacceptable to his government. There are several million such people in prison—by no means all of them behind the Iron

and Bamboo Curtains—and their numbers are growing. The newspaper reader
feels a sickening sense of impotence. Yet if these feelings of disgust all over the
world could be united into common action, something effective could be done.
(p. 21)

Benenson begins with an experience very commonplace for his audience—
the act of reading a newspaper. He briefly but vividly depicts a social need or
problem and describes its magnitude. Alluding to the Cold War, he emphasizes
that the problem is worldwide and growing. The problem, he bluntly states,
makes his readers feel sick and impotent. He implicitly assumes that these
feelings result from shared values—human dignity, freedom of opinion and
belief, and concern for one's fellow men. In this paragraph, he suggests a very
general solution, "common action," and proclaims its potential efficacy.

The remainder of his article elaborates the problem and proposed solutions.
Included are the stories and photographs of six prisoners of conscience from
Romania, the United States, Angola, Czechoslovakia, Hungary, and Greece.
Benenson legitimizes the appeal by citing articles from the Universal Declaration of Human Rights, quoting Winston Churchill and Voltaire, and noting
previous campaigns in the United States and Europe to end oppressive conditions. Finally, the article outlines clear aims for the appeal and includes a means
for readers to respond.

The article also is a compact between Benenson and his colleagues (described as "a group of lawyers, writers, and publishers in London") and the
newspaper readers. The backers of the appeal are promising to work with any
who join them to fight for the release of prisoners of conscience around the
world.

One of Benenson's great strengths was his ability to work with others to
create and communicate a compelling vision. Others in Amnesty would renew
and expand the vision in their own words, but Benenson was its progenitor.

IWRAW

The founders of IWRAW also presented a compelling vision—in this case,
a vision of women and supportive men striving for a world free of discrimination
against women. Their funding proposal to the Carnegie Corporation (Women,
Public Policy and Development Project & Development Law and Public Policy
Program, 1985) heralded the "momentum for change" generated by the international women's movement, UN initiatives, and national government programs. The proposal declared the Women's Convention "an international bill of
rights for women." IWRAW would be a vehicle for women's organizations to
promote the convention and maintain the momentum for improving women's
lives. The proposal emphasized that public policies change when citizen groups
organize around new ideas, attract media attention, gain additional supporters,
and exert pressure on government policy makers. The proposal began with

forceful quotes from Irene Cortes, a law professor at the University of the Philippines, and Norma Forde, a law professor at the University of the West Indies. Norma Forde's comment, especially, highlighted the benefits of working for improved public policies:

> Neither treaties nor municipal laws nor pronouncements nor declarations can easily change traditional attitudes. However, all these measures can generate an environment, can fashion a background against which customary and reactionary attitudes are clearly visible, by contrast with forward-thinking. Only when forward-thinking is buttressed by corresponding appropriate policy will reactionary action be diminished in application and effect. (p. 5)

The IWRAW (1990) report on the fifth annual conference of IWRAW and the tenth anniversary of the Women's Convention quoted the declaration by core network member Farida Shaheed that the convention was allowing women everywhere "to dream a different reality" (p. 4). In articles for popular and academic journals and in book chapters, IWRAW's founders have presented a clear picture of women as fully entitled world citizens, united by the fight for their rights but battling different forms of discrimination depending on their circumstances. For example, Silvia Pimentel (1993) of Brazil emphasized that Latin American women are fighting a civil law system influenced by patriarchal ideology and Roman legal concepts. In recent decades, she wrote, Latin American women have questioned "the notion of head of household, the civil law concept of *patria poder* (patriarchy), family, marriage, women's fidelity, *legitima defensa da honra* (the legitimate defense of honour), rape, and others" (p. 29).

Arvonne Fraser (1992) offered a trenchant summation of IWRAW's vision:

> Old ideas are dying, but not without a fight. Discrimination may now be contrary to international law, but equality is not automatic. The political will to change laws and behavior is still weak but in many ways and languages, women the world over are now saying: "Move over, guys, we're here to stay and we now have international law on our side." (p. 21)

DESIGNING AND USING FORUMS

Visionary leaders understand the importance of designing and using formal and informal forums to create and communicate shared meaning about public problems and their solutions. These forums can be as simple as the policy meetings that Amnesty's founders held in a London pub or as complex as the 1993 World Conference on Human Rights in Vienna or the 1995 World Conference on Women in Beijing.

Amnesty International

The use of forums by Amnesty's founders was masterful. Because of his personal connections, Peter Benenson was able to launch the Appeal for Amnesty in a nearly full-page article in one of Britain's leading newspapers on a Sunday. The man in charge of the paper's foreign news service also asked newspapers around the world to give similar space to the appeal. As a result, it was published in *Le Monde, Neue Zürchen Zeitung,* the *New York Herald Tribune,* and at least 20 other newspapers.

The founding group planned a follow-up ceremony to coincide with Human Rights Day. They sought popular appeal and drama. As the site, they chose the steps of St. Martin's in the Field Church at Trafalgar Square in London. They recruited actress Julie Christie and Cy Grant, a popular singer, to play the part of prisoners, whose bonds would be burned away with a candle held by Odette Churchill, a well-known heroine of the Resistance in World War II. They also gathered former prisoners of conscience to hold a vigil through the night following the ceremony. The event attracted British press coverage.

In the years to come, Amnesty would use Human Rights Day as an occasion for launching campaigns or focusing on particular prisoners. The event was eventually expanded to Prisoner of Conscience Week, with a different focus each year, such as human rights activists in prison or women in prison.

Through the years, Amnesty has produced numerous special reports on abuses in particular countries or regions. The main findings of these reports are transmitted to news media, which often publicize them. The organization's book-length annual report also is dominated by reports of Amnesty's work to counter abuses in specific countries. The organization has continuously prided itself on careful research to ensure that these reports are accurate, realizing that a reputation for accuracy is a vital asset in creating shared analysis of problems. For example, Martin Ennals wrote in Amnesty's 1978 annual report that "Amnesty International must continue to have the courage, as a movement, to state what it believes to be true, and to remain silent if reliable information is not available. The latter is often more difficult than the former" (Amnesty International, 1978, p. 6).

Over the years, the leadership work of designing and using forums has become widely shared in the organization. Top policy makers play a role, but staff and members provide many of the ideas for conferences to study specific issues and launch campaigns (such as the ones against torture and the death penalty). An example is the 1973 International Conference on Abolition of Torture, which produced "enormous international publicity" (Amnesty International, 1974 p. 8), program plans, and pressure for future action. Amnesty officials, members, and staff also participate in forums with other human rights organizations aimed at developing proposals for UN policies and decision making.

Amnesty's annual (and later biennial) international meetings, initiated by the founders, are important forums in which Amnesty members can reconnect with and possibly revise the organization's vision. At these meetings, in response to ideas from members, staff, and policy makers, problems are redefined, new ones are identified, and new solutions considered. Amnesty has had struggles over how representation and voting power at the meetings should be allocated among national sections, and it has adopted policies that promote participation of smaller and non-European sections at the meetings. One way of increasing non-European participation was to hold some of the meetings outside Europe, beginning in the 1980s.

The annual report and other internally distributed publications emphasize Amnesty members' extensive activities and their effects, listing numbers of cases taken up and resolved and quoting letters from prisoners of conscience who say that Amnesty campaigns gave them hope during their imprisonment or contributed to their release. Amnesty publications also illuminate the horrors that will occur if no one acts to stop them.

Annual reports also are forums for reemphasizing Amnesty's mission and its basic methods, especially its independence. In the 1968-69 report, for example, Sean MacBride noted that Amnesty had been accused of being both communist and anticommunist, pro-West and anti-West. "While we argue for release of writers in the USSR and conscientious objectors in the USA, the release of Jews in an Arab State and Arabs in a Jewish State, we will be accused by all parties of being used by others" (Amnesty International, 1969, p. 1).

Amnesty activists have used an array of additional means of communication, including Christmas cards, striking posters, video documentaries, human rights kits for use in schools, and an anthology of music and poetry. It also sends speakers to talk about Amnesty at schools, churches, and other organizations or groups.

Amnesty's founders paid attention to language. Eric Baker's idea for calling the people whom Amnesty sought to support "prisoners of conscience" helped audiences quickly understand Amnesty's moral appeal. Amnesty's founders thought carefully about the name for their campaign. They chose "amnesty" for its direct connection to the release of prisoners and its connotation of forgiveness. The name is no longer completely indicative of what the organization does, but neither is the name for Oxfam, another large international voluntary organization that has a mission embracing far more than famine relief. Semantic purity does not seem to matter very much once potent organizational names have taken root in public consciousness and the organizations have become institutions.

An early Amnesty report noted that writers attempt to keep reports "factual and unemotional" (Amnesty International, 1966, p. 8). Amnesty also tries to construct its reports and statements to hold governments and other groups responsible for violations without attacking these groups.

Amnesty continues to struggle to increase the numbers of languages in which its information is published. Not only do more languages increase the dissemination of the messages, but their use communicates Amnesty's determination to be truly global. The stationery used by the International Secretariat now is printed in English, Spanish, French, Arabic, Japanese, and Russian.

IWRAW

Important forums organized by IWRAW's leaders include the annual core network meeting and summer leadership workshops. These forums are the prime settings for the continual refinement of the organization's vision, goals, and priorities. A major public conference usually is held in conjunction with the core network meeting. IWRAW invites members of other human rights organizations, human rights scholars, and journalists to the conference. The conferences have focused on ways to increase government and public understanding of the Women's Convention, improve reporting to CEDAW, create new traditions that promote women's equality, influence the World Conference on Women in Beijing, and follow up on that gathering. Conference proceedings often are summarized in a report that can be widely distributed. The annual core network meeting and the conferences are held in the same city and near the same time as the annual meeting of CEDAW. IWRAW usually hosts a reception or lunch for CEDAW members and has often invited CEDAW members to speak at the conference.

The annual meeting, the summer workshops, and the public conference all are conducted in English. Obviously, this practice prevents many people from participating. Marsha Freeman (1993) recognized this problem but said, "If you want true networking, you have to have a common language" (interview by author, March 25, 1993). She pointed out that connections often occur in the free spaces outside formal sessions and that without a common language people would clump in national language groups as they do at UN "corridor sessions."

Women's Watch, the international newsletter published in English four times a year by IWRAW, is an important forum for reporting on progress or setbacks in achieving the group's vision. The newsletter also is translated into Spanish. Many newsletter reports include contact names and addresses for readers who want to find out more about a project or explore collaborations.

ADDITIONAL RESOURCES AND GUIDANCE
FOR VISIONARY LEADERSHIP
IN THE GLOBAL COMMONS

Essentially, visionary leadership is the work of preparing for or actually participating in forums, the settings in which people can create and communicate *shared visions* that prompt beneficial collective action on transnational public problems. Visionary individuals start with their own personal passion, insight, and foresight. They themselves can attempt to define the problem that concerns them and develop sensible solutions; they can publish stories and statistics and recommendations. But their ability to understand the problem, make it real, expand and analyze the set of possible solutions, and create shared vision can be magnified by convening forums in which many people with partial knowledge of the problem come together to share results of formal or informal research. Such forums can be as basic as an impromptu consciousness-raising session in which participants talk about their experiences. For example, a Japanese woman lawyer might host an informal gathering of her colleagues to talk about the professional barriers they have encountered. A family-planning worker in Colombia might ask a group of women visiting her clinic to tell each other about their lives. Or, a fisher might encourage other fishers to talk together about how pollution and overfishing of international waters is affecting their livelihood. On the other hand, forums can be elaborate affairs with formal agendas and prepared presentations and workshops.

To design and use forums astutely, visionary leaders

- Link formal and informal forums

- Attend to logistics and process in formal forums convened to define public problems, search for solutions, and develop action plans

- Maintain and expand the shared vision resulting from these formal forums

Let us consider each of these tasks more thoroughly. As we do so, it is important to remember that the creation and communication of a shared vision for resolving a public problem take time. This does not mean that visionary leaders counsel followers to postpone all action on a problem until the vision is clear. Especially in a crisis, visionary leaders can help people identify and pursue immediate steps to improve the situation. But in the long run, people will expect fuller explanation of how these actions fit into a coherent vision (Boal & Bryson, 1987).

Linking Informal and Formal Forums

Informal forums lay the groundwork for organizing and using more formal forums. In the case of Amnesty International, the founders had firsthand knowledge about prisoners of conscience. They brought their information to informal gatherings convened by Peter Benenson. They persuaded other early volunteers to gather more stories, more evidence. They held more small-scale meetings to plan the use of existing formal forums, such as major newspapers, and to organize new ones, such as the Human Rights Day ceremony in Trafalgar Square, to present their evidence and to galvanize collective action. As Amnesty members and staff became increasingly concerned in the early 1970s about repressive governments' use of torture, they held informal discussions that eventually led to the 1973 International Conference on the Abolition of Torture.

Informal and even small-scale formal forums lay the foundation for large formal forums. They are not just concerned with the logistics and process to be used in the larger forums that will focus wide attention on the problem that concerns them. They also take at least a preliminary crack at defining the problem, offering solutions, and outlining a desired future. I recommend using *context analysis, oval mapping,* and *problem framing* to ensure that this preliminary work connects the problem to the global context, gathers information and ideas from all participants, and identifies one or more inclusive interpretive schemes for framing the problem.

Context Analysis. Visionary leaders ask: How is the problem that concerns me connected to, caused by, or exacerbated by important aspects of the global context? What aspects might help remedy the problem?

To sort out these questions, leaders can invite participants in informal and small-scale forums to consider whether and how the global political, social, economic, and technological conditions and trends affect efforts to resolve the problem. Leaders may want to disseminate information about these conditions and trends before the forums or ask knowledgeable participants to make presentations on pertinent aspects of the global context. As part of their conversation about global conditions and trends, the participants can decide which will require the most attention to remedy the problem. At the conclusion of the conversation, the group might designate one or more members to produce a written summary of the conversation or incorporate some of the ideas into a working paper, articles, essays, reports, documentaries, or commentary that can help others see these connections.

Oval Mapping. Informal or small-scale forums can continue the work of problem definition and begin the search for solutions by using oval mapping, a process that captures a group's shared vision, or "group mind." The process facilitator guides participants in brainstorming solutions to the problem and writing their ideas on ovals, or egg-shaped cards. The ovals are then displayed on a wall. Participants cluster them into groups and then work with the clusters to identify goals and priority actions. Here is an outline of the process (described more fully in Bryson et al., 1995):

1. The basic requirements are a group consisting of no more than a dozen people (seven is optimal); a facilitator (ideally someone from outside the group); a large wall; flipchart sheets; paper ovals (in yellow or another light color) approximately 7 ½ inches long and 4 ½ inches wide, 20 per person; masking tape; black markers; and pencils with erasers. The flipchart sheets should be taped together on the wall to make a rectangular backdrop for the ovals. The rectangle should

be four to six sheets wide and two to three sheets high, depending on the size of the group.

2. The facilitator asks each group member to think of solutions or responses to the problem being considered and to write those ideas on the ovals, one idea per oval, using the black markers. If the problem were female illiteracy, the facilitator might pose the question, "What should we do to increase female literacy?" The facilitator directs the group to express their solutions as imperatives—for example, "Have reading materials with female heroes." The idea should be expressed in no more than 10 words. Group members should put their ovals on the flipchart-covered wall as they finish them.

3. The facilitator then leads participants in clustering the ovals according to common themes or subjects. Within the clusters, the more general, abstract, or goal oriented are moved toward the top and the more concrete, specific and detailed clusters toward the bottom. The facilitator asks participants to name the clusters and places a new oval with a name above each cluster.

4. The facilitator works with participants to pencil in arrows indicating linkages within and between clusters. An arrow pointing from Oval A to Oval B indicates that the action on Oval A causes, influences, or precedes the action on B; conversely, the action on Oval B is an effect, outcome, or follow-up to the action on A. Once the group agrees on the placement of the arrows, they can be drawn in permanently with a marker.

5. The group now has a map of clusters in which specific actions or options are located toward the bottom and more goal-oriented statements toward the top. The facilitator can then encourage the group to think further about what they hope to achieve by carrying out the actions on the map. The responses, or "higher" goals, can be placed on new ovals at the top of the map, and arrows can be drawn from ovals that would contribute to those goals.

6. Finally, the group may want to prioritize the actions and goals on the map. The facilitator might give everyone five red dots to place on the five ovals he or she deems most vital.

This process can be much more elaborate, but the simple version presented here should be adequate for constructing a preliminary vision of what the group should be doing about a problem and why. The map produced can be preserved as is, translated into an outline, or reproduced using computer graphics.

Besides brainstorming, other methods can be used to generate creative ideas for solutions to be placed on the ovals. For example, participants might begin by making analogies: What other problems resemble this one? What solutions have been tried? What has worked? Even more creative possibilities may be opened by calling on fantasy: Do we know of myths or traditional tales that might apply to this problem? What solutions do these myths or tales suggest?

The process assumes that participants can read and write the same language. If participants do not, an alternative process would be drawing pictures that represent possible actions. The pictures can be displayed to serve as a visual backdrop for talking about the actions.

Framing the Problem. Along with linking a problem to the global context and clarifying the problem's causes and possible solutions, visionary leaders search for a problem frame, or interpretive scheme, that can connect people across boundaries of nationality, ethnicity, gender, religion, and the like by appealing to their common values and interests. The founders of Amnesty International and IWRAW adopted the human rights frame and human family frames; two other important frames are that of earth as a delicate, yet resilient system and the world citizenship frame. In deciding whether these frames are best for the problems that concern them, leaders should consider carefully their advantages and disadvantages.

The human rights frame has the chief advantage of connecting a problem-solving effort to an entire body of international law and enforcement mechanisms, even if those mechanisms are generally weak. The 31 articles of the Universal Declaration of Human Rights provide ready justification and a mandate for remedying the problem. Moreover, the 1993 World Conference on Human Rights confirmed the universality and indivisibility of these rights.

The human rights frame has three main disadvantages: its strong association with the politics and philosophy of some European countries and the United States; its deemphasis of human responsibility; and its seeming lack of concern for the earth. (See, e.g., Desmond, 1983; Mies & Shiva, 1993; Renteln, 1988; Reoch, 1994.) Especially problematic is the tendency of industrialized democracies such as the United States to support the civil and political rights contained in the Universal Declaration more strongly than the economic, social, and cultural rights. If leaders are to use this frame effectively to unite people from all parts of the world, they will have to link and support both sets of rights in their discourse. They also can follow the example of Mohandas Gandhi and contemporary communitarian philosophers in pointing out that individual rights originate in and are sustained by social responsibility—that is, that individual rights have little meaning except as they are endorsed by a citizenry that accepts responsibility for building a just and humane society. Indeed, Mohandas Gandhi argued against proclaiming human rights. He advised, "Begin with a charter of the Duties of Man and I promise the rights will follow as spring follows winter" (quoted in Nair, 1994, p. 63). Leaders using the human rights frame also need to recognize that the human right to an adequate standard of living requires protection of the earth's capacity to sustain human life.

The human family frame is supported by many spiritual traditions and biology. It draws on the natural impulse to care for people close to us. Perhaps the greatest disadvantage of this frame is the temptation to think that people are just like us, or nearly so. Thus, leaders in the global commons who use this frame should take care to highlight the diversity within the human family.

Using the "fragile, yet resilient planet" frame has the advantage of highlighting humans' dependence and impact on the earth as a giant ecosystem that does not recognize political boundaries. A popular version of this frame is "sustainable development"—the idea that economic progress can and should be coupled with concern for the earth. Critics of sustainable development argue that its proponents are still too focused on continuous economic growth and technological prowess, especially as a way of helping "developing" countries "catch up" with industrialized countries. What is needed, these critics argue, is an understanding of how human beings can live more simply and in harmony with the earth. They advocate what Mies and Shiva (1993) called a "subsistence perspective" that focuses on smaller scale, cooperative enterprise and promotes nonconsumerist paths to human happiness.

The world citizenship frame emphasizes connection among the world's people and suggests that we are mutually responsible for working out collective goals and acting on them. It can easily be tied to the global commons metaphor that highlights collective access to and responsibility for the natural environment, the international marketplace, global information networks, and universal human rights. World citizenship also is related to the global neighborhood metaphor adopted by the Commission on Global Governance (1995). Perhaps the biggest drawback to the world citizenship frame is the likelihood that some people will associate it with the specter of world government, in which some global body, such as the UN General Assembly, would begin to function along the lines of a giant nation-state. Leaders who use the world citizenship frame can respond by using Cleveland's (1993) distinction between world government and world governance. Cleveland argued that world government based on the already defective nation-state model is neither desirable nor needed. At the same time, many international and supranational governance systems already do exist, some actually function well, and more should be established along the lines of the well-functioning systems. Leaders working in the global commons to tackle public problems should concern themselves with affecting existing supranational governance systems or establishing new ones when needed.

Convening Larger Formal Forums

Leaders help participants in informal and small-scale forums to consider how to involve a broad constituency in defining and developing solutions for the public problem that concerns them. A customary approach is convening formal face-to-face conferences or electronic conferences. These conferences might be primarily educational, or they might combine education and action in a format that includes plenary sessions, workshops, and working groups. Regardless of conference type, planners must attend to logistics and process.

Logistics. Conference planners should begin by posing the question, "Who should be there?" Again, a stakeholder analysis can help. In this case, stakeholders would be persons or groups affected by, contributing to, or concerned about the problem at issue. The planners identify stakeholders and decide which are most important and likely to participate in the conference without sabotaging it. (Journalists are important stakeholders, and it may be helpful to group them by type, such as newspaper, radio, television, magazines, and academic journals. It also is important to include people who have decision-making power in the arenas that have authority over the problem.) In deciding on an invitation list, planners are laying the groundwork for a coalition that can press for new policies and programs and watch over their implementation. Thinking most ambitiously, the planners can structure their invitation list with the aim of building a transnational social movement or transnational issue network that can mobilize people and information strategically to gain leverage over powerful governments and businesses (Sikkink, 1994).

Once the invitation list is complete, the planners can think about when and where the conference should be held, with what amenities, to attract at least the most important stakeholders. One option is to piggyback on some other meeting that will involve many of the stakeholders. Planners also should think carefully about how to extend conference invitations. As for the conference itself, planners should ensure that the physical space, equipment, food, and other supplies make it possible for participants to engage effectively in the conference process.

Process. Planners should agree on a conference process that can actively engage all participants in sharing information, opinions, and ideas and developing strategies and commitments. A process used successfully in many parts of the world is the "future search" (see Weisbord et al., 1992), usually a 3-day strategy conference involving 30 to 85 people. The main ideas of the future search are

- Bringing the whole system to the conference—that is, ensuring that a broad cross-section of stakeholders attends

- Exploring the past, current reality, and probable futures in a way that engages participants' "heads, hands, hearts, guts, and unconscious data" (Weisbord et al., 1992, p. 51)

- Generating commitment to change through self-managed dialogue

Let us consider how to conduct a future search conference on the question: How do we ensure that all girls become literate? The following scenario is based on the approach developed by facilitators Marvin Weisbord and Sandra Janoff (see Flower, 1995; Weisbord & Janoff, 1995).

The conference begins in the afternoon with a review of the *past*. Before the conference begins, the facilitators construct three time lines on a conference room wall covered with flipchart paper. Each time line spans the last 30 years;

one is devoted to the participants' personal lives, one to the world, and one to female literacy. Participants are asked to identify key events in their own lives, in the world, and in the cause of female literacy over the last 30 years. Participants use marking pens to record key events along each of the time lines, then work in small groups of diverse stakeholders to construct a story about some part of the time lines. Each group then has 3 minutes to tell the story to the larger group. When the stories are done, the facilitators ask, "What did you get out of that? What did you learn? What did you hear?"

Weisbord commented:

> This task has the effect of getting everybody on the same planet very quickly. We like the symbolism: the walls belong to everybody, anybody can use the markers, everybody's information is relevant, everybody has a story to tell, it's all part of a much larger picture. We don't have to say that, because people experience it in the first few hours of the conference. (quoted in Flower, 1995)

The next step in the conference is compiling a group "mind map" of *current reality*. It could be constructed using ovals (as in the oval mapping process described above). Everyone writes on ovals the current trends that he or she believes are affecting female literacy. The ovals are then attached to a wall covered with flipchart sheets; similar ovals could be clustered. The participants explain what their ovals mean, giving concrete examples. Participants are given colored dots to place on the ovals they think are most important, and the group talks about the ones that garner the most dots.

Often, says Weisbord, the map is an "overwhelming portrait of the world's troubles, as seen through the eyes of the people in this particular room at this particular time. . . . People will often report feeling down" (quoted in Flower, 1995). By the time this exercise is done, around 5 or 6 p.m., it is time to quit for the evening and let participants "sleep on" the results so far.

On the second day, the facilitators organize participants into small groups, but this time people who have a similar stake in the problem are grouped together. In a conference on female literacy, all the teachers would be together, and likewise all youth workers, young women, educational administrators, and so on. In each small group, participants reinterpret the mind map constructed the previous day. They may even revise it on new flipchart sheets, redrawing the whole map or making a "minimap" of the issues they deem important. Each small group then reports to the whole group on their new interpretations, their current actions on the issues they selected, and their plans for future action on the issues.

Next comes a "prouds and sorries" exercise. The facilitators ask each group to talk among themselves about their feelings about the issues that have just been highlighted. The question to the group is: "Looking at what you personally or members of your stakeholder group are doing right now about these issues, what makes you really proud? What are you doing or not doing that makes you really sorry?" Each small group summarizes its conversation for the large group. Then the whole group is asked to respond: What are their feelings, reactions, insights?

Weisbord commented on this exercise:

> The point is to get people to own up, not to finger point, not to blame, not to breastbeat, not to do anything about it, but just to be in touch with what they are proud of and what they are sorry about. This is usually a pivotal step in our conference, because of what people hear other people say. And there is an amazing release that comes from taking responsibility for your feelings. (quoted in Flower, 1995)

Participants are then reassembled into mixed groups and given the task of *creating a vision* for female literacy. They are told it is a certain day, 10 years into the future. They are asked to think of their ideal scenario of what they would like to see then in terms of female literacy—what programs would be in place, what would be the results. The groups are asked to write on flipchart sheets characteristics of their ideal scenarios. Then they are asked to list on additional sheets the barriers that would have to be overcome to achieve the ideal.

At this point, the groups are given a lengthy lunch break (2 ½ hours), during which they are to prepare a creative 7-minute report to present to the entire group. Before the presentations begin, one or two people from each group are asked to take notes on common themes that emerge, especially innovative ideas for programs, projects, or policies.

Weisbord commented: "People do the most amazing presentations. All their idealism pours out. It's fun. They are often hilariously funny. Some of them are profound. Some people do ceremonies, rituals. The collective unconscious gets mobilized in a big way" (quoted in Flower, 1995).

As the final exercise for the day, each small group compiles three flipchart sheets. On the first, they list the common desires for the future that they have heard in the presentations; on the second, they note innovative ideas that might accomplish these desires; on the third, they note unresolved differences that emerged from the presentations. The small groups are then paired and asked to compare and merge their lists. Each group then cuts the agreed-on items from the old lists and places them on the wall under the headings—common futures, potential projects, unresolved differences. This exercise concludes the second day.

On the final morning, participants come back to the wall with the lists of common futures, potential projects, and unresolved differences. They rearrange the lists, grouping similar items together. Facilitators then invite the group to talk about and clarify the lists. What does everyone endorse? What should be left in the unresolved category?

The conference concludes with action planning. Stakeholder groups meet to consider what they want to do immediately about female literacy, what they want do in the next 6 months to a year, and what they want to do in the longer term. They identify needed resources, time lines, support, action steps. They then report their conclusions to the whole group.

Next, participants meet with anyone with whom they want to work to do action planning around a particular project or interest. These common interest groups then report to the whole group about what next steps they have agreed on.

To wrap up the conference, one or more participants sum up the agreed-on action steps, which might include a new coordinating structure that included many of the people at the conference. Next steps might include follow-up conferences that involved the same group or additional stakeholders.

There are many variations on the future search process. Participants might be asked before the conference to collect information about the historical and current forces affecting the problem they are considering. Participants might be invited to a preconference session to hear presentations by experts. Such a session preceded a future search conference convened in Pakistan to develop a national conservation strategy (see Weisbord et al., 1992, Chapter 16). If conference participants do not read and write the same language, skilled storytellers, translators, and artists might be able to use the process framework to help participants create a shared understanding of the problem, a desired future, ideas and action steps for programs, policies, and projects.

Leaders can gain additional guidance from such conferences about the framing of the public problem being considered. Perhaps the problem of female illiteracy was initially placed in the human family frame: "We are all responsible for our daughters." Conference participants might have shifted to a human rights frame that added new authority and different solutions to the problem-solving effort.

Maintaining and Expanding the Shared Vision

Visionary leaders develop strategies for using various media to communicate the shared vision developed in the forums described above. They identify audience and appropriate media, and they make their vision as compelling as possible, adapting it as needed for particular audiences and media.

Audience and Media. Usually, leaders concerned about a particular problem want to reach specific stakeholder groups, as well as the general public. A starting place is the initial group that comes together to focus on a public problem. Each person in the group is likely to be connected to professional groups, other voluntary organizations, and political networks that have their own newsletters, journals, web pages, radio programs, and performances that might be used to build awareness of the problem. In addition to focusing on the media connections of the group, leaders should ask what other media we must use and even create to reach specific groups and the general public and how we obtain access to them. We may need to think about producing our own newsletter and other publications, radio show, play, or documentary. Personal connections help in gaining access to existing media forums. For example, Peter Benenson's acquaintance with an *Observer* editor made it easier for him to obtain prominent space in the newspaper for launching the Appeal for Amnesty. Having something interesting to report is important—the launch of a campaign, a public event such as educational meetings and rallies, the results of an investigation, the proceedings of a conference. Most vital, however, is developing a compelling vision that explains why this problem is important, why people should do something about it, and what they can do.

Developing a Compelling Vision, or Communal Story. As noted previously, compelling visions are stories drawing on past experiences, present opportunities, fundamental values, and cultural traditions. These stories are about real people and real places. Following Benenson's example, Amnesty International staff reporting on a massacre in Rwanda do not just give numbers of people killed and wounded. They find out the stories of several individuals and tell them in vivid detail. When Marsha Freeman wants to promote understanding of how national citizenship laws discriminate against women and how women can fight back, she tells the story of Unity Dow, an IWRAW core network member who successfully challenged a Botswanan law.

The story that constitutes a compelling vision extends beyond individuals, however. It evokes a strong sense of "we" that ties together the individual stories, the teller, and the audience. The speaker or writer says, directly or indirectly, that all of us have or might have experiences like these examples; we are connected to these people; we share values that require us to fight what is wrong and strive for what is right; and here are specific things we can do. The story reflects back to the audience an image of their best selves. By contrasting current reality and a desired state or by predicting an even worse future if nothing is done, the story helps propel the audience to action. The speaker or writer can use facts and figures to help communicate these messages, but the most useful tools are metaphors and vivid images that evoke interpretive schemes such as human rights, the human family, the fragile and resilient earth, world citizenship, and the global commons. When the audience is diverse, finding metaphors and images with broad appeal can be difficult. Even in an audience of different nationalities, there will be shared human activities, spiritual traditions, or historical events (e.g., the founding of the United Nations or the UN Decade for Women) from which such metaphors and images can be drawn. The tellers of stories should communicate their own passion and hope by speaking energetically, optimistically, and expressively.

To hone your ability to communicate a vision that can inspire others to join efforts to resolve a public problem, you can study the written or oral communication of well-known visionary leaders (such as Rigobertu Menchu Tum, Martin Luther King, Jr., Nelson Mandela) or less prominent but still powerful visionaries. In oral communication, body language as well as words is important.

Written and spoken stories can be made more real or reinforced by enacting them. The form may be a play, a documentary, or a simulation. For example, several participants in a seminar I taught wanted to communicate their concern about global economic disparity and promote a sense of personal connection to the problem. These participants planned a meal for the other seminar participants and staff. They invited three of us to sit at a table with candelabra and a linen cloth. These three had a steak dinner. They seated 10 of us at another less elegant table, where everyone was served some salad and chicken casserole. The remaining 30 or so people were seated at bare tables and given thin soup and bread. The leaders of the exercise then asked the participants to talk about their reaction to this simulation of global inequality; the leaders then built on this conversation to offer their vision of a world in which everyone had enough to eat.

Leaders also should adapt their visions to the forums in which they are to be communicated. If the forum is a print medium, check the tone, format, and length of articles or essays published in this newsletter, newspaper, or journal. If you are delivering a speech, practice the rudiments of effective public speaking, such as telling people clearly what your main points will be, fleshing out the main points, and summing up; staying on time; having a moderately relaxed posture; speaking without notes if possible; and using appropriate humor. If you are being interviewed on radio or television, find out about the interviewer and format, prepare sound bites, and practice answers that get your main points across and anticipate difficult questions. If you are preparing a documentary, think about how to communicate your vision in visual images. If you are using and creating forums in a politically repressive environment, your vision may need to be expressed in subtle form—for example, the plays written by Vaclav Havel when Czechoslovakia was under the Soviet regime.

SUMMARY

Visionary leaders work with diverse stakeholders in the global commons to define public problems, develop possible solutions for them, and offer compelling visions for a better future. They are skilled in designing and using formal and informal forums for creating and communicating a shared understanding of the problem and potential solutions and commitment to action. Helpful approaches, resources, and tools for visionary leadership include attention to context, oval mapping, problem framing, future search, attention to audience and media, and communal story.

The visionary work of developing ideas and commitments for solving public problems is crucial, but leaders also must attend to the political work of turning ideas into concrete proposals that will be adopted and implemented by decision makers in executive, legislative, and administrative arenas. Let us turn now to political leadership.

CHAPTER 7

Political Leadership

There is nothing mysterious or inherently evil about politics. It is simply the art and science of governing, of participating in public life. It requires the exercise of power, which can, of course, be used for constructive or destructive purposes.

—Arvonne Fraser

The work of political leadership in the global commons is obtaining and implementing policy decisions needed to achieve the shared vision of how a transnational public problem can and should be resolved. To do this work, political leaders

- Draw on many sources of political power

- Build winning, sustainable coalitions

- Overcome bureaucratic resistance

- Astutely design and use arenas

Usually when we speak of political leadership, we focus on electoral politics. This chapter will present a much broader view: political leadership as the process of obtaining and implementing policy decisions, in which electoral politics is only one means of channeling, shaping, and altering the decision-making power exercised in arenas. Note that the focus is on a particular type of power—the power to make and implement policy decisions, or what Gareth Morgan (1986) called "the power to rule," democratically or otherwise. In this view, politics and power are not equivalent. In Chapter 1, I argue for a broader conceptualization of power—as comprising the creation and communication of meaning and the sanctioning of conduct, along with the making and implementation of policy decisions.

Let us now explore the central activities of political leadership, using examples from Amnesty International and IWRAW. Following this exploration, I will present additional resources and guidance for political leadership in the global commons.

DRAWING ON MANY SOURCES OF POWER

Citizen groups advocating global public policy changes must think broadly about the sources of power they can draw on to counter or alter the power of government, nonprofit, or economic decision makers. Leaders help these groups develop strategies for mobilizing the power of citizens; of sympathetic government, nonprofit, and business officials; and of international courts.

Amnesty International

When Peter Benenson read about the Salazar government's imprisonment of two students for toasting freedom, he considered registering a protest with the Portuguese Embassy in London. He had little hope, however, that such a protest, coming from a mere British citizen and lawyer (even a well-connected one), would have any real impact on the decision making of Portuguese legislators and government officials. He realized that, acting individually, he had little power to change the practices of a repressive government in Portugal or elsewhere. What he needed was a strategy to draw on the personal and positional power of many other like-minded individuals and channel that power strategically to affect the decisions of government officials.

Initially, Benenson drew on and expanded his personal power by recruiting colleagues from legal and political circles and his earlier civil liberties campaigns. Eric Baker, Norman and Christel Marsh, Louis Blom-Cooper, Peter Archer, Tom Sargent, Marlys and Leonard Deeds, Margaret Benenson, and others who joined Benenson in launching the Appeal for Amnesty had little formal authority, but they did have the ability to multiply their own power by using and designing forums effectively. They put their skills, connections, and money to work to tap into the power of the press and of public assemblies to spread their message to hundreds of thousands of other people who might add their skills, energies, and funds to those of the Amnesty founders.

Amnesty's founders and their successors have understood the power of organizing and organizations to counter and alter government power. Thus, when Benenson or Blom-Cooper or other prominent Amnesty members led an Amnesty delegation to meet with government officials responsible for the fate of political prisoners, they stood for an entire organization that had already made its presence known through a letter-writing campaign directed at the officials. Sometimes Amnesty representatives bolster Amnesty's pressure on a nation's government by asking officials from other nations to raise objections to the first nation's human rights abuses. Amnesty sometimes seeks similar help from multinational corporations that do business in the country.

Amnesty members and staff actually exercise a very subtle power. They have neither the authority, coercive force, nor financial resources of most government officials. What they do have is significant capacity to affect a government's image or reputation in the court of public opinion and in international arenas such as the UN General Assembly. Amnesty representatives also can and do ask formal international courts such as the UN Commission on Human Rights to sanction repressive governments. In addition, Amnesty activists have the power of appeal to conscience—that is, they remind people in government, opposition groups, and even paramilitary organizations of their own moral responsibility to refrain from torture, executions, imprisonment of people for their religious beliefs, and many other abuses. Finally, Amnesty members and staff have the power to offer visibility and hope to those who have been imprisoned, tortured, or threatened because of their beliefs, ethnicity, or other characteristics. Thus, people in Amnesty strengthen the resolve of those whom repressive governments, opposition groups, or paramilitary organizations want to silence.

IWRAW

Arvonne Fraser, Rebecca Cook, and other IWRAW founders had little or no formal authority to obtain the decisions they desired from national governments and official international bodies. They have drawn on many other sources of power, however, to influence international bodies and persuade governments to sign the Women's Convention and implement its provisions. As veterans of women's movements and political campaigns in their own countries, IWRAW's founders knew that government officials' decisions could be affected through constituent pressure, media campaigns, expert lobbying, and elections. By disseminating information about the Women's Convention, specific violations of women's rights, and methods of using the convention to stop these violations, they helped empower women's groups around the world to pressure their own public officials to sign the Women's Convention, adopt appropriate laws and administrative rules, and make accurate reports to the Commission on the Elimination of Discrimination against Women (CEDAW) about their progress in implementing the convention. IWRAW's founders also used their connections with members of CEDAW as well as their developing expertise on the Women's Convention to influence the proceedings and findings of CEDAW. These women did not have funds of their own to organize a network for gathering, analyzing, and disseminating information, so they raised money from individual benefactors, foundations, and newsletter subscribers. They used existing institutional bases at the University of Minnesota and Columbia University.

Like Amnesty, IWRAW has the power of moral appeal. It too has the power to affect a government's image or reputation, but IWRAW leaders have not been as forceful as Amnesty spokespersons and report writers in exercising this power. Instead, they have tried to build the power of women within their own countries and regions to change laws and work with and even within government to ensure that women's rights are protected. Arvonne Fraser has noted that sometimes being part of IWRAW's core network gives women not only resources for their work in their home country but outside legitimation that increases the respect they are accorded at home.

BUILDING COALITIONS

Coalitions are shared-power arrangements that allow separate organizations to share information, funds, staff and member energies, and other resources to accomplish joint aims, while preserving each organization's distinctiveness. They allow an organization to expand its constituency without having to actually incorporate new constituents.

Amnesty International

Amnesty's founders initially relied on pressure from its own members through letter writing and delegations to persuade heads of state, ministers, and other officials to release prisoners of conscience. As the years went on, however, Amnesty leaders realized the value of building or joining coalitions that might include other human rights groups, professional groups, religious organizations, and unions to work for the release of certain types of prisoners, to pressure governments to stop torture or some other abuse, or to win policy changes at the United Nations. The organizers of Amnesty campaigns recognized that these other organizations had members and staff who might not be attracted to all of Amnesty's efforts but would be interested in working on behalf of a particular prisoner because of his or her nationality or professional, union, or religious background. Similarly, a human rights group might be willing to work with Amnesty on a particular issue, such as torture or the death penalty, that was part of both groups' agendas.

Becoming one of the world's strongest human rights organizations offers Amnesty leaders advantages and disadvantages in forming coalitions. Obviously, the organization will bring tremendous assets to the coalition; at the same time, smaller organizations, especially those based outside Europe and North America, will worry that Amnesty will dominate coalition activities.

IWRAW

IWRAW is itself a loose coalition of groups around the world that support women's rights but are working on different parts of the struggle to achieve them. IWRAW's core network meetings are the forums in which leaders of these groups come together to plan common initiatives and offer assistance to each other's separate projects.

IWRAW core network members frequently organize or join coalitions in their own countries, as exemplified by the work of core network members Isabel Plata, Miren Busto, Miriam Habib, and Hadja Soumare. For example, Isabel Plata's Colombian feminist group was part of a coalition that helped shape her country's new constitution. In Chile, Miren Busto's social action group has participated in the Reproductive Rights Forum, the Network of Women's Nongovernmental Organizations, and the National Consumer's Union. In Pakistan, Miriam Habib's All Pakistan Women's Association has been joined by the Women's Action Forum, women's professional groups, and union groups in spearheading women's rights campaigns. In Mali, Hadja Soumare has helped create a "coordination" of women's associations and nongovernmental organizations.

OVERCOMING BUREAUCRATIC RESISTANCE

Political leaders are well aware that getting treaties signed, laws passed, programs approved, or rules promulgated will have little impact if resistant or disinterested bureaucrats are in charge of implementing them. Thus, leaders of transnational citizen initiatives promote strategies for influencing and working with government bureaucrats.

For example, Amnesty delegations often meet with government ministers responsible for national security and corrections. Very early in its history, Amnesty put together a "prisoner of conscience" code of conduct for governments (Amnesty International, 1963). The code, issued on Human Rights Day, 1962, was translated into several languages and sent to every national government. The code spelled out safeguards for arrest, remand, trial, appeal, imprisonment, and detention of prisoners of conscience. In 1994, Amnesty's Brazilian section actually conducted a course for Brazilian police. As another example, Amnesty staff and members work with the UN bureaucracy to monitor and improve human rights mechanisms adopted by the United Nations.

Once a country signs the Women's Convention, IWRAW focuses on the bureaucrats responsible for reporting to CEDAW on the country's progress in implementing the convention. IWRAW staff and members keep track of the reporting process. They identify who in a particular government is responsible for compiling and presenting the report and either offer assistance or submit comments on draft reports. One means of assisting governments is an IWRAW manual (IWRAW, 1996) that advises them on gathering and analyzing information on the status of women in any country or community. IWRAW also files independent reports with CEDAW to accompany the country reports.

Both Amnesty International and IWRAW keep the publicity spotlight trained on countries to let the world know whether adopted treaties, laws, policies, and rules are being observed. This publicity heightens top government officials' interest in prodding bureaucrats to produce at least some evidence of compliance.

DESIGNING AND USING ARENAS

Political leaders identify the government, nonprofit, and business arenas in which decision makers have the power to approve and implement policies, programs, and projects necessary to carry out a shared vision of how to resolve a public problem. Political leaders also help constituents develop strategies for obtaining desired decisions in particular arenas.

Amnesty International

Amnesty's founders focused mainly on national government arenas but also sought UN consultative status so they could affect the UN decision-making process. The main techniques that Amnesty's founders and their successors have adopted to influence government decision makers are

- Continually monitoring and carefully documenting human rights abuses

- Directing letter-writing and postcard campaigns at heads of state, government ministers, other officials, and prisoners of conscience

- Making Urgent Action appeals

- Sending Amnesty delegations to a country to investigate human rights abuses and/or to meet with government officials. Sometimes the meetings are publicized, sometimes not

- Adhering to a nonpartisan stance to lessen the tendency of governments to see Amnesty as part of the opposition

- Generating pressure from religious and professional groups, unions, other governments, and businesses

- Cultivating the court of public opinion through wide publication of proven human rights abuses in the countries involved

- Appealing to regional intergovernmental arenas such as the European Parliament and the Organization of African Unity to promote human rights and censure governments that violate them

- Working to strengthen international courts and quasi-judicial bodies such as the UN Commission on Human Rights

- Publicizing the release of prisoners of conscience and improved human rights records as well as abuses

At the United Nations, Amnesty representatives work through UN committees to develop proposals for consideration by the General Assembly; members of national sections lobby assembly members to support the proposals, which range from new treaties to improvements in UN monitoring and sanctioning mechanisms. In 1994, Amnesty had six staff members—two at the International Secretariat, two in New York, and two in Geneva—working continually on human rights in the UN system. In addition, Amnesty sends special delegations including members and researchers to meetings of human rights bodies such as the UN Commission on Human Rights.

At times, Amnesty has taken a more populist approach to the United Nations. For example, on Human Rights Day, 1982, Amnesty launched a petition campaign for a Universal Amnesty for Prisoners of Conscience. After obtaining more than 1.5 million signatures from people in 122 countries, Amnesty presented the petition to the UN General Assembly and to heads of state.

Amnesty members also make appeals to leaders of opposition groups and paramilitary organizations that are responsible for "disappearances," extrajudicial executions, and the like. Amnesty representatives try to persuade the governments that supply arms to these groups to stop doing so.

Since its founding, Amnesty's work has probably contributed to the release of many thousands of prisoners of conscience. Although it is often difficult to know whether pressure from Amnesty members and staff led to the release of a particular prisoner, Amnesty staff members have collected plenty of anecdotal evidence that Amnesty efforts have impact on government officials. Prisoner accounts are often the most compelling. The following testimony of a released prisoner of conscience from the Dominican Republic, taken from a 1996 Amnesty promotional brochure, is just one example:

> When the first two hundred letters came, the guards gave me back my clothes. Then the next two hundred letters came, and the prison director came to see me. When the next pile of letters arrived, the director got in touch with his superior. The letters kept coming and coming: three thousand of them. The President was informed. The letters still kept arriving, and the President called the prison and told them to let me go.

IWRAW

IWRAW's founders sought to affect decision making in national government arenas by helping women in those countries become more politically powerful. Thus, core network members and staff have focused on

- Educating women about their rights under the Women's Convention and other international treaties

- Disseminating information about successful efforts to change national laws and constitutions

- Urging women to become involved in public life

- Organizing leadership workshops

- Helping set up projects and regional networks aimed at changing national laws and policies

- Assisting with court cases challenging national laws

Arvonne Fraser, in particular, has urged women to consider running for public office or obtaining government appointments in order to affect government decisions. In keeping with her own advice, she accepted an appointment from President Clinton to head the U.S. delegation to the UN Commission on the Status of Women. Marsha Freeman emphasizes the need for women who have helped an opposition group win public office to remain vigilant so that women retain clout once the opposition group is in power.

IWRAW also tries to affect national government arenas by providing CEDAW with independent assessments of national governments' progress in implementing the Women's Convention. In addition, it makes recommendations for strengthening CEDAW and provides the UN Center for Human Rights with analysis of international treaties in relation to gender issues.

IWRAW core network members and staff joined other nongovernmental activists in trying to affect the wording of the documents hammered out by government representatives at the 1993 World Conference on Human Rights in Vienna. IWRAW's most intense campaign to shape an international document was its participation in the 1995 World Conference on Women in Beijing and in the 2 years of preparatory meetings leading up to the conference. Much of the January 1994 IWRAW core network meeting was devoted to exchanges with UN staff, national government representatives, and other nongovernmental groups that were overseeing or trying to shape preparations for the Beijing conference. The IWRAW core network committed itself to ensuring that the action program adopted at the conference would have a strong human rights flavor.

At the regional preparatory meetings for Beijing, IWRAW core network members focused on the language in the preliminary platform for the conference. They sought to replace what they considered objectionable language with words that more forcefully proclaimed women's rights. According to Freeman, IWRAW and other nongovernmental organizations active in the preparatory conferences benefited from the groundwork that the Women's Environment and Development Organization (WEDO) laid at the 1992 World Conference on the Environment in Rio (interview by author, December 20, 1995). An international network organized by U.S. activists Bella Abzug and Mim Kelker, WEDO set an example at Rio of how nongovernmental organizations could affect official documents by carefully analyzing drafts, bracketing offending language, and recommending substitute language. Computer technology helped too.

Nongovernmental activists were able to show up at preparatory meetings for Beijing with laptop computers, printers, and the preliminary platform on disk. They could quickly generate new versions of the platform as the drafting proceeded.

At Beijing, IWRAW representatives continued the work of pressing government representatives to insert language supporting women's rights into the action plan to be adopted at the conference. (In several cases, an IWRAW member was part of a government delegation.) The critical thing, according to Freeman, was to approach government representatives with a piece of paper containing the language you hoped they would insert into the particular part of the document they were working on at the moment. Sometimes, government representatives approached her for help because they knew she was well informed about the document and background issues (interview by author, December 20, 1995).

At Beijing, nongovernmental activists also benefited from a new willingness of UN officials to allow them to attend not only the conference plenary sessions but meetings of working groups that were drafting different parts of the action plan. Being at these drafting sessions allowed IWRAW representatives to hear what government representatives were actually saying to each other. "What an enormous breakthrough," noted Freeman (interview by author, December 20, 1995). Sometimes small "contact groups" spun off from the drafting sessions to deal with very difficult issues. Freeman said these groups usually closed their meetings to the nongovernmental groups, but "We often knew their position because we had friends in the delegations [that participated in the meeting]." At Beijing, women's rights organizations organized a human rights caucus that met daily to allow them to pool information and strategize together. Nongovernmental organizations gained increased access to the Beijing drafting sessions in large part because the nongovernmental organizations attending the 1993 Human Rights Conference had fought hard, with some success, to be admitted to such sessions.

It may seem that spending so much energy on shaping the official declarations issued by a world conference is misguided because declarations will mean little unless they are bolstered by new policies, laws, and programs in the countries whose representatives approved the declaration. IWRAW leaders and other women's rights activists believe, however, that the action plan approved by delegates to the Beijing conference gives women a powerful new instrument to use in fighting for policy change in their countries. Women, energized by the adoption of the action plan, can hold it up to their legislators and say, "Here's what government delegates committed themselves to. Now we expect you to adopt policies that make it happen."

ADDITIONAL RESOURCES AND GUIDANCE FOR POLITICAL LEADERSHIP IN THE GLOBAL COMMONS

Political leadership is concerned mainly with the operation of arenas, just as visionary leadership is concerned mainly with the operation of forums. Moreover, the effective design and use of forums lays the groundwork for effective design and use of arenas. Political leadership overlaps into forums as forum organizers consider how to effectively link a forum focusing on a public problem to the arenas that have vital decision-making authority over proposed remedies to the problem. Thus, as suggested in the previous chapter, organizers of a future search or visioning conference may invite those with decision-making power in key arenas to participate in the conference. If they want these decision makers to attend, they also will time the conference to fit their schedules.

Once forum participants develop a shared vision, political leadership will be needed to

- Transform the solutions embraced by the vision into concrete, viable proposals that can be submitted to government, voluntary, and business arenas
- Develop strategies for actual adoption of the proposals
- Ensure effective implementation of adopted proposals

Let us explore how political leaders can help constituents accomplish each of these tasks. The guidance offered is designed for proposals that are fairly complex, but some of the advice also should be useful to advocates of simple proposals.

Developing Viable Proposals

After a large forum generates solutions to a public problem, the immediate assignment for political leaders is convening a steering committee or working groups to develop concrete, viable proposals for consideration by decision makers in arenas. A working group can be organized around a particular solution or around arenas. These groups may emerge rather naturally from the forum itself. Take the example of a conference focusing on female literacy. At the conclusion of the conference, one group of participants may have agreed to develop proposals for mentoring programs, another group may be generating proposals for replacing girls' labor in their households so that they can be freed to attend school. Other groups may be developing proposals for submission to international arenas, others may be focusing on democratic governments as a group, and still others may be focusing on nondemocratic governments or a particular government. A steering committee may be established to coordinate the working groups—to foster intergroup communication, avoid needless duplication, and sustain the continuing coalition necessary to gain adoption of the resulting proposals.

In steering committees, working groups, and task forces, political leaders help other group members identify which government, voluntary, and business arenas have the power to adopt and implement remedies for a particular public problem. Political leaders then help group members develop high-quality proposals that are clearly connected to competent sources and supported by a broad coalition. Such proposals should evoke the vision that inspired them; be technically feasible, politically acceptable, and legally and ethically defensible; and include implementation plans. Finally, political leaders should schedule review sessions to allow key stakeholders to critique the proposal.

Identifying Arenas. The arenas can be in the government, economic, or voluntary spheres; the government arenas can be executive, legislative, or administrative. Thus, in the female literacy example, a group working on proposals for making households less dependent on girls' labor might focus on legislators who could consider a law giving tax benefits to families to send their girls to school, and they might seek support from the education ministry for starting more preschools (to relieve older daughters from caring for young siblings). The group might focus on a foundation that funds programs helping girls and women, and it might identify businesses and unions likely to consider proposals for flexible work days.

Also important is identifying the actual people in the arenas who will consider the proposal. Is it a legislative committee, a board of directors, a management team, a union council, the director of a government agency, the membership of a voluntary organization, the citizenry? Do new arenas need to be created—for example, a new government department specifically dedicated to promoting female literacy?

Proposals should be geared to the arena and people to whom they will be directed. For example, the most effective proposals for submission to a legislature will be draft legislation. Proposals to foundations should be formatted according to foundation guidelines. A proposal to a group of venture capitalists should include a business plan. The group developing a proposal may need to add people skilled in using these formats—for example, legislative staff or grant writers—as well as specialists in the substance of the proposal.

Evoking the Vision. The proposal should highlight the problem it addresses and explain why the proposed solutions will remedy it. The proposal also should be inspiring, even if it has to include technical, legal, and budgetary language. Such language can be introduced by and interwoven with vivid depiction of the problem being attacked and with optimism about the prospects of beneficial change. Thus, the proposal that Arvonne Fraser and Stephen Isaacs submitted to the Carnegie Corporation to begin IWRAW depicted policy change as a drama in which individuals, groups, media, and policy makers play a part. The proposal detailed the "momentum for change" generated by the UN Decade for Women and presented the proposed Women's Rights Action Watch as a means of building on that momentum.

Assessing Technical Feasibility. The developers of a proposal must ask themselves if the proposal can be carried out at reasonable cost, given available technology and social systems. For example, no one was likely to get very far in 1950 with a proposal urging the United Nations to sponsor a forum bringing together thousands of ordinary women from around the world because it was not very feasible, given the state of air transportation at the time. By 1975, when the global conference initiating the International Decade for Women was held in Copenhagen, advances in air transportation made such a forum feasible.

The developers of a proposal should include credible evidence that the solutions it embodies are feasible—for example, by including expert endorsements. To promote feasibility, solutions should be as easy to administer as possible. Proposal developers also should identify what resources will be needed to implement it and how these can be provided.

Assessing Political Acceptability. A proposal can be technically workable and still have little chance in an arena unless it is politically acceptable—that is, unless it accomplishes the objectives of key stakeholders, including decision makers. A technique for assessing and improving the political acceptability of a proposal is *stakeholder mapping* (described in Bryson & Crosby, 1992, pp. 377-379). The mapping exercise presented here uses a two-dimensional matrix adapted from the work of Patton (1997). To begin the exercise, the working group first identifies the key stakeholders for the proposal. Group members then locate each stakeholder within the matrix. One dimension, the importance of the stakeholder to proposal adoption and implementation, is divided into "high," "moderate," and "low." The second dimension, the stakeholder's likely position on the proposal, is divided into "favorable," "neutral or unknown," and "antagonistic" (see Figure 7.1). Once stakeholders are placed on the map, the working group has a picture of who is likely to participate in a coalition supporting the proposal, who might be part of an opposing coalition, and who might be recruited to both camps. The working group can then consider how to make arguments for the proposal that will win over potential supporters and low-priority stakeholders and neutralize opponents. Especially vital is support from people who must implement the proposal once it is adopted.

It may be necessary to rework the proposal (e.g., by increasing benefits or reducing costs) to increase the numbers of likely and potential supporters. Proposal developers also may improve the proposal's political acceptability by including a range of solutions and indicating cost-benefit ratios of each, thus giving decision makers options and providing incentive to adopt at least those with the most favorable cost-benefit ratios.

The stakeholder mapping can help the working group decide whether a "small win" or "big win" strategy is best. In other words, should the group seek a number of incremental changes that will eventually add up to fundamental and widespread change, or should it try now for far-reaching change? The attraction of the "small win" strategy is that opposition may not be as strong to incremental changes and that an innovation can be tested on a small scale before proceeding to systemwide change. The disadvantage of this strategy is that a

Estimate of Stakeholders' Initial Likely Position on the Proposal

Importance of Stakeholder▼	Favorable	Neutral or Unknown	Antagonistic
High			
Moderate			
Low			

Figure 7.1. Mapping Stakeholders

SOURCE: From *Utilization-Focused Evaluation,* by M. Q. Patton, 1997, Thousand Oaks, CA: Sage. Copyright 1997 by Sage Publications. Adapted by permission.

supportive coalition will need to stay together for a long period to maintain the change effort, and problems may be too severe to wait. If the prospects of building a coalition large enough to achieve a big win are favorable and the need is pressing, astute political leaders urge the group to develop a proposal for fundamental and comprehensive change. If not, political leaders help the group decide which series of small wins to pursue over the long haul to accomplish the group's vision.

Amnesty International has pursued both types of strategy. Campaigning for an international treaty to abolish torture was a "big win" approach. Advocacy for individual prisoners usually focuses on small wins. For example, Amnesty members may first try to obtain a stay of execution, then work for better conditions of imprisonment, and finally work for the prisoner's release.

Assessing Legality. To ensure that their proposal is legally defensible, the working group should assign one or more members to study laws related to the problem addressed by the proposal. If the proposal is counter to those laws, it may be necessary to make repeal of those laws part of the proposal. In general, the working group should craft proposals so that if they do become law, they will withstand the scrutiny of formal courts.

Assessing Ethical Implications. To make their proposal ethically defensible, a working group should consider whether it accords with widely accepted ethical principles, especially those that undergird the group's vision. Thus, a group working on proposals to ensure that girls receive education should be able to answer yes to questions such as these:

- Is the proposal just—for example, does it help the girls most in need?

- Does the proposal promote social responsibility—for example, by developing communities' resources for supporting girls' education?

- Does the proposal foster individual development and freedom—for example, by giving girls instruction about citizenship?

- Is it truthful?

The *ethics impact statement* recommended by Lewis (1991) is a more sophisticated method of considering the ethical implications of a policy proposal.

Planning Implementation. The proposal should include guidelines, incentives, and resources for implementation and evaluation. The general aim should be to make implementation as easy and flexible as possible. Evaluation (see Patton, 1997) should include assessments that monitor changes in midstream and indicate needed adjustments and assessments that measure how well a change that has been substantially implemented has accomplished its goals.

Reviewing the Proposal. Political leaders also plan review sessions for the proposals developed by working groups. Sometimes the review is required—for example, when a working group has been established with the understanding that it will submit its draft proposal for approval by a steering committee or a plenary session of a conference. In addition, political leaders can convene informal review sessions at which key stakeholders (including representatives of arenas expected to act on the proposal) have a chance to critique the proposal. Such sessions can be especially helpful when leaders know that the proposal will not be easily approved in the arenas.

Participants in review sessions should be divided into groups of five to nine people and asked to identify strengths of the proposal and modifications that would improve it. (The snow card exercise described in Appendix D can be used.) Political leaders ensure that the final proposal incorporates those suggestions that actually do improve it.

Well-planned review sessions have several benefits. They can reveal new information or bring up unanticipated effects. They promote stakeholder buy-in and thus can expand and strengthen the coalition that supports the proposal. In addition, they allow legislators and other decision makers to offer their views before the proposal becomes a matter of hot debate in formal arenas.

Getting the Proposal Adopted

In addition to overseeing the development of a strong proposal, political leaders help other proposal advocates develop strategies for persuading decision makers to adopt it. Effective strategies must be based on an understanding of how the pertinent arenas operate. The strategies should also include

- Assessing needed changes in arenas

- Cultivating relationships with sympathetic decision makers

- Reducing uncertainty

- Monitoring opponents

- Building and sustaining the coalition that supports the proposal

- Negotiating, compromising, and copromoting

- Attracting favorable media coverage

- Attending to agendas, timing, strategic voting, issue dimensions

- Turning to courts if necessary

- Reassessing a failed proposal

Understanding the Arenas. Political leaders must be knowledgeable about the structure and processes of the arenas that will consider their proposals. Does the arena operate through committees that consider and modify proposals before sending them to the ultimate decision-making body? If so, which ones will consider the particular proposal being advanced? Who are the powerful people on those committees? Will the committees hold hearings at which supporters and opponents of the proposal can testify? Which members and groups in the ultimate decision-making body will have the most impact on the proposal's chances of adoption? What is the arena's schedule? What decision-making procedures—consensus, majority vote, and so on—does the arena use? What types of lobbying are possible, permissible, and ethical? What other procedures and rules are important?

Is the arena really controlled by outside powers, such as a military dictator, political party bosses, or a cartel? If so, which powerful allies—other governments, international bodies, news media, churches, multinational corporations—can proposal advocates recruit to put pressure on these decision makers on their behalf? When two or more arenas must act on the proposal, is there a process for reconciling different outcomes? If a proposal is defeated in one arena, is there recourse in other arenas (e.g., proposal advocates who are unsuccessful in the national legislature may do better in a popular referendum)?

Assessing Needed Changes in Arenas. Sometimes the rules or composition of an arena must be changed before a proposal even has a chance for adoption. This is especially true for proposals that call for fundamental change in a policy regime. To achieve adoption of such proposals, advocates should seek to build or join coalitions that can supplant the existing dominant coalition in the pertinent arena (Browning, Marshall, & Tabb, 1984; Sabatier & Jenkins, 1993).

Political leaders help their groups decide how to achieve necessary changes. Do we ally with other groups that are trying to reform the arenas—for example, by agitating for democratic elections of the decision makers or pressing for limitations on the power of affluent special interest groups to shape policy decisions? Do we try to place our own people in decision-making positions? Do we need new arenas altogether? (For dealing with transnational problems, the creation of new arenas at both the supranational and local levels may be very important. See, e.g., Cleveland, 1993, and Ostrom, 1990.)

IWRAW leaders, Arvonne Fraser especially, have urged women to become a part of government arenas in order to bolster women's rights. In another example, political leaders in Amnesty have worked hard over many years for the creation of a High Commissioner for Human Rights who would oversee all human rights activities within the United Nations System. Pressure from Amnesty and other nongovernmental organizations resulted in UN General Assembly approval of the new office in 1993.

Cultivating Relationships With Sympathetic Decision Makers. Politically minded leaders know that personal connection with decision makers is often crucial for winning their support. If the decision makers have been involved in drafting the proposal, this connection already exists. Otherwise, advocates of a proposal may request meetings with the decision makers, especially those with substantial authority or following. Such meetings can help decision makers gain additional evidence that the proposal is being advanced by competent and sincere people. Meetings with decision makers or their staff also provide opportunities to give decision makers additional information about the proposal, advance practical and moral arguments, and demonstrate widespread support for the proposal. Once a proposal is taken up by the arena, political leaders should continue to feed supportive decision makers information, arguments, and even language for new versions of the proposal.

Proposal advocates should try to persuade at least one sympathetic decision maker, preferably a powerful one, to sponsor their proposal. (In some cases, such sponsorship will be required.) In addition to finding a sponsor who endorses and possibly introduces the proposal, proposal advocates should persuade at least one decision maker to champion the proposal—that is, to educate other decision makers about it and negotiate their support throughout the adoption process.

Unsympathetic decision makers should not be ignored. It may be possible to win them over or at least reduce their hostility by meeting them and presenting the case for the proposal.

Sometimes, the proposal advocates will be among the decision makers. This would be true, for example, when a group of delegates to Amnesty's international membership meeting is pressing for a change in the organization's mandate because changes to the mandate are decided by all of the delegates. In such cases, proposal advocates may play the sponsor and champion roles, but they still should cultivate relationships with other key decision makers.

Reducing Uncertainty. Decision makers need as much reassurance as possible that the proposal, if adopted, will actually produce promised results. As Patton (1997) noted, decision makers seek to retain power over outcomes and seek the information that can assure them that other powerful groups and forces will not defeat their intentions. Proposal advocates may need to marshal additional supportive evidence from credible sources as decision makers raise new questions. (This is especially true when the decision makers discount proposal advocates because of the advocates' gender, ethnicity, age, class, or other characteristics.) The advocates also should demonstrate that the proposal is aligned with the decision makers' objectives. For example, a leader trying to persuade legislators to adopt a female literacy program might present—if the legislators have made economic development a priority—research showing a close correlation between increases in female education levels and economic productivity. If possible, proposal advocates might use opinion polls to convince decision makers that citizens will approve their adopting the proposal. Proposal advocates also may need to woo stakeholder groups that are the decision makers' key supporters.

Monitoring Opponents. Politically astute leaders remember that people who oppose the proposal's adoption also may work hard to alter the arena in their favor, develop relationships with decision makers, increase doubts about the benefits of the proposal, or promote their own counterproposals. Proposal advocates should monitor opponents' activities in order to counter their efforts, especially any dissemination of misinformation. This is the kind of watchfulness that Amnesty activists, for example, must exhibit as they try to convince the UN General Assembly to take action on a proposal or that IWRAW core network members needed as they tried to shape the agenda for the Beijing Conference on Women.

Building and Sustaining the Supportive Coalition. As noted in the preceding chapter, the work of building a supportive coalition begins in the forums convened to define a public problem and generate solutions. Indeed, an outcome of a forum such as the future search conference may well be an agreement to organize a coalition consisting initially of organizations represented at the conference. As the focus turns to arenas, political leaders attempt to strengthen and expand the initial coalition with the goal of developing an ultimate coalition that has enough collective clout to persuade policy makers to adopt their proposals. The stakeholder mapping is a helpful technique for expanding the coalition beyond initial participants.

To give the coalition visibility and structure, political leaders may want to press for agreement on a formal name and mission statement, a formal structure of officers or coordinating committee, and possibly a process for accepting new members and ongoing consultation with coalition members. If such an agreement is too hard to obtain because of the diversity of coalition members or the lack of time and other resources, political leaders can opt for informal arrangements. For example, they may build an informal coalition of organizations that endorse proposed policies, programs, or projects and make a commitment to work on specific parts of the campaign for their adoption. Coalitions work best when the participants agree on what issues or areas the coalition covers and how work will be conducted and coordinated, and when the participants perceive that the benefits of participating in the coalition outweigh costs (Roberts-DeGennaro, 1986).

Once a coalition is assembled, political leaders must work hard to sustain it, especially when the battle to have a proposal adopted is prolonged. Leaders must keep coalition members informed of progress and call on them for additional expertise and needed demonstrations of support—such as well-timed rallies at the legislature. Leaders also coordinate the efforts of different groups in a coalition through mechanisms such as the human rights caucus at the Beijing conference.

Leaders should keep the unifying vision alive by updates on the problem to be remedied and the urgency of proposed solutions. They should celebrate small wins and spread credit among coalition members.

Although maintaining unity among coalition members is important, uniformity is not. Leaders should play on the advantages of the groups' diversity, so that, for example, a more radical group carries out the most confrontational tactics while moderate groups work carefully behind the scenes to build consensus for change.

Negotiating, Compromising, and Copromoting. Politically astute leaders know that they must be prepared to negotiate on the particulars of their proposal to gain enough votes for its adoption. They should be open to compromise and what Thomas Fiutak (1996) called "copromotion," while being sure that the core of their proposal is preserved.

In the art of compromise, two parties agree to accept an outcome that satisfies neither party completely but that partially satisfies the aims of each. Thus, the supporters of a national female literacy program, faced with legislators determined to control public spending, may agree to prune their ambitious proposal for serving all girls and settle for a pilot project that will establish programs in several regions of the country. At the Beijing Conference on Women, human rights advocates were unable to convince government delegates to commit themselves to protecting women against discrimination based on sexual orientation. Although the final conference statement did not mention sexual orientation, the human rights groups endorsed the statement and look ahead to future opportunities to promote the rights of lesbians and others who are discriminated against because of their sexual orientation.

An important element of wise compromise is leaving the door implicitly or explicitly open to renegotiation. For example, the supporters of a national female literacy program might ask that the legislation setting up pilot programs include a requirement that the ministry of education will develop a plan for expanding the programs if they are successful.

Copromotion, whereby two parties develop an agreement that gives both what they want, is more appealing than compromise, but it can be much harder to obtain. The main danger is that adding too many new policies, projects, or programs to a proposal may make it so cumbersome, complicated, and costly that it is susceptible to attack for precisely those characteristics.

Attracting Favorable Media Coverage. In many cases, proposal advocates can improve the chances that their proposal will be adopted by using various news media to keep attention focused on their cause. They can issue news releases, plan newsworthy events, maintain ongoing contacts with media representatives, and send messages on the Internet to build and maintain public awareness of the changes they are advocating and developments in related arenas. They also may need to publicly reveal and challenge opponents' efforts to defeat the proposal.

Attending to Agendas, Timing, Strategic Voting, and Issue Dimensions. Within arenas, certain pervasive practices—agenda control, timing, strategic voting, and control of issue dimensions (see Riker, 1986)—are crucial to a proposal's fate. Leaders help proposal advocates use these practices to their advantage.

Politically astute leaders know that their proposal has to get on the decision makers' formal agenda before it will even be considered. They know when the agenda will be finalized and who will decide what is on it. If the proposal must be placed on the agenda of one or more committees before reaching the ultimate decision-making body, the proposal advocates should try to ensure that their proposal will go to the most favorable committees.

Proposal advocates also know that timing is important. Arenas usually have decision-making cycles tied to calendar and fiscal years, holidays and vacations, budgets, and allocations. The plan for managing a proposal through the adoption process must accord with the arena's decision-making cycle. Also, proposal advocates should adjust their timing in relation to competing proposals. If the arena's decision-making cycle is likely to be crowded with more urgent and popular matters in one session, it may be wise to put off one's own proposal to a future session.

Proposal advocates also must be alert to the use of strategic voting within arenas. That is, decision makers may use their vote as a resource that is deployed in the service of aims that have little to do with the proposal at hand. Thus, in the UN General Assembly, the representative from the United Kingdom may actually favor a proposal opposed by the United States but may abstain or vote against the proposal because the British government deems its alliance with the United States more important than the proposal. Conversely, the U.S. representative might be persuaded to support a proposal backed by the British government more because of the alliance than because of the proposal's merits. To take another case, one decision maker may agree to support a proposal solely as a means of acquiring future support for his or her own favored policies.

The manipulation of issue dimensions is another means of altering a proposal's chances of adoption in an arena. In some cases, proposal advocates will be wise to expand the dimensions of the issue at the heart of their proposal; in other cases, the wisest course will be to resist expansion. Expanding an issue's dimensions—for example, presenting a proposed female literacy initiative as an economic development program—may increase the base of support for the proposal without adding significant new opposition. But what if opponents of the proposal try to expand the issue dimensions to include religion and culture by arguing that the program will lead girls to challenge or reject the roles and practices that their religion or culture requires? Proposal advocates should attempt to defuse these arguments quickly to prevent issue expansion in which debates over religion and culture overshadow attention to the needs of girls and threaten the cohesiveness of the coalition favoring the proposal.

Turning to Courts. When an arena is so corrupt, so divided, or so hostile to a proposal that prospects for adoption are extremely dim, proposal advocates should consider whether courts might be more hospitable to their cause. Moving toward ethical leadership (to be discussed in the next chapter), proposal advocates should ask themselves whether they might be able to convince a court to overrule the arena on the basis of the harm being done to individuals or groups and the constitutional and legal principles that guide the court.

Reassessing a Failed Proposal. If proposal advocates are unable to convince decision makers to adopt the proposal, they should analyze why the proposal failed and consider whether different strategies, a new version of the proposal, or changes in the arena might make adoption more likely in the future. After such an analysis, leaders of the proposal adoption effort may conclude that their groups need to turn again to studying the problem that prompted the proposal and come up with more appealing solutions.

Implementing the Proposal

Once government, voluntary, or business arenas adopt a proposal, its advocates still have considerable work remaining. To ensure that the proposal is effectively implemented, leaders should

- Keep the supporting coalition together

- Plan, manage, or monitor implementation

- Win over the implementers

- Stay alert for court challenges or new attempts to alter or repeal the proposal in arenas

- Use news media to publicize progress or foot dragging

- Possibly promote a vision of success

Keeping the Supporting Coalition Together. It is all too tempting for a coalition to disband once its proposal has been adopted. Coalition members may have other matters on their agendas, and they want to declare victory and move on to them. Very often, however, the implementation of an adopted proposal simply will not happen unless coalition members either do it themselves or carefully monitor the bureaucrats given implementation responsibility.

For example, Mel James, Amnesty International staff person in charge of UN relations, was pleased when the UN Commission on Human Rights, responding to pressure from Amnesty and other human rights groups, agreed in the mid-1990s to pay more attention to violations of women's rights. She knew, however, that she and her allies would have to monitor and assist the mechanisms that the commission created for protecting women's rights in order to make them effective.

Sometimes proposal advocates must assume the main responsibility for implementation. Consider the example of a proposed national female literacy program. The national legislature might approve several pilot projects and even make money available for them, but rather than turning the projects over to a government department, the legislature might invite nonprofit groups to apply for grants to begin the projects. In this case, leaders of the coalition that supported the female literacy program would want to rally coalition members to organize these projects, both because they otherwise might not happen and because they offer coalition members a chance to more surely realize their vision.

Planning, Managing, and Evaluating Implementation. Ideally, the adopted proposal will include implementation guidelines, but an implementation team should produce a more detailed plan that assigns responsibilities and resources, spells out incentives, establishes timetables, and specifies how outcomes will be evaluated. There are advantages to planning implementation from the ground up (see Bryson & Crosby, 1992, pp. 289-291; Goggin, Bowman, Lester, & O'Toole, 1990). That is, planners should ask: Who or what organization should be responsible for implementing the new policies, programs, or projects at the ground level? What outcomes are realistic and desirable at that level? What resources, incentives, and timetables and other strategies will ground-level implementers need to produce these outcomes? How can these resources and incentives be provided? What information needs to be gathered about results? Who will oversee the ground-level implementers? What policies and account-ability systems should the oversight groups establish? What resources and incentives will they need to establish these policies and systems?

Often implementation will require considerable interorganizational coordi-nation. Planners should set up coordination systems that fit the mission of the change effort and the number, independence, and other characteristics of the organizations involved (Alexander, 1995).

Planners should try to implement simple or easy changes as early as possible so that some visible progress can be achieved before supporters lose interest, or even faith, in the project. Planners also should incorporate evaluation throughout the implementation process to judge the success of the change efforts and make necessary adjustments. (See Patton, 1997, for excellent guid-ance on program evaluation.)

If the advocates of a proposal are not themselves directly responsible for implementation, their leaders should ensure that they develop plans for moni-toring and possibly assisting the implementation. Thus, leaders in IWRAW synchronize the network's reports and meetings with the work of CEDAW, which is responsible for implementing the Women's Convention. IWRAW representatives attend CEDAW sessions, and IWRAW makes recommendations for strengthening CEDAW, provides independent information to CEDAW about conditions in countries that have signed the convention, and educates women and their advocates about the convention.

Winning Over the Implementers. Implementers of the change who are not members of the supportive coalition may see the newly mandated policies, programs, or projects as a nuisance, just one more burdensome task. As noted earlier, proposal advocates should take the concerns of implementers into account as they are drafting the proposal. Once it is adopted, they should work hard to ensure that implementation responsibility is assigned to people who are competent, sympathetic to the proposal's aims, and given adequate authority to carry out their responsibility.

Coalition leaders can devise ways to help the implementers do their jobs. They can cooperate with implementers in planning training sessions, or forums, that explain the changes in terms of the implementers' objectives and allow implementers to develop their own shared meaning about the changes. Such forums can offer implementers a chance to fill in the details of the implementation plan outlined in the adopted proposal. The forums also can provide specialized training in implementation strategies. For example, Amnesty International, in the wake of adding attention to women's rights in its mandate, offers members and staff needed coaching in interviewing women whose human rights may have been violated. In the case of a new female literacy initiative, implementers might be trained in using a reading series aimed at teenage girls who have little schooling.

In addition to training, coalition members can provide implementers with information and expertise as needed. Thus, Marsha Freeman has prepared IWRAW to be the organization to which UN agencies turn for information about gender issues and international treaties.

Staying Alert for Challenges in Courts and Arenas. Those who opposed adoption of the proposal may try to stop implementation by challenging it in court or persuading an arena to override the proposal's adoption. Once changes are being implemented, some opponents may decide that the changes are beneficial and drop their opposition; on the other hand, some people who were previously unconcerned about the change or mildly supportive may become opponents once they begin losing some advantage because of the changes.

If opponents are planning to challenge adopted policies, programs, or projects in court, the supporters of the changes should help build a strong legal case that will defeat the opponents in court or cause them to drop their challenge. Supporters also should be prepared for appeals to higher courts.

If opponents are trying to persuade an arena to overturn the new policies, programs, or projects, supporters of the changes will need to employ many of the strategies necessary to adopt the proposal in the first place. Especially important is keeping supportive decision makers informed about and credited with benefits that the new policies, programs, or projects already are producing.

Using News Media. Politically minded leaders use a variety of news media to build support for adopted policies, programs, and projects in the court of public opinion. They publicize progress as well as foot dragging by implementers. Amnesty International, for example, issues reports and news releases that assess how well governments are living up to their human rights commitments.

Promoting a Vision of Success. Those leading the implementation process should consider summoning visionary leadership to develop a vision of success. The vision would describe the new regime resulting from full implementation of the adopted proposal. It would encompass the resulting new behaviors, new products and services, and new conditions but would connect the changes to past and present experience. It would include basic strategies, performance criteria, decision rules, and ethical standards. It would be recorded in inspiring language and imagery so that it could be disseminated widely to everyone involved in the implementation process.

A vision of success for policy change can be developed in much the same way as a vision of success for an organization (see Chapter 5). The vision of success should build on the vision that animated the proposal development, but it will be somewhat different and certainly more detailed. It will be different because of alterations in the proposal during the adoption process and because the vision of success will be shaped more strongly by people involved in implementing the proposal. It will be more detailed in order to provide practical guidance to implementers.

To begin constructing the vision of success, implementation leaders can assemble a team that includes representatives of key stakeholder groups involved in the implementation. The team then puts together a draft vision of success based on answers to the following questions (taken from Bryson & Alston, 1995):

- What is the mission of the implementation effort?
- What are the core philosophies and values of the effort?
- What basic strategies should the implementers pursue?
- What performance criteria should be applied to implementers?
- What processes and procedures should be used to make major implementation decisions? To make minor decisions?
- What should be decided at the ground level?
- What should be decided by oversight groups?
- Are there important exceptions to the decision-making procedures?
- What ethical standards should implementers follow? (p. 93)

Once the team has drafted a vision of success, it is probably best if one person who has a good command of inspirational communication develops the next draft, which can then be reviewed by the original team, by various groups of implementers, by the decision makers who adopted the proposal being implemented, by the proposal's advocates, and by the people the proposal was designed to benefit. Review sessions should identify strengths of the vision and modifications that would improve it.

Ideally, the outlines of consensus will be clear from these review sessions, and a talented communicator can draw up a final vision of success that can be disseminated as a booklet, poster, videotape, or some other useful form. If consensus does not develop, implementation leaders may decide that it is too early to create the vision, and indeed at least some actual implementation may need to occur before people begin to agree on what success might look like.

Implementation leaders should not be terribly discouraged if a vision of success is impossible. Even if key stakeholders cannot reach consensus on a vision of success, they still can often agree on some aspects of mission and some strategies. Their areas of disagreement provide valuable information to implementers about possible trouble spots they will need to overcome or avoid.

SUMMARY

In the global commons, political leadership is required to translate shared visions for resolving global problems into concrete proposals that are adopted and implemented by decision makers in government, voluntary, and business arenas. To influence those decision makers, political leaders draw on many sources of power; build winning sustainable coalitions; avoid bureaucratic resistance; and tailor their proposals and strategies to particular arenas. They also attempt to alter arenas and establish new ones as necessary.

To sustain implementation of proposals adopted in arenas, leaders in the global commons also must ensure that formal and informal courts resolve residual disputes and provide ethical and legal sanctions that discourage conduct undermining implementation and that encourage conduct contributing to implementation. This ethical leadership work will be explored in the next chapter.

CHAPTER 8

Ethical Leadership

Always do what's right. That will gratify some and surprise the rest.
—Mark Twain

Mark Twain suggests that human conduct rarely jibes with "what's right." Even if we are less cynical than he, we must recognize that it takes more than exhortations and admonitions to persuade large numbers of people to comply with new policies and rules established to remedy a public problem. In the global commons, ethical leadership is needed to ensure that people actually act in accordance with policy and implementation decisions designed to remedy a global public problem. Ethical leadership also may be needed to change policy and implementation decisions that conflict with ethical principles, laws, and norms.

Ethical leaders help constituents judge or evaluate policy decisions and conduct in relation to ethical principles, laws, and norms. Ethical leaders focus on sanctioning conduct and resolving residual conflicts in formal and informal courts.

The main tasks of ethical leadership are

- Educating others about ethics, laws, and norms
- Promoting awareness of how ethical principles, laws, and norms apply to specific cases
- Adapting principles, laws, and norms to changing times
- Resolving conflicts among principles, laws, and norms
- Attending to the design and use of formal and informal courts

There are, of course, ethical aspects to all the types of leadership we have considered up to this point. I identify ethical leadership with the sanctioning of conduct and resolution of residual conflicts in courts, however, because in this process, questions of what is ethical and legitimate are fundamental, whereas in organizational leadership, for example, the fundamental question is how we build effective and humane organizational structures.

Ethical leadership has been very important in the work of Amnesty International and IWRAW, and I will offer examples from these organizations to illuminate the central tasks of ethical leadership. I also will offer extended guidance on the design and use of courts.

EDUCATING OTHERS ABOUT ETHICAL PRINCIPLES, LAWS, AND NORMS

To build support for their cause in formal and informal courts, leaders in the global commons seek out and explain the moral and legal ground for what citizens, either on their own or within organizations, should and should not do. As they try to ensure that citizens' conduct accords with adopted policies or plans—or as they try to persuade courts to overrule arenas that have refused to adopt their proposed policies—they emphasize in word and deed the ethical principles, laws, and norms that legitimate their cause, their actions, and the sanctioning of citizens' conduct. They find these principles in "higher law" (religious or philosophical traditions), in international treaties and other documents, in constitutions, and in codes of conduct. International treaties, national constitutions, and national to local legislation constitute the laws that various courts use to decide what conduct is permitted and not permitted. Norms are the behavioral standards enforced by informal courts, especially the court of public opinion.

Amnesty International

At the most abstract level, Amnesty's founders held up ethical ideals of justice and freedom. Most powerfully, they have helped people understand the meaning of those ideals in particular areas of human behavior.

Reports and public statements by Amnesty officials and members continually emphasize the ethical principles, laws, and norms that sanction human behavior related to free expression. For example, in one of the earliest annual reports, Sean MacBride wrote, "We base ourselves on a broad and basic human principle: that everyone, if he will concede the same to others, has the right to nonviolent expression of his beliefs" (Amnesty International, 1963, p. 1). Amnesty's leaders have viewed the violation of these rights as unjust.

Amnesty officials, members, and staff have constantly promoted public awareness of the articles of the Universal Declaration of Human Rights (United Nations, 1948/1983d) that undergird its work. The organization urges governments to sign treaties, conventions, and protocols that bind them to respect the rights that Amnesty upholds. Amnesty also has formulated an ethical code for professionals who might be caught up in the practice of torture.

In 1968, René Cassin, former chair of the UN Commission on Human Rights, applauded the contribution of Amnesty and other nongovernmental human rights organizations. These organizations, he stated,

> have provided a link between, on the one hand, human beings—ordinary men and women, all members of the world community—and on the other, official bodies, national and international. They were the first to make the principles of the Universal Declaration of Human Rights widely known in circles informed inadequately or not at all through official channels. (Amnesty International, 1976, p. 168)

By "making the rights of human beings known and respected," these organizations were providing "education for citizenship" (p. 168).

Peter Benenson and his successors have emphasized particularly Articles 18 (proclaiming the right to freedom of thought, conscience, and religion) and 19 (proclaiming the right to freedom of opinion and expression) of the Universal Declaration. Article 5, which prohibits torture and "cruel, inhuman, or degrading treatment or punishment," and Article 9, which prohibits arbitrary arrest, detention and exile, were added to Amnesty's mission in 1968.

The inclusion of Article 5 resulted from ethical leadership by Amnesty investigators Anthony Marreco and James Becket and by people in Amnesty's Swedish section. Anthony Marreco and James Becket, British and U.S. lawyers respectively, went to Greece in 1967 to investigate the plight of Greek citizens imprisoned by the reigning military junta because they opposed or refused to endorse the junta's rule. They found not only that thousands of people were being imprisoned and denied trial merely because of their beliefs but that many also were being terribly tortured, despite the fact that Greece had signed the European Convention on Human Rights, which banned "inhuman or degrading treatment." The two lawyers compiled a report, issued by Amnesty to extensive press coverage, documenting abuses by the Greek rulers. People in Amnesty's Swedish section then added the practice of torture to the list of complaints the section filed against the Greek junta at the European Commission on Human Rights. Leaders in the Swedish section also successfully worked for incorporation of Article 5's prohibition into Amnesty's mandate. (For a fuller description of this initiative, see Larsen, 1978.)

Amnesty campaigners cited Article 5 in their efforts in the mid-1970s to persuade the UN General Assembly to adopt a resolution protecting every human being from torture and other cruel, inhuman, or degrading treatment or punishment. Amnesty campaigners also have cited Article 5, along with Article 3 (declaring the right to life) and provisions of the International Covenant on Civil and Political Rights, as the ground for their opposition to capital punishment or the death penalty.

Perhaps the norm most emphasized by Amnesty leaders has been impartiality. In his 1961 article announcing the Appeal for Amnesty, Peter Benenson declared that the people behind the appeal shared "the underlying conviction expressed by Voltaire: 'I detest your views, but am prepared to die for your right to express them' " (p. 21). He emphasized that prisoners of conscience would be selected impartially and called for the appeal to be inclusive, international and "politically impartial" (p. 21). As noted earlier, Benenson's secret agreement to channel British government funds to people imprisoned in Rhodesia undermined this norm. Subsequently, the organization's policy makers decided to accept no government funds except to assist refugees. Official Amnesty statements highlight the organization's impartiality and independence from "any government, political persuasion or religious creed" (Amnesty International, 1994, frontispiece).

IWRAW

IWRAW's core network members also promote the ethical ideals of justice and freedom. Justice, explained Marsha Freeman and Arvonne Fraser (1993), requires the removal of all barriers to women's free and full participation in economic and political spheres.

IWRAW's leaders continually emphasize the human rights principles contained in the Women's Convention and other international treaties. Indeed, they refer to the convention as an international bill of rights for women. In most general terms, IWRAW leaders proclaim the right of women to be treated as full-fledged human beings and to be free of discrimination. Freeman and Fraser (1993) declared, "The human enterprise must include recognition of women's full status as adult human beings, entitled to human rights and freedoms and particularly to education for participation in economic, political, and social activity" (p. 103). They added that

the Universal Declaration [of Human Rights], the International Covenants on Civil and Political Rights and on Economic, Social and Cultural Rights, and regional instruments all declare that people are entitled to human rights and fundamental freedoms without discrimination on the basis of sex. (p. 110)

In conjunction with IWRAW's annual meeting, Fraser, Freeman, and other core network members have held public seminars to educate participants about the Women's Convention and specific articles. At these seminars, participants hear many examples of how the rights explicitly or implicitly declared in the articles—for example, the right to vote, the right to equal remuneration for work, and the right to equal access to education—apply to women in different countries and cultures. IWRAW publishes reports that summarize the seminars' contents. The IWRAW newsletter also highlights progress and problems in implementing particular articles of the convention.

Core network members in their own countries carry out projects to educate women from diverse backgrounds about the convention and its articles. For example, Isabel Plata wrote a book on the convention and circulated it throughout Latin America; she uses workshops, videos, and booklets to educate Colombian women about basic human rights.

The norm most emphasized by Fraser, Freeman, and other IWRAW leaders is equality. As they see it, the "central concern of women's human rights is equality in the family, the law, and everyday situations" (Humphrey Institute of Public Affairs, 1993, p. 1). Fraser, however, emphasizes that she and her allies are not seeking mere equality with men, especially when men are deprived of their full rights. Instead, she advocates the ideal, embodied in the Women's Convention, of "partnership between women and men, making them equal citizens" (Fraser, 1993, p. i). Freeman and Fraser (1993) critiqued "structural inequality," noting that even if women are granted full civil and political rights, they are in an unequal position to exercise them. They argued:

> While women now have rights to vote and to participate in civic life in most countries, their representation in elected bodies remains minimal. This is a direct result of their systematic exclusion, by custom and by law, from access to key elements of empowerment: education, physical and social freedom of movement, and mentorship by those already in power. . . . Structural inequality results in the perpetuation of injustice and ignorance despite all efforts to enact and enforce legal rights. (p. 105)

APPLYING ETHICAL PRINCIPLES, LAWS, AND NORMS TO SPECIFIC CASES

Simply educating people about ethical principles, laws, and norms is not enough to obtain desired behavioral changes. Ethical leaders also must explain how these principles, laws, and norms apply in individual cases or to classes of individuals.

Amnesty International

Peter Benenson's 1961 *Observer* article began what was to become Amnesty's unremitting effort to connect human rights principles to specific cases. He denounced the following examples of government officials' attempts to stifle nonviolent expression:

- In Angola, members of the Portuguese Political Police beat and arrested Dr. Agostino Neto for attempting to improve health services for African people. He was then imprisoned "without charge or trial" (p. 21).

- In Romania, a philosopher, Constantin Noica, was sentenced to 25 years in prison in order to halt his teaching.

- The Spanish government imprisoned without trial Antonio Amat, a lawyer who had tried to form a coalition of democratic groups.

- In the United States, Ashton Jones, a minister, was imprisoned in Louisiana and Texas "for doing what the Freedom Riders are now doing in Alabama" (p. 21).

- The South African government forbid Patrick Duncan, son of a former South African governor-general, from attending or addressing a meeting for 5 years.

In the more than 30 years since Benenson's article, Amnesty activists have highlighted the cases of tens of thousands of individual prisoners whose treatment has contravened international law. They also have publicized the plight of specific communities or groups that have been threatened with or have experienced random or wholesale killings and "disappearances" because of their politics, religion, ethnicity, or the like. They, in effect, have defined what constitutes the violation of the human right to freely express one's beliefs and to be free of torture.

IWRAW

IWRAW's reports and newsletters describe case after case of discrimination against women, whether sexual harassment at the United Nations, female circumcision in African societies, abuse of domestic workers in numerous countries, forced prostitution of Filipinas and other women, or discriminatory hiring practices in Japan and elsewhere. Although IWRAW tends to highlight abuses against groups of women, it also reports individual cases—for example, those of Wambui Otieno, a Kenyan woman, and Unity Dow, an IWRAW core network member from Botswana. Otieno waged an unsuccessful battle in Kenyan courts to be able to bury her deceased husband on their farm near Nairobi, rather than in his clan's homeland, as his family of origin wished. Dow successfully challenged Botswana law that had prevented her from conferring Botswanan citizenhood on her children because her husband was not a citizen of Botswana.

ADAPTING ETHICAL PRINCIPLES, LAWS, AND NORMS TO CHANGING TIMES

Either because technology has changed, new information has emerged, or new issues have developed, the existing ways of applying ethical principles, laws, and norms often become inadequate or even harmful. Thus, ethical leaders often must reinterpret or adapt ethical principles, laws, and norms to changing conditions.

Amnesty International

Amnesty officials, members, and staff have been in the forefront of applying international laws to new forms of human rights violations. Whereas these laws were initially viewed as applying to government actions, Amnesty has insisted that they be applied to extrajudicial killings and disappearances that are carried out by political opposition groups and paramilitary organizations. Amnesty also raised public awareness of the need for special attention to human rights violations aimed at certain categories of people, such as women, children, gay and lesbian people, and indigenous tribes.

Tracy Ulltvit-Moe, a veteran Latin America researcher at the International Secretariat, was among those who prompted the organization to give special attention to treatment of indigenous people. As Amnesty members and staff gathered information about human rights violations in Latin America, they realized that people were being targeted for massacres and other abuses because they were indigenous or lived in a particular place. For example, government-backed forces in El Salvador and Guatemala attacked indigenous people in certain areas of these countries because "they wanted to get rid of them as potential support for guerillas or because they lived in a village where there were [government] opponents or suspected sympathizers with opponents" (T. Ulltvit-Moe, interview by author, May 25, 1994). Usually, these people were being tortured and killed, not because of expressing their political beliefs, but because people in power suspected them of sympathizing or potentially sympathizing with government opponents. Ulltvit-Moe took the lead in preparing a report in 1992 on this type of abuse. She and others led the campaign to ensure that Amnesty would add to its mandate such attempts to stifle even potential expression of beliefs and opinion.

IWRAW

Under the banner of "Women's Rights Are Human Rights," IWRAW's leaders (along with leaders in other human rights and women's rights organizations, including Amnesty) have been at the forefront of efforts to make human rights principles contained in international treaties specifically applicable to women. For too long, they have argued, the interpretation of various articles in these treaties has been geared to the experience of men. Thus, wife battering or systematic rape of whole populations of women was not identified as a human rights abuse.

Freeman and Fraser (1993) emphasized that

> women's rights are neither a separate category nor a subcategory of human rights. They are, fundamentally, the rights proclaimed in the Universal Declaration of Human Rights and subsequent international and human rights instruments. The ultimate goal of the human rights endeavor does not differ by sex; both women and men are entitled to full civil, political, economic, social, and cultural rights.

But because most women in the world live in situations of structural inequality, even subservience, special attention must be given to overcoming the obstacles that stand in the way of full achievement of their human rights. (p. 104)

IWRAW leaders joined in the efforts led by the Center for Women's Global Leadership and the International Women's Tribune Center to make women's human rights a focal point at the 1993 World Conference on Human Rights in Vienna. Having served as an official delegate to the conference, Fraser (1993) pointed with special pride to the incorporation of women's concerns into the Declaration and Programme of Action adopted by consensus at the Vienna Conference. She quoted several specific statements on women's rights in the document; probably the strongest was:

The human rights of women and of the girl-child are an inalienable, integral and indivisible part of universal human rights. The full and equal participation of women in the political, civil, economic, social and cultural life, at the national, regional and international levels, and the eradication of all forms of discrimination on grounds of sex are priority objectives of the international community. (p. i)

RESOLVING CONFLICTS AMONG PRINCIPLES, LAWS, AND NORMS

As they attempt to apply ethical principles, laws, or norms to particular cases, ethical leaders often face the dilemma of reconciling competing ethical or legal claims. When such claims collide, ethical leaders can decide that one claim clearly outweighs the others, that all have merit and thus should be balanced, or that the dilemma can be resolved by reframing.

Amnesty International

Amnesty's founders and their successors have argued that ethical principles, laws, and norms supporting individual rights are more important than laws and norms supporting a national government's sovereignty over internal affairs. At the same time, Amnesty's leaders have emphasized that they have no intention to overthrow any particular government and indeed have suggested that governments actually protect their stability by respecting the rights of their citizens.

Perhaps the toughest ethical dilemma for Amnesty has been the conflict between the right of expression and the right to "life, liberty, and the security of person" (United Nations, 1948/1983d, p. 64). In other words, is each of us entitled to express political beliefs in ways that would deprive others of life, liberty, or security? At the outset, Peter Benenson in the 1961 *Observer* article emphasized that Amnesty's definition of *political prisoner* would exclude people who had advocated or condoned "personal violence" (p. 21). At the same time, Amnesty officials, members, and staff have defended the right of everyone to a fair trial, even if he or she is charged with advocating or engaging in antigovernment violence.

Amnesty leaders also have struggled with the question of whether there are fundamental conflicts between political and civil rights, on the one hand, and economic, social, and cultural rights on the other. In particular, Amnesty as an organization has refused to buy the argument that promotion of economic, social, and cultural well-being sometimes requires the abrogation of civil and political rights. In 1977, Thomas Hammarberg, then chair of the International Executive Committee, also emphasized that Amnesty's focus on civil rights does not mean that Amnesty "downgrades other basic rights, such as social and economic ones." Both types of rights are needed, he added. "If a people is deprived of one right, its chance of securing others is usually in danger" (Amnesty International, 1977, p. 12).

IWRAW

IWRAW leaders have responded forcefully to those who claim that the right to privacy in the home and the right to engage in cultural and religious observances outweigh women's rights to equal treatment. They argue that neither the sanctity of the family, nor religion, nor culture can rightfully be used as a smokescreen to hide oppression and abuse of women. Besides, they add, women's rights are compatible with strong families and freedom of religion and cultural integrity.

According to Freeman (1993),

> Because the claims of culture and family are a primary obstacle to establishment of women's human rights, the challenge for the international community, including governments, individual citizens, and nongovernmental organizations, is to recognize that protecting the rights of women within families as well as within society is not inimical to family life or cultural integrity. In fact, family life and societies are strengthened when the capacity of all family members to function with respect between themselves is fully developed. And a strong culture is never static. It is the expression of how people live, which changes in response to changing conditions. Cultures maintain themselves only by incorporating and adapting to change.
>
> The use of cultural preservation as a justification for discrimination against women is no more acceptable than the now discredited use of national sovereignty as a justification for other human rights abuses. (p. 3)

Unity Dow echoed Freeman: "Culture is changing all the time. The world is changing all the time" (interview by author, January 15, 1994). She urged African women to critically examine attempts to cloak discriminatory practices with the mantle of custom and ask whether these practices really derive from the culture's values. Women's rights, she argued, are not foreign to African cultural traditions. Similarly, core network member Farida Shaheed, a founder

of Women Living Under Muslim Laws, emphasizes that her group's championing of women's rights in Islamic countries is by no means anti-Muslim. The
group, she explains, strives for more enlightened interpretation of the Koran
and Muslim laws and practices.

THE DESIGN AND USE OF COURTS

Formal and informal courts are the primary social settings in which ethical
principles, laws, and norms are applied to specific cases and in which conduct
is sanctioned accordingly. Formal courts include government-created local,
provincial, national, and military courts; international courts such as the International Court of Justice or the European Court of Human Rights; quasi-judicial
bodies such as the UN's Human Rights Commission; religious courts; and
professional boards. The most pervasive informal court is the court of public
opinion. Also important are tribal or communal mediation arrangements.

Amnesty International

Amnesty's leaders have appealed to the court of public opinion throughout
the organization's history. Peter Benenson's 1961 *Observer* article launching
Amnesty cited the importance and effectiveness of mobilizing "world opinion"
against repressive government actions. In Amnesty's 1969-70 report, Sean
MacBride stated:

> One hopeful feature of the present period of world history is that public opinion
> is now becoming more powerful. Because of the mass media of communications
> there is a growing awareness of world happenings. This growing awareness leads
> to the formation of public opinion on a world-wide basis. In turn, governments
> can no longer act in secret: they are dependent on their own image both nationally
> and internationally and therefore must heed world opinion. (Amnesty Inter-
> national, 1970, p. 1)

In Amnesty's 1972-73 report, Secretary-General Martin Ennals declared that
international law is "virtually dependent on public opinion for its renovation
and enforcement" (Amnesty International, 1973, p. 7). During its campaign
against torture, Amnesty declared its reports exposing the practice of torture in
specific countries to be "a powerful moral weapon in the hands of world
opinion" (Amnesty International, 1976, p. 101). Ian Martin, when he was
secretary general, noted that the court of opinion within the United Nations is
especially important. National officials, he said, are "quite sensitive to their
reputations at the UN" (interview by author, June 29, 1987).

Amnesty officials, members, and staff also work with formal national and
international courts to obtain the release of prisoners of conscience or to ensure
timely, fair trials and humane treatment of all prisoners. In addition, Amnesty's

founders initiated Amnesty's emphasis on designing more effective international courts. Early on, Benenson and MacBride convened meetings of nongovernmental organizations to review international mechanisms for the protection of human rights. In subsequent years, Amnesty officials, members, and staff worked especially to strengthen and augment the will and power of the UN Human Rights Commission to enforce human rights provisions contained in international law. Especially important is the independent information that Amnesty supplies the commission on human rights abuses in particular countries.

IWRAW

IWRAW's core network members defend women's rights in formal courts as well as the court of public opinion. They also try to change the courts so that they can be stronger defenders of women's rights.

Unity Dow, for example, brought before the Botswana courts a groundbreaking test case based on the Women's Convention. She cited the principles of the convention in challenging Botswana law that permitted women citizens to confer citizenhood on their children only if the children were born outside marriage. Because her husband is not a citizen of Botswana, the country would not recognize her children as citizens, even though the entire family was living permanently in Botswana. Although her country had not ratified the Women's Convention, Dow argued successfully before the Appeals Court that it had become accepted international law and should have bearing on her case. The IWRAW staff (assisted by the Minnesota Lawyers International Human Rights Committee) supported Dow's efforts by sending her information about favorable precedents and legal arguments. The staff also helped generate international news coverage of the case. Once the case was decided in Dow's favor, the staff urged women to write to the Botswana government to oppose a rumored government effort to pass legislation that would undermine the decision.

Hadja Soumare's Comité d'Action pour les Droits de L'Enfant et de la Femme provides human rights training for lawyers and judges in Mali, educates women about the legal system, and provides legal assistance for poor women. Isabel Plata's Legal Services for Women informs women of their rights to challenge discriminatory practices in Colombian courts.

IWRAW's leaders also have sought to help the UN Committee on the Elimination of Discrimination Against Women (CEDAW) operate more effectively as a court. Because CEDAW has no direct enforcement power (although it can make recommendations to the United Nations), it must rely on nongovernmental organizations to appeal to various other courts to maintain pressure on governments to comply with the Women's Convention. The committee issues its reviews of country reports, but the reviews, Marsha Freeman noted, are written in "UN-ese," making them less than riveting reading (interview by author, March 25, 1993). The commission is "understaffed and overwhelmed," preventing it from promoting its findings. Freeman added that CEDAW only documents what countries report. It does not conduct an independent analysis. "That's left to groups like ours." IWRAW offers its own information about countries' progress in implementing the Women's Convention and makes recommendations to CEDAW.

ADDITIONAL RESOURCES AND GUIDANCE FOR LEADERSHIP IN THE GLOBAL COMMONS

Ethical leadership is mainly about influencing people, processes, and outcomes in courts, just as visionary and political leadership are concerned with people, processes, and outcomes in forums and arenas respectively. To implement solutions to global problems, leaders in the global commons must attend to courts for the following reasons:

- Court decisions provide guidance about what specific behavior is required, permitted, or forbidden in implementing new policies, programs, or projects.

- Opponents of new policies, programs, and projects may challenge them in court.

- The courts may be part of the problem—that is, the courts may be enforcing laws and norms that undermine the new policies, programs, and projects.

As leaders in the global commons help constituents obtain favorable verdicts in formal and informal courts, they should

- Identify, update, and reconcile the main ethical principles, laws, and norms that support their claims

- Recognize the connections between informal and formal courts

- Identify appropriate courts for arguing their case

- Seek changes in courts or establish new courts

To do this as part of a particular policy change effort, leaders can convene one or more working groups that are the same as, or coordinated with, the working groups that are constructing policy proposals for arenas. As working groups focus on courts, leaders should ensure that the groups either include or consult experts on ethics and law.

Identifying, Updating, and Reconciling Ethical Principles, Laws, and Norms

Ethical leaders help their constituents clearly identify the sources of legitimacy for the policies they support so that these ethical, legal, and normative grounds can be emphasized and interpreted in appeals to formal and informal courts. Let us first consider sources of legitimacy for efforts to resolve global public problems and then explore how ethical leaders can help their groups articulate ethical principles, laws, and norms important to their cause. Finally, we will examine methods of reconciling contradictions among ethical principles, laws, and norms in formal and informal courts.

Sources of Legitimacy. Efforts to resolve global public problems must be grounded in ethical principles, laws, and norms that have transnational and transcultural acceptance. Many thinkers have struggled with whether there can be a universal, or global, ethic and whether international laws and norms can be globally valid. I do not intend to repeat the debates here: I acknowledge the many different ethical schemes and approaches prevalent in the world's societies, but my focus will be on the numerous ethical principles, laws, and norms that have clear evidence of strong support around the world.

One approach to discovering ethical principles with global appeal is to distill common themes from the main world religions. Such was the enterprise of British writer Aldous Huxley (1945) in compiling *The Perennial Philosophy.* The core message in Huxley's explorations is that all human souls partake of the divine, God, or the "Ground of Being."

Another approach is to consult philosophers who derive ethical principles from their understanding of human commonality and diversity. According to the French philosopher Maurice Merleau-Ponty (1964), for example, all human beings are meaning seekers, yet each person will develop different meanings because his or her perspective is inherently limited. Each human being requires interaction with other human beings to develop a more comprehensive, more truthful view of the world. This argument is a powerful justification for the ethical principle that each person should be free to express his or her opinion or belief.

U.S. philosopher Cornel West (quoted in von Sternberg, 1996) espoused what he called the "radical democratic tradition" that views each person as "unique and distinctive and singular and irreproducible and thereby warranting a certain kind of dignity, and even sanctity" (p. A24). This common and holy diversity also requires that each person have some influence in the governance of society.

For feminist philosopher Nel Noddings (1984) of the United States, the most powerful human commonality is our urge to care for other human beings, especially our children and others closest to us. We also have in common other urges that pull us toward uncaring behavior. Ethical principles based on her analysis would include an imperative to care for other human beings and to accept or respond to caring, while secondarily protecting one's ability to care.

U.S. liberation theologian Matthew Fox (1983) extended this caring imperative to the earth itself. All humans, he contended, are cocreators of the Universe with God; thus, everyone has a responsibility to join with other human beings to care for the natural world and for each other, especially for those who suffer injustice and misfortune.

Robert Terry (1993) found human commonality in our existence simultaneously as individuals and social beings and in our existence as actors in the world. At the heart of his ethical system is the concept of authenticity, the call for human beings to be true to self and true to world. Terry tied ethical principles to six main categories of human action: existence, resources, structure, power, mission, and meaning. The principles are

- *Dwelling,* or the affirmation of human existence and development, as well as ecological diversity and survival (tied to existence)

- *Freedom,* or the requirement that everyone have the necessities of living and be allowed to fulfill his or her potential (tied to resources)

- *Justice,* or the affirmation of fairness, especially in distribution of resources (tied to structure)

- *Participation,* or the affirmation of engagement and shared power (tied to power)

- *Love,* or the affirmation of care, respect, and forgiveness toward self and others (tied to mission)

- *Responsibility,* a combination of wise judgment and accountability for authentic action (tied to meaning)

A common way to summarize the ethical principles described above is to see human beings as bearing certain important rights and responsibilities. Widely acknowledged statements of those rights are the Universal Declaration of Human Rights; the International Convenant on Civil and Political Rights; and the International Covenant on Economic, Social, and Cultural Rights; and the Convention on the Elimination of All Forms of Discrimination Against Women (United Nations, 1979/1983a, 1966/1983b, 1966/1983c, 1948/1983d). These documents, all important international laws, are signed by representatives of national governments, but the documents declare the promotion and protection of these rights to be both an individual and societal responsibility. The preamble to the Universal Declaration (United Nations, 1948/1983d) proclaims it to be

a common standard of achievement for all peoples and all nations, to the end that every individual and every organ of society, keeping this Declaration constantly in mind, shall strive by teaching and education to promote respect for these rights and freedoms and by progressive measures, national and international, to secure their universal and effective recognition and observance. (p. 63)

The preamble to each covenant cites the obligation of UN member countries to promote human rights and freedoms and emphasizes that "the individual, having duties to other individuals and to the community to which he belongs is under a responsibility to strive for the promotion and observance of the rights recognized in the present Covenant" (United Nations, 1948/1983d, p. 63).

There are many other international resolutions and treaties that spell out rights and responsibilities in international trade, use of natural resources, treatment of refugees, and other matters. Advocates of particular transnational policy changes can find out more about the international resolutions and treaties related to their concerns by consulting appropriate UN offices, experts in international law, and transnational citizen organizations knowledgeable about treaties in a particular area.

Important norms that support global ethical principles and laws are

- Respect and care for other human beings and the earth

- Tolerance of different opinions and beliefs

- Concern for future generations

- Fairness

- Abiding by one's word (a helpful norm in persuading nations to honor treaty obligations)

Specifying and Updating Ethical Principles, Laws, and Norms. How can ethical leaders help their groups articulate the cross-cultural ethical principles that underlie their mission? One method is to return to the personal passions and concerns that prompted group members to be involved in the first place and then probe for the underlying cross-cultural ethical principles. For example, the women in IWRAW's core network became active in the women's rights movement mainly because they were determined to fight injustice directed at women and children. Their determination was rooted in the general feminist philosophy that all human beings should have dignity, the essentials of a decent life, equal opportunity, and full citizenship in their societies. In the case of Amnesty International, religious beliefs very clearly underlay several of the founders' commitment to the Amnesty mission of championing freedom of belief and opinion. (For Peter Benenson, it was Catholicism; for Eric Baker, Quakerism; for Tom Sargent, Methodism.) The founders appealed, however, to broader ethical principles embedded in the Universal Declaration of Human Rights and Enlightenment political philosophy.

Once group members identify the ethical principles that support their cause, they should ask what laws help apply those principles to the problem that concerns them. Finally, the group should consider what norms would reinforce those ethical principles in formal and informal courts.

The group also should ask if the principles, laws, and norms need reinterpreting to take account of new information, new technology, and new practices or issues. Thus, groups such as IWRAW have fought to reinterpret human rights principles so that the principles would clearly apply to women. To take another example, a group supporting female literacy works hard for a new law requiring girls to be sent to school. The legislative debate indicates that the law is intended to ensure that girls and boys have equal education. The group finds that a year after the law is enforced, most girls are being sent to school, but they are being assigned to classes that train them in traditional female skills and are excluded from courses that prepare young men for other careers. The supporters of the law then will need to argue in informal courts and formal courts that the intent of the law is equal education, not just sending girls to school.

Reconciling Conflicting Ethical Principles, Laws, and Norms. What happens when these principles, laws, and norms conflict with each other or with other valid principles, laws, and norms? As noted earlier, ethical leaders can help groups resolve these conflicts by deciding that one competing claim outweighs another, by balancing the claim, or by reframing the conflict. For example, those opposed to a new law that requires sending girls to school may argue that it interferes with parental authority over children or with the parents' right to economic security. Ethical leaders might argue that children's right to education is so important that parental rights and needs are secondary. Ethical leaders who desire to more strongly recognize the needs of parents (and win their support for change) might argue that the rights can be balanced, by giving parents who send their children to school a tax credit, for example. Or they might reframe the conflict, pointing out that well-educated girls will be better prepared to help their parents in their old age.

Ethical leaders also should stay alert to the reality of human imperfection and the danger of rigidity and self-righteousness in the pursuit of ethical behavior. Many sages and philosophers remind us that rigid adherence to particular ethical principles and laws and overreliance on laws can actually undermine the common good. Lao-tzu declared:

> The more prohibitions you have, the less virtuous people will be. . . .
> The master says: I let go of the law, and people become honest.
> I let go of economics, and people become prosperous.
> I let go of religion, and the people become serene.
> I let go of all desire for the common good and the good becomes as common
>   as grass.
>
>   (Mitchell, 1988, No. 57)

Recognizing Connections Among Informal and Formal Courts

Ethical leaders help constituents recognize the importance of combining appeals to informal courts, especially the court of public opinion, with appeals to formal courts. Widespread implementation of new solutions to public problems will require mutually reinforcing decisions by both types of courts.

Both types of courts have advantages and disadvantages. Take for example, the important informal court, the court of public opinion. Its advantages include its pervasiveness and its low-cost enforcement mechanisms. Its verdicts consist of norms that are widely internalized and, when necessary, enforced by numerous authority figures. Probably the most severe sanction employed by the court of public opinion is shunning. For example, consider a town in which public opinion is strongly opposed to torture. The townspeople find out that a soldier from the town has been a member of an army unit suspected of torturing opponents of the government. When this man returns to the town, hardly anyone will speak to him, and no one will hire him or do business with him. Not only is the man punished for his conduct, but he and everyone else in the town are given incentives to never torture anyone in the future.

Relying on the court of public opinion also has disadvantages. The court operates effectively only when there is very strong societal consensus about right and wrong behavior. Except for shunning, its sanctions tend to be weak—tacit or expressed reprimands for disagreeable behavior, praise for approved behavior. (These sanctions are especially ineffective when the incentives for wrong behavior are strong—for example, when a polluter makes higher profits or when a commanding officer threatens to shoot any soldier who refuses to torture his prisoners.)

Often verdicts of formal courts are crucial in providing strong sanctions and nudging emerging public opinion toward a consensus for enforcing new behavioral norms. Consider, for example, the implementation of female literacy projects in a society that has previously condoned parents' keeping girls at home to work instead of sending them to school. Even though many people are beginning to question the old norm of allowing parents to decide whether girls should be educated, and even though the national legislature has passed a law requiring girls to attend school, it may take one or more decisions by a formal court to finally sway the court of public opinion in favor of sending girls to school. Thus, emerging opinion is reinforced by the sanctions, such as fines or imprisonment, meted out by formal courts. If formal courts begin to fine parents who resist sending their girls to school, then the emerging norm of guaranteeing girls' schooling is likely to become widely shared much more quickly than it would have been without the formal court action.

It is not always necessary to go through the full judicial process in formal courts to influence the implementation of a new policy. Even attempting to bring a case (such as a challenge of girls' assignments to traditional classes) to a court can prompt implementers to change their behavior (see Forsythe, 1989, p. 46).

Identifying Appropriate Courts

For any major policy change, an array of informal and formal courts—each with its own jurisdiction, judges, and decision-making methods—is potentially important for policy implementation. For policies dealing with global problems, leaders will need to pay attention to courts at many levels from local to national to international.

To help their groups identify these courts and decide whether and how to influence them, ethical leaders could ask group members to begin by brainstorming answers to the following questions:

- For informal courts:
    1. Which local informal courts should we seek to influence? (e.g., community opinion, a group of elders, a religious council, vocational or professional councils, local mediation systems)
    2. Which provincial and national courts should we seek to influence? (e.g., national public opinion, provincial and national professional or vocational councils, national religious councils)
    3. Which international courts should we seek to influence? (e.g., public opinion in southern Africa or other multicountry regions, world opinion, and transnational religious, professional, or vocational councils)

- For formal courts:
    1. Which local courts should we seek to influence? (e.g., district or municipal courts, military courts, tribal courts, religious courts)
    2. Which provincial and national courts should we seek to influence? (e.g., arbitration boards, appellate courts, national supreme courts, national military tribunals, religious courts)
    3. Which international courts should we seek to influence? (e.g., the UN Human Rights Commission, the International Court of Justice, CEDAW, the Inter-American Commission on Human Rights, the European Court of Justice)

More research often will be needed after initial brainstorming to fill in courts unknown to the group.

Once courts are identified, the group (or subgroups) can do necessary research to compile a basic profile for each one. The profile should include

- The court's jurisdiction—the geographic territory covered by the court, the types of disputes it handles
- Access rules (e.g., who can bring disputes to the court, who can attend trials, who can serve on a jury)
- The court's decision-making methods (e.g., consensus among judges, majority vote by judges, jury trial, prompt or delayed trial, reliance on precedent, reliance on bribes or political influence, mediation, arbitration)
- The court's enforcement methods—fines, reprimands, imprisonment, expulsion, reliability and uniformity of punishment
- Characteristics of the judges, other officers of the court, and jury members— fairness, honesty, indicators of possible bias (e.g., gender, training, religion,

ethnicity, past decisions, political affiliation) in favor of or against the policy advocates' position

- Resources required for influencing the court (e.g., lawyers, excellent communicators, travel money)

- Advantages and disadvantages of attempting to influence the court

- Likelihood of obtaining a favorable verdict from the court

Ethical leaders can use these profiles to help their groups decide where to direct their efforts. Let us assume that a group of teachers trying to promote female literacy in southern Africa compiled such profiles. The profiles might indicate that several courts, such as CEDAW, the South African Supreme Court, urban public opinion, and religious and professional councils, would probably produce favorable verdicts. The teachers may most easily triumph in teachers' professional councils, but if they allied with a group such as IWRAW, they might obtain necessary expertise to influence CEDAW or to win a case in the South African Supreme Court.

Seeking Changes in Courts or New Courts

Ethical leaders also help their groups consider what changes may be needed in formal and informal courts to improve the chances that the court will endorse the policy changes the group supports. The profiles developed in the previous section can be a starting place for this assessment. The profiles might reveal that the group needs to work for expanding or narrowing a court's jurisdiction or fight for public trials or for the right of individual claimants (not just government officials) to bring a case before a court. Or the group might seek to replace certain judges or alter the training for judges and other court officers. A legal aid system might be needed for indigent citizens.

The process of identifying and assessing existing formal and informal courts also might reveal that there was no court, or at least no court powerful enough, to supply needed sanctions or resolve residual conflicts connected with a policy change. In this case, ethical leaders would help their groups develop strategies for establishing such courts. Starting new courts also may be the best approach when needed changes in existing courts would be very difficult to accomplish.

In designing new courts, a helpful guideline is to create the least coercive court that will obtain the desired results at a reasonable cost. A voluntary mediation system would be low on the coercion scale; a criminal court with authority to imprison people would be high on the scale. For example, the advocates of national laws requiring parents to send their daughters to school may realize that in communities where resistance is widespread, school officials will have to rely in many cases on courts to enforce the law. They could turn to a formal court that could fine or imprison parents, but that level of coercion could cause great harm to the families involved. Instead, the supporters of girls' education might establish local mediation offices that could bring together resistant parents and school officials to work out mutually acceptable solutions, such as finding alternative care for preschoolers that was now provided by the girls or developing a school schedule that was more convenient for the families. Such a mediation system probably would need to be backed up by a formal court that imposed penalties on parents who still refused to send their girls to school.

Plans for altering existing courts or creating new ones often must be approved by official decision makers in government, nonprofit, and business arenas. Thus, ethical leadership must overlap with political leadership to incorporate these changes into proposals that have an optimal chance of adoption and implementation in arenas.

SUMMARY

Ethical leaders in the global commons focus on the design and use of courts to ensure that people actually comply with adopted policy changes that help resolve global public problems. These leaders also may turn to courts to try to override arenas that have resisted a policy change that has legitimacy under current law. It is especially important that ethical leaders help their groups identify and interpret the ethical principles, laws, and norms that provide legitimacy for their cause.

Ethical leadership is the last of the seven main types of leadership that are vital for tackling global public problems. The next and final chapter will examine how all seven types of leadership are linked together over a policy change cycle. It also will offer additional counsel and caveats for those answering the call to leadership in the global commons.

CHAPTER 9

Putting It All Together

Thus times do shift, each thing his turn does hold;
New things succeed, as former things grow old.
                                                    —Robert Herrick

Everything the Power of the World does is done in a circle. . . . The life of
a [person] is a circle from childhood to childhood, and so it is in everything
where power moves.
                                                    —Black Elk

Leaders in the global commons need to think systematically and holistically about the process of tackling public problems that spill beyond national boundaries. They especially need to realize that in a shared-power world, major change hardly ever proceeds along a linear path. The pattern of change is more cyclic, and even chaotic, as public attention to a particular problem waxes and wanes; as groups frame and reframe the problem; as some solutions are rejected, only to be resurrected when accepted solutions fail; as new policies are adopted in arenas, only to be altered or stymied by implementers; and as elected decision makers reject policies, only to be overruled by courts.

The change cycle (Figure 9.1) is a way of representing this nonlinear, recursive, chaotic process. The cycle consists of seven interrelated phases: (a) the initial agreement, (b) problem definition, (c) the search for solutions, (d) policy or plan formulation, (e) proposal review, (f) adoption, implementation, and evaluation, and (g) maintenance, succession, or termination.

The change cycle offers a systematic way to think about leadership and problem solving in the global commons. Leaders in the global commons need

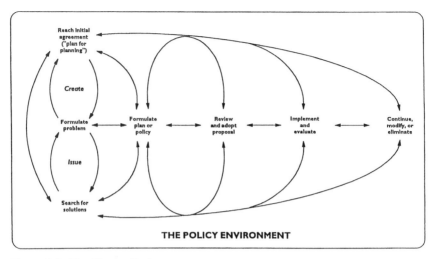

Figure 9.1. The Change Cycle

SOURCE: From *Leadership for the Common Good: Tackling Public Problems in a Shared-Power World* (p. 58), by J. M. Bryson & B. C. Crosby, 1992, San Francisco: Jossey-Bass. Copyright 1992 by Jossey-Bass. Adapted by permission.

to understand how the change cycle works and how to link different types of leadership to the different phases of the cycle.

Let us look more closely at the cycle and its phases, using illustrations from Amnesty International and IWRAW. We will then see how the different types of leadership, from personal to ethical, weave through the cycle. Finally, we will consider the key pitfalls and possibilities that leaders in the global commons should keep in mind as they try to combine all the types of leadership in a successful change effort.

THE CHANGE CYCLE

Probably the easiest way to understand the change cycle is to think about it as a story with beginning, middle, and end. The beginning would comprise the phases of initial agreement, problem definition, and search for solutions; the middle would be the proposal development and proposal review and adoption phases; and the end would be implementation and evaluation, followed by the maintenance, succession, or termination phase.

The Beginning

The first three phases of the change cycle together result in issue creation—that is, the placement of a public problem and one or more solutions on the agenda of many people beyond a small group of concerned activists. Ideally, the problem will be framed in a way that appeals to a broad array of stakeholders.

Initial Agreement. In the initial agreement phase, one or more groups of people come together in forums and agree to do something about a problem, or "a difficult matter requiring a solution" (*Pocket Oxford Dictionary*, 1992). The problem previously may have been a condition that was taken for granted, not really seen as a problem to be worked on or solved. Or the problem may have been previously defined and solutions proposed or even adopted, but the solutions may not be working.

The founders of Amnesty International agreed to work on the global problem of people's being imprisoned because of their political or religious beliefs. The problem had been identified previously, but existing solutions—for example, the provisions of the Universal Declaration of Human Rights and foreign observers at trials of political dissidents—were not having much impact. Thus, Amnesty's founders agreed to seek new solutions.

Similarly, IWRAW's founders agreed to work on the problem of global discrimination against women. A solution—the Convention on the Elimination of All Forms of Discrimination Against Women—was in place. What was missing was some method of making the convention effective.

Often a "triggering mechanism" (Cobb & Elder, 1983, p. 84) prompts an agreement to do something about a public problem. Important triggering mechanisms are

- Changes in key indicators, such as unemployment rates or immunization levels

- Focusing events, such as a natural disaster, a glaring injustice, or significant markers (e.g., the end of the millenium or the International Year of the Child)

- Crises, such as famine or war

- Manipulation of powerful symbols, such as the nation or "Mother Earth"

The agreement to launch Amnesty was triggered by the imprisonment of two Portuguese students. IWRAW was founded as the end of the International Decade for Women prompted Rebecca Cook, Arvonne Fraser, and others to strategize about how to continue the decade's momentum for improving women's status.

Problem Formulation. The problem formulation phase overlaps with the initial agreement phase because a group must have some understanding of a problem to agree to do something about it. The main purpose of this phase, however, is to deepen the group's understanding of the problem and define it in a way that can appeal to a broad array of stakeholders. In this phase, groups gather information about the problem and organize forums to share the information and experiment with different problem frames.

Amnesty's founders began with awareness of several political prisoners: the *Observer* article (Benenson, 1961) mentioned nine. Once the campaign was launched and offers of support began pouring into the makeshift Amnesty office, the small staff—Christel Marsh especially—scanned newspapers and monitored the BBC to find additional prisoners of conscience around the world. Christel Marsh also drew on her own connections and those of her husband Norman Marsh and of Peter Benenson to identify these prisoners. Through the years, Amnesty staff developed increasingly sophisticated methods of information gathering about individual prisoners of conscience. The organization has never actually abandoned the problem definition phase, for it is always adding new prisoners and new abusers to its statements of the problem.

In addition, Amnesty officials, staff, and members have contended with each other through the years over expansion of the problem's dimensions. The majority have accepted the argument that Amnesty should be concerned not solely about governments' unjust imprisonment of their citizens but also about several other grievous human rights abuses aimed at silencing personal opinion and belief. The majority also have accepted the argument that the problem's dimensions should be expanded to include the particular forms of such abuse directed at groups such as women, gay and lesbian people, and indigenous people.

Benenson and other founders disagreed over the framing of the problem that concerned them. Benenson cited the Universal Declaration of Human Rights in support of Amnesty's cause, he maintained that it was better to view the problem as a violation of civil liberties than as a human rights abuse. He was not able to convince his colleagues, however, and the human rights frame, which had stronger international resonance than civil liberties, prevailed.

The founders of IWRAW did not initially concentrate on finding out more about the problem of global discrimination against women. Indeed, they had been a part of an international decade that had explored that problem deeply. They did provide, however, a clear framing of discrimination as a women's rights problem—for example, by their choice of the network's name and by their characterization of the Women's Convention as an "international bill of rights for women."

With the creation of IWRAW's newsletter, the network did begin gathering and disseminating reports of many different types of discrimination against the world's women. By the 1990s, Arvonne Fraser and other IWRAW leaders also increasingly framed discrimination against women as a human rights problem, partly in response to the opportunity that the Vienna World Conference on Human Rights offered for promoting that interpretation.

Search for Solutions. In the search-for-solutions phase, change advocates work mainly in forums to find optimal solutions for the problem that concerns them. The search-for-solutions phase almost always overlaps the other two beginning phases. When a group decides something should be done about a problem, members already have at least a vague or preliminary idea of what that something might be. If the problem is imprisonment of political dissidents, the solutions generally must be aimed at keeping them from being imprisoned in the first place or getting them out of prisons.

The easiest approach to finding solutions for a public problem is adapting solutions already known to the group. Thus, as Benenson and other founders discussed ways of using volunteers to work for the release of political prisoners, they readily turned to the idea of forming adoption groups, an idea derived from Benenson's earlier humanitarian activities. As IWRAW's founders planned their organization, they were attracted to the idea of a network, highly popular in feminist circles as an alternative to hierarchical structures associated with male domination. Solutions already known to the group have extra appeal because they have often been tested, albeit in a different context.

To increase its chances of finding effective solutions, the group can do the research to identify solutions beyond its knowledge. The group also can try to develop new and innovative solutions. Such efforts to move beyond solutions known to the group are often prompted by awareness that the known solutions are inadequate or highly flawed.

Just as change-oriented groups continue expanding their understanding of a public problem after it has been formulated, the groups may frequently cycle back to the search-for-solutions phase. The solutions that once seemed promising may have failed, or new understandings of the problem may reveal that existing solutions are inadequate. For example, when Amnesty workers realized that Latin American paramilitary groups were executing large numbers of political opponents without trial, they knew that they needed a more rapid response than careful case-by-case research, followed by campaigns pressuring government officials. Thus, the Urgent Action idea was born.

IWRAW remained open to new solutions by welcoming new people into the core network. When Arvonne Fraser heard about someone who was doing interesting and important work for women's rights, she invited her or him to a core network meeting. Unity Dow was one who brought a new solution to IWRAW. Originally, IWRAW focused on building a global network that would educate people about the Women's Convention, build public support for the convention, monitor implementation of the convention, and provide technical assistance to government officials responsible for implementing the convention. Unity Dow brought an additional solution to IWRAW—the use of court suits to force governments to comply with specific provisions of the Women's Convention.

Issue Creation. When a group has successfully passed through the first three phases at least once, it has created a public issue—that is, a widely visible public problem linked to one or more clear solutions that have advantages and disadvantages from the standpoint of various stakeholder groups. (The best solutions

are those that have high likelihood of remedying the problem and that appeal
to as many of the stakeholders as possible.)

Less than a year after Peter Benenson began talking to his colleagues and
acquaintances about the possibility of organizing a campaign on behalf of
political prisoners, the readers of mass circulation newspapers around the world
received the message in May 1961 that numerous governments were imprison-
ing, torturing, or executing citizens whose views the governments abhorred.
Moreover, these readers were offered an initial solution—joining with a group
of English writers, lawyers, and publishers to "work impartially" for the fair
trial and release of specific "prisoners of conscience," to assist political refugees, and to "urge effective international machinery to guarantee freedom of
opinion." By the time the first annual report was published in 1962, additional,
more concrete solutions were offered. The report declared that the Appeal for
Amnesty was now an "international movement for freedom of opinion and
religion" (Amnesty International, 1962). Members had formed 70 groups,
mainly in Britain but also in Australia, Finland, Switzerland, Norway, and
Sweden. Anyone concerned about prisoners of conscience could join the organization and become involved in the work of setting up adoption groups,
sending missions to countries where abuses were suspected, focusing public
attention on the prisoners and their families, and organizing conferences. The
annual report emphasized advantages for the key stakeholders, political prisoners, by noting that general or partial amnesties for such prisoners had been
declared in many countries since the Appeal for Amnesty campaign began.

In the IWRAW case, about 6 months after Lois Brunott, Rebecca Cook, Jane
Connors, Norma Forde, Arvonne Fraser, Silvia Pimentel, and Isabel Plata
agreed to form an international women's rights network, the fledgling IWRAW
held its first public seminar in conjunction with the February 1986 meeting of
the Committee on the Elimination of Discrimination against Women (CEDAW)
in New York. Those invited to the seminar—lawyers, scholars, and representatives of women's and other organizations—worked with IWRAW's founders to refine the founders' initial ideals for ensuring that the Women's Convention was implemented around the world. By the seminar's end, an issue was
emerging for a group beyond IWRAW's founders. For seminar participants, the
problem of global discrimination against women was now linked to several
solutions—educating people around the world about the Women's Convention,
assessing signatory countries' progress in implementing the convention, and
working closely with CEDAW. The chief beneficiaries of these solutions were
to be women in every nation and CEDAW. Opposition might be expected from
government officials who hoped to ignore or merely give lip service to the
convention.

By the spring of 1987, IWRAW's staff and volunteers had further expanded
awareness of the issue by distributing numerous materials to more than 4,000
individuals and organizations around the world. Materials included the full and
condensed text of the Women's Convention, a report on the 1986 seminar, a

report on CEDAW's reviews of reports from various countries, a bibliography, and reprints of articles about the convention. IWRAW workers also issued studies and "easy-to-read" booklets on women's rights in various countries, established "working relationships and potential projects" in several countries, and participated in international conferences in Jamaica, Indonesia, Zimbabwe, Egypt, Canada, Singapore, Australia, Europe and the United States (IWRAW, n.d.). IWRAW also began a quarterly newsletter and garnered publicity in organizational newsletters and major media.

The Middle

In the middle phases of the change cycle, change advocates focus on putting the issue developed in the previous three phases on the agenda of policy makers in appropriate government, business, and nonprofit arenas. They press for policy makers' approval of specific proposals embodying the advocates' preferred solutions.

Proposal Development. Change advocates may be able to implement some of their preferred solutions directly, but usually they will need to obtain specific decisions from nonprofit, government, or business arenas that control various resources needed to implement the solutions. In the proposal development phase, change advocates identify which arenas are crucial to their cause and craft proposed policies, programs, or projects that will deploy the arena's funds, authority, or personnel to implement the advocates' proposed solutions. The proposed policies, programs, or projects may be as complicated as development of a draft international treaty or as straightforward as the request that a nation's president order the release of a political dissident from jail. No matter what, change advocates must carefully tailor their proposal to the decision makers who will consider it and to the procedures and timetables the decision makers employ.

Beginning in Amnesty International's early years, Amnesty officials, volunteers, and staff have, in effect developed a proposal for each prisoner of conscience they have adopted. Researchers at the secretariat compile evidence that a person has been jailed for his beliefs and identify who has authority to release the person or guarantee him a fair trial. The evidence, along with provisions of the Universal Declaration of Human Rights, can then be cited in letters, postcards, and in-person presentations directed at the officials who have power over the prisoner's fate. The evidence also provides support when Amnesty representatives ask government officials in countries other than the one in which an abuse is occurring to put pressure on those responsible for the abuse.

As Amnesty members and staff have expanded the dimensions of the problem that concerns them, and thus the range of solutions, they have put together additional types of proposals. For example, Amnesty representatives propose new initiatives at the United Nations, and they ask governments to protect groups of people—for example, citizens from a particular ethnic group—as well as individuals. Amnesty members and staff also prepare proposals seeking decisions from other nonprofit groups (e.g., trade unions, foundations, lawyers) and businesses.

IWRAW staff and members put together proposals for foundation funding, for changes in particular countries' laws, and for improving particular countries' reports on implementation of the Women's Convention. Proposals to foundations and individual contributors have been especially important to IWRAW because it does not collect membership fees (although it does sell subscriptions to its newsletter). Rebecca Cook, Stephen Isaacs, Arvonne Fraser, Marsha Freeman, and others have identified which foundations and contributors might be interested in the issue presented by IWRAW and have then developed proposals that carefully tailored the problem definition and preferred solutions to the philanthropists' priorities and requirements.

Proposal Review and Adoption. In this phase, decision makers in government, nonprofit, or business arenas consider the proposals developed by the change advocates and decide whether to adopt them entirely or partly. The advocates must continue working for their proposal at this stage—by being available to supply additional information, by directly lobbying decision makers if permitted, and by reminding the decision makers of the importance, popularity, or morality of the proposal.

For example, an Amnesty group that has adopted a particular prisoner of conscience does not simply send officials a bunch of letters asking that the prisoner be released and then wait to see what happens. They continue to collect information about the prisoner's condition, they send additional letters, and they activate other groups that might put pressure on the officials.

Similarly, IWRAW leaders did not just submit proposed language to the framers of the platform for the 1995 World Conference on Women. They lobbied for their proposals at regional preparatory meetings and at the conference itself. They coordinated their efforts with other human rights organizations to maximize their impact.

The End

In the last two phases of the change cycle, change advocates focus on implementing changes that have been adopted by government, nonprofit, and business arenas. Advocates also must assess whether the new policies, projects, or programs being implemented are working well—that is, whether they are effective remedies for the problem that prompted them.

Implementation and Evaluation. Once policy makers approve a new policy, project, or program, advocates of the change often must be responsible for actual implementation. If other people are charged with implementing new policies, the change advocates should remain involved, advising and monitoring the implementers. Reliable evaluations should be built into the implementation process. That is, at certain intervals—perhaps every month, every 6 months, or every year—implementers should be required to demonstrate their progress in achieving the goals of the policy change.

For example, a country's policy makers may agree to release all political prisoners in response to pressure from Amnesty and other human rights groups. Amnesty researchers continue collecting information about the prisoners to track how many are actually released; staff will publicize the results in press releases, Amnesty's annual report, and other forums. Amnesty representatives may try to invoke sanctions from international courts if the country's officials do not live up to their commitments.

Members of IWRAW were very pleased that government representatives at the 1995 World Conference on Women approved a Platform of Action that seeks "to promote and protect the full enjoyment of all human rights and the fundamental freedoms of all women throughout their life cycle" (Freeman, 1995, p. 1). The platform, Marsha Freeman noted, "unequivocally asserts women's rights to full participation in society and outlines what must be done for those rights to be realized" (p. 1). At the same time, she did not expect most government representatives to rush home and ensure that the actions outlined in the platform were implemented. The platform, she said, "will only mean something when women make it mean something" (p. 1). For IWRAW members, the platform is one more set of official commitments that women and advocacy organizations can use as they press for rights of citizenship, equal employment opportunity, education, health care, and the like.

Policy or Plan Maintenance, Succession, or Termination. Once a new policy, plan, program, or project has been substantially implemented, leaders should reevaluate it. They should engage the main stakeholders in exploring to what extent the change effort has produced a regime of mutual gain, in which measurable, significant, and widespread improvements have been made at reasonable costs. Leaders can begin by convening the stakeholders to review outcomes, compare costs and benefits of the change effort, and assess the status of the problem that prompted the effort. Then they can initiate a dialogue among the stakeholders about strengths and weaknesses of the policy, plan, program, or project; needed improvements; and lessons learned from the change process.

These conversations may indicate that a change effort is no longer needed or is so badly flawed that it should be terminated. Leaders will then have the task of arranging appropriate celebrations or funerals, depending on whether the change effort succeeded or failed. Alternatively, stakeholders may agree that the policy, plan, program, or project is generally successful (i.e., has produced a regime of mutual gain) and should be maintained. The ensuing work of leaders then will be to keep policy makers and citizens aware of the regime's benefits and promote minor modifications that would strengthen it. Finally, the stake-holders may agree that the policy, plan, program, or project is highly flawed but that it has produced some gains that can serve as a starting place for a successor regime, just as the failed League of Nations was succeeded by the United Nations. If a group does decide that a policy or plan should be revamped, leaders will have the task of returning to the earlier phases of the policy change cycle to begin developing new understandings of the public problem and possible solutions and then to develop new proposals based on the most promising solutions.

The efforts of nongovernmental organizations such as Amnesty International and IWRAW, along with supportive officials in national governments and intergovernmental organizations, have produced a global human rights regime that is a remarkable achievement over the past half-century. The foundation of the regime was laid with the adoption of the UN Charter and the Universal Declaration of Human Rights. Pillars of the regime are subsequent international treaties, such as the International Covenant on Civil and Political Rights; the International Covenant on Economic, Social and Economic Rights; and the Women's Convention. The regime has been enlivened by human rights activists who showed how these documents applied to actual people and cases and insisted that governments and other organizations uphold the provisions of these documents. These activists also have worked successfully for strengthen-ing intergovernmental structures that contribute to the regime—for example, the UN Commission on Human Rights and the Inter-American Commission on Human Rights. The capstone of the new regime is the 1993 World Conference on Human Rights, which produced a Declaration and Programme of Action "strongly reaffirming the universality, indivisibility, and interdependence of all human rights" (Amnesty International, 1994, p. 32). The document includes recognition of the rights of women, children, indigenous people, refugees, disabled people, and other groups. Although the document falls short from the perspective of human rights organizations, the conference was a powerful rallying point for supporters of human rights and a powerful forum for commu-nicating the principles, laws, procedures, and norms that are part of the global human rights regime.

Of course, the implementation of international human rights law is highly imperfect. Success stories are matched by reports of continued abuses and new violations. Global human rights problems have not gone away; the regime that has emerged to deal with them has many weaknesses. Human rights advocates thus are continuing to work for strengthening and maintenance of the regime.

Multiple Entry Points

Although the change cycle can be understood as a story with beginning, middle, and end, a person or group may become involved at any point in the story. Indeed, the beginning of policy change might be somewhere other than initial agreement. For example, the emergence of a solution, such as new technology or a munificent bequest, may prompt a group to reformulate existing problems to take advantage of the new solution.

It is also important to recognize that different change cycles often intersect each other. In the mid-1940s, voluntary organizations, international jurists, and government officials who were concerned about global human rights managed to win almost unanimous approval of the Universal Declaration of Human Rights by the countries joining the new United Nations. The policy change represented by the declaration was in a slow-paced implementation phase when Peter Benenson cited the declaration as legitimizing the attempts of Amnesty's founders to draw attention to the problem of political prisoners. Amnesty's founders, in effect, took part of the Universal Declaration of Human Rights and initiated a new change cycle around it. Similarly, the efforts to fight global discrimination against women via a comprehensive international treaty had reached the implementation phase with UN adoption of the Women's Convention. The founders of IWRAW cycled back through the policy change cycle to build public awareness of violations of women's rights, the solutions legitimized by the Women's Convention, and means of pressuring governments to implement the convention.

LEADERSHIP AND CHANGE

All six major types of leadership are vital for successful navigation of the change cycle. Some are more important than others, however, in particular phases. For example, personal leadership is crucial in initiating change, visionary leadership is especially important in the phases of problem formulation and the search for solutions, and political leadership is prominent throughout proposal development, review and adoption, and implementation. To more fully describe how the different types of leadership are woven through the change cycle, let us consider a possible scenario of an effort to promote female literacy throughout the world.

Initial Agreement

A woman—because of her values, experiences, or profession—feels the need to respond to a new report that shows that many girls throughout the world remain illiterate. She believes this problem must be remedied if women are to have any chance of being full citizens of their countries, finding decent jobs, and adequately supporting their children. She is most committed to girls and women in her own country but also feels some responsibility for girls and women in other parts of the world. She thinks a transnational campaign for female literacy would foster information exchange among existing literacy programs, attract new attention and resources to the needs of girls, and perhaps foster more effective approaches to girls' education.

As this woman begins to think about the possibility of finding other people to join her in a transnational campaign for female literacy, she is poised at the beginning of a change cycle. The time is right for thinking about personal leadership. For example, she should ask herself, Why am I concerned about this? How does the plight of illiterate girls connect to my personal passions and commitments? What strengths and weaknesses do I bring to an effort to do something about this problem? Do I have the courage to go forward even when this gets controversial?

The work of leadership in context can begin as well. The woman can do preliminary investigation of social, political, economic, and technological conditions and trends that are affecting female literacy in her own country and providing opportunities or even demands for leadership. She also can explore the global context by, for example, learning more about how the UN system handles issues affecting women and children.

To move into the initial agreement phase of the policy change cycle, this woman asks, "Who can I persuade to join me in informal meetings to talk about the problems of girls and women who cannot read or write adequately?" Because even such preliminary meetings lay the groundwork for future phases of the policy change cycle, she should seek to involve people who understand diverse groups of girls and women and who have access to resources (including their personal energies) that might be employed in a female literacy effort.

Let us assume that the woman convenes the informal meetings and that at their conclusion several participants have agreed that something needs to be done and that they will stay involved. These participants agree to work as a team to organize additional meetings, or forums, that will bring as many key stakeholders as possible together to explore and further define the problem of female literacy.

At this point, the group should think about team leadership. One or more team members should help the team decide on its purpose, the way it will operate, who will do what, and how decisions will be made.

Problem Formulation

As the team moves fully into the problem formulation phase by organizing stakeholder forums to explore the problem of female literacy, one or more members should exercise visionary leadership. They are the ones who ask: How can we frame this problem so that key stakeholders will feel included? Who are insightful speakers who can help us see what's really going on? How do we design these forums so that the people we want to be there can attend?

Search for Solutions

As the original or an expanded team moves into the search-for-solutions phase, visionary leadership is still needed to elicit and support promising ideas for remedying the problem. The team can convene forums in which solutions can be presented, debated, and ranked. To prepare for these meetings, the team members may do or commission research to find out more about existing literacy programs or other efforts to help women and girls. In designing the forums, team members should foster an atmosphere in which practical visions can flourish and participants can evaluate the strengths and weaknesses of each idea in order to decide which ones to pursue.

Among the solutions that may emerge is the need for a new organization or for improvements in existing organizations. Thus, organizational leadership will come into play as participants start designing or planning improvements in organizations that will play a part in the campaign for female literacy.

Proposal Review and Adoption

Once forum participants have developed consensus around one or more solutions to female illiteracy, visionary leaders among the change advocates can help larger audiences see how their support of these solutions can produce a better future. Change advocates also must focus on proposal development. They can assign a working group the task of translating the solutions into concrete proposals that can be adopted by appropriate government, business, and non-profit arenas.

Political leadership becomes vital as the working group considers how to draft a proposal that can be supported by a broad coalition and to which policy makers can say yes—that is, the proposal must be politically acceptable. The proposal also should be technically feasible and legally and morally defensible. In other words, the proposal must stand up in the court of public opinion and other courts, and thus ethical leadership will be needed.

The focus on political leadership continues in the proposal review and adoption phase as the advocates of female literacy work with people who have control over the arenas' agendas, committees, and scheduling of votes. The advocates must keep policy makers supplied with information and evidence of support for the proposal. They also must keep members of their coalition informed and active. Visionary leadership may still be needed in this phase to emphasize the possibility of a better future resulting from adoption of the proposal.

Implementation and Evaluation

If new female literacy programs are approved, their advocates should con-tinue to exercise political leadership in order to shape administrative decisions in the implementation and evaluation phase. The coalition that backed the new programs should be maintained so that it can oversee or monitor implementa-tion. Organizational leadership is likely to be needed as new organizations come into existence or as old ones take on new responsibility for serving girls and women. Change advocates also should exercise ethical leadership in this phase to ensure that, for example, teachers and parents are actually complying with a program that requires them to educate girls on an equal basis with boys.

If all goes well, the implementation phase will produce a regime of mutual gain. At some point, the supporters of female literacy should assess the effectiveness of the regime. If the problem of female literacy has not changed substantially and if the regime is working well, the regime should be maintained. If, however, previous leaders or a new group sees that conditions have changed, visionary leadership may come into play again. Perhaps girls are being educated on an equal basis with boys in many countries; then visionary leaders should highlight the success of special female literacy programs and urge that they be concluded. Meanwhile, in other countries, economic shifts or political turmoil may have rendered the new programs ineffective, and visionary leaders will call for returning to the early stages of the change cycle to reinterpret the problem of female literacy and find more effective solutions.

Admittedly, this scenario is a simplistic description of how various forms of leadership are woven through the change cycle. It is important to remember that even though one type of leadership may be more prominent than others in a particular phase, the other types are usually needed as well.

In tackling a particular public problem, leaders may need both macro and micro views of the change cycle. For example, at the macro level, IWRAW's leaders likely would see the effort to combat worldwide discrimination against women as a change effort mainly in the implementation phase, where the primary leadership challenge is how to use provisions of the Women's Convention and other international law to end discrimination. At the micro level, IWRAW's leaders consider particular change efforts within the global campaign. For example, Marsha Freeman will need to focus on the initial agreement phase if she is advising a group of women just beginning to consider how to persuade their country to ratify the Women's Convention.

CONCLUDING COUNSEL AND CAVEATS

Leadership in the global commons requires the exercise of all the major types of leadership over the course of change cycles. The types—leadership in context, personal leadership, team leadership, organizational leadership, visionary leadership, political leadership, and ethical leadership—have been explored at length in previous chapters. This chapter has described the change cycle and showed how the different types of leadership are woven through it.

It should be clear by now that leadership in the global commons is no simple undertaking. Tackling global public problems ethically and effectively requires people with many kinds of leadership talents over long periods. At the same time, leadership in the global commons is a hopeful undertaking. Those who engage in this work can learn from the insights and experiences of theorists and practitioners, such as those introduced in this book. The examples of leadership in Amnesty International and IWRAW demonstrate that committed world citizens acting in concert have been able to achieve considerable progress on major transnational problems.

Before concluding, I want to review key lessons for those seeking to exercise leadership in the global commons. They are organized by the main leadership categories.

Leadership in Context

Leaders in the global commons should attempt to understand the social, economic, political, and technological context in which the changes they seek will occur. At the same time, they must not be trapped by the way things are; instead, they must see how shifts in social, economic, political, and technological systems provide openings for leadership. Leaders can expect that, for the foreseeable future, global interdependence and the importance of supranational organizations and activities will continue to increase, although people will still be attached to their countries. Some public problems are worsened by this increasing globalization; at the same time, new opportunities for connecting people around the world can make solving the problems easier.

Personal Leadership

Those aspiring to leadership in the global commons need to claim their policy passions, strengthen their spirituality, and understand their own strengths and weaknesses and those of others who will be involved in the leadership endeavor. Leaders in the global commons need to be continually learning and realistically optimistic. The personal capacity most needed by these leaders is the ability to appreciate similarities and differences among those involved in the leadership work. Leaders in the global commons especially need to understand that everyone, including themselves, is a product of his or her national culture. If they are to work with people from other national cultures, they must respect the strengths of those cultures and adopt a multicultural outlook in their leadership work. At the same time, they should recognize that there are many common characteristics and interests among people affected by a public problem that spills across national boundaries.

Most leaders in the global commons are not saints or paragons. Peter Benenson, whose formidable strengths were accompanied by considerable flaws, is a prime example. Other leaders in Amnesty International and IWRAW had or have flaws that sometimes make life difficult for their colleagues. This is not to excuse petty, paranoid, or abusive behavior on the part of people with otherwise admirable traits. It is to warn leaders and constituents alike that the people pursuing grand causes are human—we all have our failings and areas of ignorance. Leaders and constituents should be alert to the shadow side of leadership. We should challenge each other to remember our own limitations and the dangers of intense commitment to even the greatest cause. We should strive to match words and deeds and seek forgiveness when we fall too short.

Team Leadership

Leaders in the global commons should build on their understanding of themselves and others to develop teams that can launch and sustain the effort to tackle global public problems. Team members should be unified around a common purpose but diverse enough to contribute different perspectives, connections, and other resources that will be vital to accomplishing the team's mission. Leaders need to be skilled in communication methods that elicit and honor multiple perspectives, in team empowerment (through attention to team mission, goals, decision-making rules, norms, and resources), and in leadership development of team members.

Organizational Leadership

In shaping organizations that can effectively muster and direct considerable person power and other resources toward resolving global public problems, leaders in the global commons should help their organizations keep their mission clear and alive. Alteration of the mission should be deliberate and strategic—that is, the change should be carefully considered, designed to help the organization more effectively tackle the problems central to its mission, and related to the organization's core competencies.

Leaders must ensure that the design and culture of their organizations support the mission and that organizational structure and systems prepare the organizations to adapt to internal and external changes. Leaders should encourage a reasonable amount of organizational opportunism in the service of their organization's mission—that is, they should help their organizations take advantage of unexpected occurrences or of events organized or caused by others in order to carry out organizational aims. Organizational leaders also should foster supportive and synergistic internal relationships and build interorganizational networks.

Visionary Leadership

Leaders in the global commons should pay careful attention to the design and use of forums, in which they help others frame transnational public problems and find solutions for them. Leaders should promote problem frames that appeal to diverse stakeholders—for example, the "human rights," "human family," "earth as delicate but resilient system," and "world citizenship" frames. Visionary leaders weave together understandings of context, social needs, interpretations of problems, and promising solutions into visions that help followers develop a sense of what they have in common with each other and the larger world.

Political Leadership

Leaders in the global commons should help followers draw on many sources of power to obtain desired decisions from policy makers in nonprofit, government, and business arenas. Leaders help their groups multiply their power by allying with other groups to form sustainable coalitions committed to common objectives.

Ethical Leadership

Leaders in the global commons should uphold ethical principles, laws, and norms that legitimize their efforts to remedy transnational public problems. They should emphasize, reconcile, and update these principles, laws, and norms as they press various courts to reward conduct that reduces the problems and punish conduct that perpetuates the problems.

Putting It All Together

Leaders in the global commons can use the change cycle to develop a comprehensive view of how the various types of leadership can be woven together to resolve a public problem. The cycle is really a leadership device for making sense of a change effort; fostering a long-term, complex perspective; and developing strategies. When problems are simple, and solutions easy to implement, leaders may be able to move swiftly through the early phases of the cycle. When problems are complex or solutions are difficult to implement, however, leaders must resist the temptation to truncate the early phases. A thorough search for solutions will be especially vital to ensure that change advocates do not settle on a solution because it is available or favored by influential people or factions.

Working with the change cycle takes persistence and faith. Grand hopes that surround solutions developed in forums may be dissipated as leaders and followers grind their way slowly through the decision-making process in arenas. The proposals that emerge from arenas may have slight resemblance to original drafts. Leaders in the global commons have faith that no matter what the outcome in a particular phase of the change cycle, there are always opportunities to improve matters by acting wisely in a subsequent phase or cycling back through earlier phases.

Leaders may well think of the cycle as a developing drama. They help constituents draft the initial script and refine it as the story unfolds. They pay attention to players, props, needed resources, and how these must be orchestrated to keep the drama moving to a successful conclusion. Leaders invite cast members and audience alike into the action and help them reflect on enduring lessons of the experience.

In this book, I have described an extensive array of approaches and tools that can help leaders in the global commons as they answer and transmit the call to world citizenship. Not all will be needed in any particular effort to tackle a global public problem. Nor do leaders in the global commons need to perform perfectly any of the leadership tasks emphasized here. They just have to do the tasks well enough that they succeed in helping others find and enact policies, plans, programs, and projects that actually remedy the problem and promote the common good.

As the 20th century comes to a close, the opportunities to be leaders in the global commons will only increase. Indeed, the nurturing of world citizenship, as an urgently needed complement to national citizenship, must surely be among the highest callings in the years to come.

The Case Studies of
Amnesty International and IWRAW

Since the mid-1980s, I have studied the history and operation of numerous citizen organizations founded by people who are committed to working on transnational public problems. Most of these organizations—for example, Oxfam, Save the Children, Friends of the Earth, the Red Cross, and Greenpeace—were founded and have their headquarters in the United States and Europe. Of these organizations, I selected two—Amnesty International and the International Women's Rights Action Watch (IWRAW)—for in-depth study, not because they are representative of transnational citizen organizations, but because they have a record of achievement and offer opportunities for contrast and comparison. Both focus on human rights, but one (Amnesty) now has a 37-year history, whereas the other has just celebrated its 10th anniversary. Although both organizations have a global membership, their structure and operation are very different. Thus, despite their common human rights focus, they offer contrasting models of organizational design.

An important consideration in choosing these two organizations was access. While living in London for 2 years, I was able to spend many days interviewing Amnesty staff and reading reports, interview transcripts, and other documents at Amnesty's international headquarters. At the University of Minnesota, I had access to the Human Rights Center and David Weissbrodt, its director and former member of Amnesty's International Executive Committee. IWRAW's headquarters is at the Humphrey Institute of Public Affairs, and Arvonne Fraser, IWRAW's director until 1994 and an IWRAW founder, gave me access to IWRAW files and core network members.

I prepared extensive qualitative case studies of leadership in each organization, with an emphasis on the first 10 years of the organizations' history. In designing the two studies, I was guided by Yin's (1984) work on case study research and by Reinharz's (1992) investigation of feminist research methods. The research questions explored in my study of Amnesty International and IWRAW are:

- How have people in these organizations exercised leadership to promote global human rights?

- What are the leadership implications for other citizen organizations working on global problems?

I used several methods to collect information about Amnesty International and IWRAW. They are listed below, in order of their importance:

- Interviewing people who have occupied leadership positions or exercised "non-positional" leadership in the organizations

- Developing and distributing a questionnaire to IWRAW's core network members

- Reviewing transcripts of interviews conducted for the Amnesty International Oral History Pilot Project, conducted mainly by Andrew Blane, a U.S. historian who served on Amnesty's International Executive Committee, and, in several cases, by Amnesty member Priscilla Ellsworth

- Reviewing annual reports, bulletins, and other organizational documents, publications, and training materials spanning the organizations' history

- Reviewing books, articles, theses, and news accounts referring to the organizations' work

- Attending IWRAW's core network meeting in January 1994

Some results of my research on Amnesty and IWRAW are presented in two papers (Crosby, 1993, 1996a). The questionnaire I used to survey IWRAW core network members is in Appendix B. In the personal interviews, I asked similar questions, but with much additional probing into details and experiences. I sometimes began those interviews by simply saying, "Tell me the story of your involvement with Amnesty International [or IWRAW]."

To some extent, I have been what Patton (1990) called a participant observer of these organizations. I am a member, though not an especially active one, of Amnesty; I collected some of my information on IWRAW while serving as an intern for its staff. I strongly support the aims and activities of both organizations. Additional explanation of my case study methodology is in the contextual essay "A Framework and Methodology for *Leadership in the Global Commons*" (Crosby, 1996b).

IWRAW Questionnaire

Name

1. What does leadership mean to you?

2. Why did you become active in the women's rights movement?

3. In your family, who supported you in your work for women's rights, and what kind of support did each person give?

4. Who in your family opposed your work for women, and how did they oppose it?

5. How have friends and colleagues supported or opposed your work for women?

6. Have role models helped motivate and sustain you in your work? If so, who are they, how old are they, and how have they motivated and sustained you?

7. Were there any people whom you consider to be the heroes or heroines in women's rights work? Who are they, why do you consider them to be heroes, and how have they affected you?

8. What books, films, or other materials motivated and sustained you in your work? How have they been important to you?

9. Please describe your formal and informal education, beginning in early childhood.

10. In which women's rights organizations (besides IWRAW) have you worked? Please describe your involvement with each organization, including dates. How did you help the organization accomplish its goals?

11. What have you learned about organizational leadership as you have worked with IWRAW and other organizations?

12. What is the vision you seek for women in your country and around the world?

13. How do you think that vision can be achieved?

14. How do you influence decision making in IWRAW and other women's rights organizations?

15. How do you try to influence your government and other groups or organizations that affect women's rights in your country? How successful have you been?

16. Have you built coalitions to improve women's rights in your country? If so, which groups were involved, and how have you done this?

17. What ethical principles are important to you in your work on behalf of women's rights?

18. How do you help educate others about these ethical principles?

19. What difficulties or challenges have you experienced in acting ethically yourself or inspiring ethical behavior in others?

20. Any other comments about IWRAW, leadership, or work on behalf of women's rights?

21. Any comments about the questionnaire?

Guidelines for Assessing Personal Highs and Lows

1. Take out a sheet of paper, turn it sideways, and draw a line from left to right that divides the paper into top and bottom halves of equal size.

2. At the right-hand end of the line, write in the current year. At the left-hand end of the line, write in the date of your first involvement in dealing with organizational or societal problems.

3. Think about the organizational or societal problems you have worked on over the time span you have marked out.

4. Leadership highs: In the appropriate place above the time line, mark, date, and label the times when your personal leadership helped remedy these problems. The distance of each mark above the time line should represent just how high it was.

5. Leadership lows: In the appropriate place below the time line, mark, date, and label times when you were unable to help remedy these problems. The distance of each mark below the time line should represent just how low it was.

6. At the appropriate points on the time line, fill in as highs or lows any important events that have occurred in your personal life, such as weddings, births, divorces, deaths of relatives or friends, the establishment or breakup of important relationships, graduations, layoffs, and so forth.

7. What themes are common to the "highs"?

8. What themes are common to the "lows"?

9. What conclusions do you draw from this analysis? What guidance would you give yourself for the future?

10. Share these results with someone who knows you well and whose friendship, support, and insights you value. Ask for observations and feedback.

Using Snow Cards to Identify
and Agree on Norms

1. Ask the group the question: What norms or standards would be good for us to establish to help us accomplish our work together? Think of things that might improve performance, inspire commitment, or enhance satisfaction.

2. Have individuals in the group brainstorm as many ideas as possible and record each idea on a separate "snow card," such as a
   - Post-it note
   - 5″ × 7″ cards
   - Oval
   - Square of paper

3. Have individuals share their ideas in round-robin fashion.

4. Tape the ideas to the wall. As a group, remove duplication and cluster similar ideas in categories. Establish subcategories as needed. The resulting clusters of cards may resemble a "blizzard" of ideas—hence the term *snow cards*.

5. Clarify ideas.

6. Once all the ideas are on the wall and included in a category, rearrange and tinker with the categories until they make the most sense. Place a card with the category name above each cluster.

7. As a group, decide how to monitor and reinforce the norms.

After the exercise, distribute a copy of the norms listed by categories to all members of the group.

References

Albert, R. D. (1983). The intercultural sensitizer or culture assimilator: A cognitive approach. In D. Landis & R. Brislin (Eds.), *Handbook of intercultural training* (Vol. 2, (pp. 186-217). New York: Pergamon.

Alexander, E. (1995). *How organizations act together: Interorganizational coordination in theory and practice.* Amsterdam: Gordon & Breach.

Allport, G. W. (1954). *The nature of prejudice.* Reading, MA: Addison-Wesley.

Almond, G., & Powell, G. B., Jr. (1992). *Comparative politics today: A world view* (5th ed.). New York: HarperCollins.

Amnesty International. (1963). *Amnesty International report, 1962-63.* London: Author.

Amnesty International. (1966). *Amnesty International report, 1965-66.* London: Author.

Amnesty International. (1969). *Amnesty International report, 1968-69.* London: Author.

Amnesty International. (1970). *Amnesty International report, 1969-70.* London: Author.

Amnesty International. (1974). *Amnesty International report, 1974.* London: Author.

Amnesty International. (1976). *Amnesty International report, 1976.* London: Author.

Amnesty International. (1977). *Amnesty International report, 1977.* London: Author.

Amnesty International. (1978). *Amnesty International report, 1978.* London: Author.

Amnesty International. (1979). *Amnesty International report, 1979.* London: Author.

Amnesty International. (1994). *Amnesty International report, 1994.* London: Author.

Anzaldúa, G. (Ed.). (1990). *Making face, making soul/Haciendo caras.* San Francisco: aunt lute.

Archer, P. (1986, May 31). Interview by A. Blane and P. Ellsworth [Transcript]. Amnesty International Oral History Project. Amnesty International, International Secretariat.

Baker, J. (1983, June). Interview by A. Blane and P. Ellsworth [Transcript]. Amnesty International Oral History Project. Amnesty International, International Secretariat.

Baldwin, C. (1990). *Life's companion: Journal writing as a spiritual quest.* New York: Bantam.

Baldwin, C. (1994). *Calling the circle: The first and future culture.* Newberg, OR: Swan Raven.

Barber, B. (1984). *Strong democracy: Participatory politics for a new age.* Berkeley: University of California Press.

Bates, C. (1991). *When pigs eat wolves.* St. Paul, MN: Yes International.

Becker, E. (1973). *The denial of death.* New York: Free Press.

Benenson, P. (1984, June 6). Interview by A. Blane [Transcript]. Amnesty International Oral History Pilot Project. Amnesty International, International Secretariat.

Benenson, P. (1961, May 28). The forgotten prisoners. *London Observer,* p. 21.

Bennis, W. (1989). *On becoming a leader.* Reading, MA: Addison-Wesley.

Bennis, W., & Nanus, B. (1985). *Leaders: The strategies of taking charge.* New York: HarperCollins.

Boal, K. B., & Bryson, J. M. (1987). Charismatic leadership: A phenomenological and structural approach. In J. G. Hunt, B. R. Balinga, H. P. Dachler, & C. A. Schriescheim (Eds.), *Emerging leadership vistas* (pp. 11-28). Elmsford, NY: Pergamon.

Bohm, D. (1994, Summer). On dialogue. *Kettering Review,* pp. 35-39.

Bolman, L. G., & Deal, T. (1991). *Reframing organizations: Artistry, choice and leadership.* San Francisco: Jossey-Bass.

Bolman, L. G., & Deal, T. (1995). *Leading with soul.* San Francisco: Jossey-Bass.

Bradsher, K. (1995, April 18). America, land of inequality. *Minneapolis Star Tribune,* p. 4A.

Brislin, R. W. (1981). *Cross-cultural encounters.* New York: Pergamon.

Brown, L. D., & Covey, J. G. (1987). Organizing and managing private development agencies: A comparative analysis. *IDR Reports [Institute for Development Research], 4*(1), 1-63.

Brown, C. R., & Mazza, G. (1992). *Peer training strategies for welcoming diversity.* Unpublished manuscript, National Coalition Building Institute, Washington, DC.

Browning, R. P., Marshall, D. R., & Tabb, D. H. (1984). *Protest is not enough: The struggle of blacks and Hispanics for equality in urban politics.* Berkeley: University of California Press.

Bruce, J., Lloyd, C. B., & Leonard, A. (1995). *Families in focus: New perspectives on mothers, fathers, and children.* New York: Population Council.

Brudney, J. L. (1994). Designing and managing volunteer programs. In R. D. Herman & Associates (Eds.), *Jossey-Bass handbook of nonprofit leadership and management* (pp. 279-302). San Francisco: Jossey-Bass.

Bryson, J. M. (1995). *Strategic planning for public and nonprofit organizations* (Rev. ed.). San Francisco: Jossey-Bass.

Bryson, J. M., Ackermann, F., Eden, C., & Finn, C. B. (1995). Using the "oval mapping process" to identify strategic issues and formulate effective strategies. In J. M. Bryson (Ed.), *Strategic planning for public and nonprofit organizations* (Rev. ed., pp. 257-275). San Francisco: Jossey-Bass.

Bryson, J. M., & Alston, F. K. (1995). *Creating and implementing your strategic plan: A workbook for public and nonprofit organizations.* San Francisco: Jossey-Bass.

Bryson, J. M., & Crosby, B. C. (1992). *Leadership for the common good: Tackling public problems in a shared-power world.* San Francisco: Jossey-Bass.

Burns, J. M. (1978). *Leadership.* New York: HarperCollins.

Campbell, J. (1949). *The hero with a thousand faces.* Princeton, NJ: Princeton/Bollingen.

Carse, J. P. (1995). *Breakfast at the Victory: The mysticism of ordinary experience.* San Francisco: HarperSanFrancisco.

Center for Creative Leadership. (1995). New survey measures creativity in the workplace. *Issues and Observations, 15*(3), 9.

Cleveland, H. (1990). *The global commons.* Lanham, MD: University Press of America.

Cleveland, H. (1993). *Birth of a new world: An open moment for international leadership.* San Francisco: Jossey-Bass.

Cobb, R. W., & Elder, C. D. (1983). *Participation in American politics: The dynamics of agenda-building.* Baltimore: Johns Hopkins University Press.

Cohen, S., & Brand, R. (1993). *Total quality management in government: A practical guide for the real world.* San Francisco: Jossey-Bass.

Collins, J. C., & Porras, J. I. (1994). *Built to last: Successful habits of visionary companies.* New York: HarperBusiness.

Commission on Global Governance. (1995). *Our global neighborhood.* Geneva: Author.

Covey, S. R. (1991). *Principle-centered leadership.* New York: Simon & Schuster.

Crane, P. (1985, June 17). Interview by A. Blane and P. Ellsworth [Transcript]. Amnesty International Oral History Project. Amnesty International, International Secretariat.

Crosby, B. C. (1993, April). *Women's transnational leadership: A case study.* Paper presented at the 51st annual meeting of the Midwest Political Science Association, Chicago.

Crosby, B. C. (1996a). *A case study in transnational leadership: Amnesty International.* Working paper, Reflective Leadership Center, University of Minnesota, Minneapolis.

Crosby, B. C. (1996b). *A framework and methodology for* Leadership in the Global Commons. Unpublished manuscript, Reflective Leadership Center, University of Minnesota, Minneapolis.

Crossette, B. (1995a, March 5). In low-key Denmark, U.N. talks will discuss all the ways the world hurts. *New York Times,* p. A6.

Crossette, B. (1995b, March 6). U.N. parley ponders ways to stretch scarce aid funds. *New York Times,* p. A6.

Daly, H. E., & Cobb, J. B., Jr. (1989). *For the common good: Redirecting the economy toward community, the environment, and a sustainable future.* Boston: Beacon.

de Bono, E. (1970). *Lateral thinking.* New York: HarperCollins.

de Oliveira, M. D. (1995). The case for global civil society. *National Civic Review, 84,* 130-132.

De Pree, M. (1992). *Leadership jazz.* New York: Dell.

Delbecq, A., Van de Ven, A., & Gustafson, D. (1975). *Group techniques for program planning.* Glenview, IL: Scott-Foresman.

Desmond, C. (1983). *Persecution East and West: Human rights, political prisoners, and amnesty.* New York: Penguin.

Drath, W. H., & Palus, C. J. (1994). *Making common sense: Leadership as meaning-making in a community of practice.* Greensboro, NC: Center for Creative Leadership.

Drucker, P. (1994, November). The age of social transformation. *Atlantic Monthly,* pp. 53-80.

Emmott, B. (1993, March 27). Multinationals back in fashion. *Economist,* pp. 5-20.

Estés, C. P. (1992). *Women who run with the wolves.* New York: Ballantine.

Evans, S. M., & Boyte, H. C. (1986). *Free spaces: The sources of democratic change in America.* New York: Harper & Row.

Farazmand, A. (1990). *Handbook of comparative public administration and development.* New York: Marcel Dekker.

Fields, B. J. (1992, January). *Ideology and race in American cultural dialogue.* Paper presented at the annual meeting of the American Association of Colleges, Washington, DC.

Fisher, J. (1998). *Nongovernments: NGOs and the political development of the third world.* West Hartford, CT: Kumarian.

Fisher, R., & Brown, S. (1988). *Getting together: Building a relationship that gets to yes.* Boston: Houghton Mifflin.

Fisher, R., & Ury, W. (1981). *Getting to yes: Negotiating agreement without giving in.* New York: Penguin.

Fiutak, T. R. (1996, January). *Working together.* Speech presented at the Humphrey Institute of Public Affairs, University of Minnesota, Minneapolis.

Flower, J. (1995). Future search: A power tool for building healthier communities. *Healthcare Forum Journal, 38*(3).

Forsythe, D. P. (1989). *Human rights and world politics.* Lincoln: University of Nebraska Press.

Forsythe, D. P. (1991). *The internationalization of human rights.* Lexington, MA: Lexington.

Fox, M. (1983). *Original blessing.* Santa Fe, NM: Bear.

Fraser, A. (1990, August 28). Letter to Isabel Plata. Archives, International Women's Rights Action Watch headquarters, Humphrey Institute, University of Minnesota, Minneapolis.

Fraser, A. (1991a, February 3). Letter to Miren Busto. Archives, International Women's Rights Action Watch headquarters, Humphrey Institute, University of Minnesota, Minneapolis.

Fraser, A. (1991b, February 3). Letter to Isabel Plata. Archives, International Women's Rights Action Watch headquarters, Humphrey Institute, University of Minnesota, Minneapolis.

Fraser, A. (1992). Feminism: It's not just for America anymore. *Law and Politics, 7*(1), 19-21.

Fraser, A. (1993, June). *CEDAW #12 and women's human rights.* Minneapolis: International Women's Rights Action Watch.

Freeman, J. (Ed.). (1983). *Social movements of the Sixties and Seventies.* New York: Longman.

Freeman, M. (1993). Women, development and justice: Using the International Convention on Women's Rights. In J. Kerr (Ed.), *Ours by right* (pp. 93-105). London: Zed.

Freeman, M. (1995, September 25). *Home from Beijing* [2-page news brief]. Minneapolis: University of Minnesota, Humphrey Institute of Public Affairs.

Freeman, M., & Fraser, A. (1993). Women's human rights: Making the theory a reality. In L. Henkin & J. L. Hargrove (Eds.), *Human rights: An agenda for the next century* (pp. 103-133). Washington, DC: American Society of International Law.

Goggin, M. L., Bowman, A. O., Lester, J. P., & O'Toole, L. J., Jr. (1990). *Implementation theory and practice: Toward a third generation.* Glenview, IL: Scott-Foresman.

Goleman, D. (1995). *Emotional intelligence.* New York: Bantam.

Gudykunst, W. B., & Kim, Y. Y. (1984). *Communicating with strangers.* Reading, MA: Addison-Wesley.

Hall, E. T. (1959). *The silent language.* New York: Doubleday.

Hall, N. (1990). African-American women leaders and alliances of power. In L. Albrecht & R. M. Brewer (Eds.), *Bridges of power: Women's multicultural alliances* (pp. 74-94). Philadelphia: New Society.

Hammer, M., & Champy, J. (1993). *Reengineering the corporation.* New York: HarperBusiness.

Hamminck, D. (1993). *Nonprofit organizations in a market economy.* San Francisco: Jossey-Bass.

Heifetz, R. A. (1994). *Leadership without easy answers.* Cambridge, MA: Belknap.

Helgeson, S. (1994). *The female advantage: Women's ways of leading.* New York: Doubleday.

Herman, R. D., & Associates. (Eds.). (1994). *The Jossey-Bass handbook of nonprofit leadership and management.* San Francisco: Jossey-Bass.

Hersey, P., & Blanchard, K. H. (1988). *Management of organizational behavior: Utilizing human resources* (5th ed.). Englewood Cliffs, NJ: Prentice Hall.

Humphrey Institute of Public Affairs. (1993, March 8). A closer look: Women's rights as human rights. *Happenings,* p. 1.

Hunsaker, J., & Hunsaker, P. (1986). *Strategies and skills for managerial women.* Cincinnati, OH: South-Western Publishing.

Huxley, A. (1945). *The perennial philosophy.* New York: Harper & Row.

International Women's Rights Action Watch. (n.d.). *What and who is IWRAW?* Minneapolis: Humphrey Institute of Public Affairs, University of Minnesota.

International Women's Rights Action Watch. (1990, January). *Dreaming a different reality: Report on the Fifth Annual Conference of the International Women's Rights Action Watch.* Minneapolist: University of Minnesota, Humphrey Institute of Public Affairs.

International Women's Rights Action Watch. (1996). *Assessing the status of women: A guide to reporting under the Convention on Elimination of All Forms of Discrimination Against Women.* Minneapolis: University of Minnesota, Humphrey Institute of Public Affairs.

Jacobs, R. (1994). *Real time strategic change: How to involve an entire organization in fast and far-reaching change.* San Francisco: Berrett-Koehler.

Jeavons, T. H. (1994). Ethics in nonprofit management: Creating a culture of integrity. In R. D. Herman & Associates (Eds.), *Jossey-Bass handbook of nonprofit leadership and management* (pp. 184-207). San Francisco: Jossey-Bass.

Johnson, D. W., & Johnson, F. P. (1994). *Joining together* (5th ed.). Englewood Cliffs, NJ: Prentice Hall.

Kellerman, B., & Barrilleaux, R. J. (1991). *The president as world leader.* New York: St. Martin's.

Kelly, K. (1994). *Out of control: The rise of neo-biological civilization.* Reading, MA: Addison-Wesley.

Kets de Vries, M. F. R. (1993). *Leaders, fools, and imposters: Essays on the psychology of leadership.* San Francisco: Jossey-Bass.

Klandermans, B. (1992). The social construction of protest and multiorganizational fields. In A. D. Morris & C. M. Mueller (Eds.), *Frontiers in social movement theory* (pp. 77-103). New Haven, CT: Yale University Press.

Kluckhohn, F. R., & Strodtbeck, F. L. (1961). *Variations in value orientations.* Evanston, IL: Row, Peterson.

Korten, D. (1995). *When corporations rule the world.* San Francisco: Berrett-Koehler.

Kouzes, J. M., & Posner, B. Z. (1987). *The leadership challenge: How to get extraordinary things done in organizations.* San Francisco: Jossey-Bass.

Kouzes, J. M., & Posner, B. Z. (1993). *Credibility: How leaders gain and lose it, why people demand it.* San Francisco: Jossey-Bass.

Kretzmann, J. P., & McKnight, J. L. (1993). *Building communities from the inside out: A path toward finding and mobilizing a community's assets.* Evanston, IL: Center for Urban Affairs.

Kristof, N. D. (1996, September 22). Aging world, new wrinkles. *New York Times,* p. 1E.

Lakey, B., Lakey, G., Napier, R., & Robinson, J. (1995). *Grassroots and nonprofit leadership.* Philadelphia: New Society.

Land, G., & Jarman, B. (1992). *Breakpoint and beyond: Mastering the future today.* New York: HarperBusiness.

Larsen, E. (1978). *A flame in barbed wire: The story of Amnesty International.* London: Frederick Muller.

Lewis, C. W. (1991). *The ethics challenge in the public sector.* San Francisco: Jossey-Bass.

Light, P. (1995, February 22). *Innovation in public organizations.* Paper presented at the Humphrey Institute of Public Affairs, University of Minnesota, Minneapolis.

Lindblom, C. E. (1977). *Politics and markets.* New York: Free Press.

Luke, J. S. (1994). Character and conduct in public service: A review of historical perspectives and a definition for the twenty-first century. In T. L. Cooper (Ed.), *Handbook of administrative ethics* (pp. 391-412). New York: Marcel Dekker.

Luke, J. S. (1998). *Catalytic leadership.* San Francisco: Jossey-Bass.

Mandela, N. (1994). [A 1994 inaugural speech, written by Marianne Williamson]. http://members.aol.com/hermitsoul.

Marsh, C. (1984, June). Interview by A. Blane and P. Ellsworth [Transcript]. Amnesty International Oral History Project. Amnesty International, International Secretariat.

Merleau-Ponty, M. (1964). *Signs* (R. C. McCleary, Trans.). Chicago: Northwestern University Press.

Mies, M., & Shiva, V. (1993). *Ecofeminism.* London: Zed.

Miner, M. (1995, November 3). Presentation to the Missing Page Club.

Mitchell, S. (Trans.). (1988). *Tao Te Ching.* New York: Harper & Row.

Moen, J. K. (1995). Women in leadership: The Norwegian example. *Journal of Leadership Studies, 2*(3), 3-19.

Moore, T. (1992). *Care of the soul: A guide for cultivating depth and sacredness in everyday life.* New York: HarperCollins.

Morgan, G. (1986). *Images of organization.* Newbury Park, CA: Sage.

Morrison, A. (1992). *The new leaders: Guidelines on leadership diversity in America.* San Francisco: Jossey-Bass.

Murdock, M. (1990). *The heroine's journey.* Boston: Shambala.

Myers, I. B. (1980). *Gifts differing.* Palo Alto, CA: Consulting Psychologists Press.

Nair, K. (1994). *A higher standard of leadership.* San Francisco: Berrett-Koehler.

Nelson, B., & Chowdhury, N. (1994). *Women and politics worldwide.* New Haven, CT: Yale University Press.

Noddings, N. (1984). *Caring: A feminine approach to ethics and moral education.* Berkeley: University of California Press.

O'Toole, J. (1995). *Leading change: Overcoming the ideology of comfort and the tyranny of custom.* San Francisco: Jossey-Bass.

Osborne, D., & Gaebler, T. (1992). *Reinventing government.* Reading, MA: Addison-Wesley.

Ostrom, E. (1990). *Governing the commons.* New York: Cambridge University Press.

Patton, M. Q. (1990). *Qualitative evaluation and research methods* (2nd ed.). Thousand Oaks, CA: Sage.

Patton, M. Q. (1997). *Utilization-focused evaluation* (3rd ed.). Thousand Oaks, CA: Sage.

Pearson, C. (1986). *The hero within: Six archetypes we live by.* San Francisco: Harper & Row.

Pimentel, S. (1993). Special challenges confronting Latin American women. In J. Kerr (Ed.), *Ours by right* (pp. 27-31). London: Zed.

Pocket Oxford Dictionary of Current English. (1992). Oxford, UK: Clarendon.

Power, J. (1981). *Against oblivion: Amnesty International's fight for human rights.* UK: Fontana.

Quinn, R. E. (1988). *Beyond rational management: Mastering the paradoxes and competing demands of high performance.* San Francisco: Jossey-Bass.

Reinharz, S. (1992). *Feminist methods in social research.* New York: Oxford University Press.

Renteln, A. D. (1988). The concept of human rights. *Anthropos, 83,* 343-364.

Reoch, R. (Ed.). (1994). *Human rights: The new consensus.* London: Regency.

Riker, W. H. (1986). *The art of political manipulation.* New Haven, CT: Yale University Press.

Roberts-DeGennaro, M. (1986). Factors contributing to coalition maintenance. *Journal of Sociology and Social Welfare, 8,* 248-264.

Roseau, H. A., & Associates. (1992). *Achieving excellence in fundraising.* San Francisco: Jossey-Bass.

Rost, J. C. (1991). *Leadership for the twenty-first century.* New York: Praeger.

Rusk, T. (1993. *The power of ethical persuasion.* New York: Viking.

Sabatier, P. A., & Jenkins, H. C. (1993). *Policy change and learning: An advocacy coalition approach.* Boulder, CO: Westview.

Sagan, C. (1995). *Pale blue dot.* New York: Random House.

Samovar, L., & Porter, R. (Eds.). (1994). *Intercultural communication: A reader* (7th ed.). Belmont, CA: Wadsworth.

Sané, P. (1994). Fundamental freedoms. In R. Reoch (Ed.), *Human rights: The new consensus* (pp. 38-42). London: Regency.

Sargent, T. (1985, June 21). Interview by A. Blane and P. Ellsworth [Transcript]. Amnesty International Oral History Project. Amnesty International, International Secretariat.

Schein, E. H. (1993, Autumn). On dialogue, culture, and organizational learning. *Organizational Dynamics,* pp. 40-51.

Schein, E. H. (1992). *Organizational culture and leadership* (2nd ed.). San Francisco: Jossey-Bass.

Schwartz, H. (1990). *Century's end.* New York: Doubleday.

Seligman, M. E. P. (1991). *Learned optimism.* New York: Knopf.

Senge, P. M. (1990). *The fifth discipline: The art and practice of the learning organization.* New York: Doubleday.

Senge, P., Kleiner, A., Roberts, C., Ross, R. B., & Smith, B. J. (1994). *The fifth discipline fieldbook: Strategies and tools for building a learning organization.* New York: Doubleday.

Shaver, T. (1995). *When the people lead . . . How to create leaders in grassroots organizations.* Unpublished master's thesis, School of International Training, Brattleboro, VT.

Shirts, R. G. (n.d.). *BaFa BaFa* [Game]. Del Mar, CA: Simile.

Shively, W. P. (1995). *Power and choice: An introduction to political science* (4th ed.). New York: McGraw-Hill.

Sikkink, K. (1994, June). *Memo to participants in MacArthur Summer Workshop on Effective Democratization and Popular Empowerment, University of Minnesota, Minneapolis* [Memo]. University of Minnesota.

Stephan, W. G. (1985). Intergroup relations. In G. Lindzey & E. Aronson (Eds.), *Handbook of social psychology* (3rd ed., Vol. 2, pp. 599-658). New York: Random House.

Tannen, D. (1990). *You just don't understand: Women and men in conversation.* New York: Ballantine.

Taylor, S., & Novelli, L., Jr. (1991). Telling a story about innovation. *Issues and Observations [Center for Creative Leadership], 11*(1), 6-9.

Terry, R. (1993). *Authentic leadership: Courage in action.* San Francisco: Jossey-Bass.

Terry, R. (1996, January 10). *Views of leadership.* Paper presented at the Hubert H. Humphrey Institute of Public Affairs, Minneapolis.

Treacy, M., & Wiersema, F. (1995). *Discipline of market leaders.* Reading, MA: Addison-Wesley.

Triandis, H. C., & Albert, R. D. (1987). Cross-cultural perspectives. In F. M. Jablin, L. L. Putnam, K. H. Roberts, & L. W. Porter (Eds.), *Handbook of organizational communication* (pp. 264-295). Thousand Oaks, CA: Sage.

United Nations. (1983a). Convention on the Elimination of All Forms of Discrimination Against Women. In U.S. Congress, Committee on Foreign Affairs (Ed.), *Human rights documents* (pp. 139-149). Washington, DC: Government Printing Office. (Original work published 1979)

United Nations. (1983b). International Covenant on Civil and Political Rights. In U.S. Congress, Committee on Foreign Affairs (Ed.), *Human rights documents* (pp. 79-95). Washington, DC: Government Printing Office. (Original work published 1966)

United Nations. (1983c). International Covenant on Economic, Cultural, and Social Rights. In U.S. Congress, Committee on Foreign Affairs (Ed.), *Human rights documents* (pp. 69-78). Washington, DC: Government Printing Office. (Original work published 1966)

United Nations. (1983d). Universal Declaration of Human Rights. In U.S. Congress, Committee on Foreign Affairs (Ed.), *Human rights documents* (pp. 63-68). Washington, DC: Government Printing Office. (Original work published 1948)

United Nations. (1995). *Basic facts about the United Nations.* New York: Author.

United Nations Development Programme. (1995). *Human development report 1994.* New York: Oxford University Press.

von Oech, R. (1983). *A whack on the side of the head: How to unlock your mind for innovation.* New York: Basic Books.

von Sternberg, B. (1996, May 2). Heart, backbone, mind and faith. *Minneapolis Star Tribune,* p. A24.

Waldemar, C. (1983, September 14). Leading by her own example. *Twin Cities Reader,* p. 12.

Wallace, D., & White, J. B. (1988). Building integrity in organizations. *New Management, 6*(1), 30-35.

Waring, M. (1988). *If women counted: A new feminist economics.* San Francisco: Harper.

Weisbord, M., et al. (1992). *Discovering common ground.* San Francisco: Berrett-Koehler.

Weisbord, M., & Janoff, S. (1995). *Future search.* San Francisco: Berrett-Koehler.

Wheatley, M. J. (1992). *Leadership and the new science: Learning about organization from an orderly universe.* San Francisco: Berrett-Koehler.

Winer, M. (1996). *Abundance: Partnering in power, passion, and politics.* Unpublished manuscript, Synoptics, St. Paul, MN.

Winer, M., & Ray, K. (1994). *Collaboration handbook.* St. Paul, MN: Amherst H. Wilder Foundation.

Women, Public Policy, and Development Project, & Development Law and Public Policy Program. (1985, October 22). *Women's Rights Action Project: Proposal to the Carnegie Corporation.* Minneapolis: University of Minnesota.

Wood, M. M. (1995). *Nonprofit boards and leadership.* San Francisco: Jossey-Bass.

Yin, R. K. (1984). *Case study research: Design and methods.* Beverly Hills, CA: Sage.

Index

About the Author

Barbara C. Crosby is a Senior Fellow at the Hubert H. Humphrey Institute of Public Affairs, University of Minnesota. As a staff member of the Institute's Reflective Leadership Center, she has taught and written extensively about leadership and public policy, women in leadership, media and public policy, and strategic planning. She is the coauthor with John M. Bryson of *Leadership for the Common Good: Tackling Public Problems in a Shared-Power World,* which won the 1993 Terry McAdam Award from the Nonprofit Management Association and was named the Best Book of 1992-93 by the Public and Nonprofit Sector Division of the Academy of Management. She was Coordinator of the Humphrey Fellowship Program at the University of Minnesota from 1990 to 1993. A frequent speaker at conferences and workshops, she has conducted training for senior managers of nonprofit and government organizations, local officials, and business people in the United States, the United Kingdom, and Poland. She is a former press secretary for Governor Patrick Lucey of Wisconsin and a former speech writer for Governor Rudy Perpich of Minnesota. She also has been a newspaper reporter and editor and has written several book chapters and articles for national journals, including the *National Civic Review* and *Social Policy.* She has a BA degree, with a major in political science and a minor in French, from Vanderbilt University and an MA degree in journalism and mass communication from the University of Wisconsin-Madison. She has a PhD in leadership studies from the Union Institute, where she concentrated on leadership, political philosophy, international relations, social movements, and intercultural communication.